Supervising Postgraduates from Non-English Speaking Backgrounds

SRHE and Open University Press Imprint
General Editor: Heather Eggins

Supervising Postgraduates from Non-English Speaking Backgrounds

Edited by
Yoni Ryan
and
Ortrun Zuber-Skerritt

The Society for Research into Higher Education
& Open University Press

Published by SRHE and
Open University Press
Celtic Court
22 Ballmoor
Buckingham
MK18 1XW

email: enquiries@openup.co.uk
world wide web: http://www.openup.co.uk

and 325 Chestnut Street
Philadelphia, PA 19106, USA

First published 1999

A catalogue record of this book is available from the British Library

ISBN 0 335 20371 X (pbk)   0 335 20372 8 (hbk)

Library of Congress Cataloging-in-Publication Data
Supervising postgraduates from non-English speaking
backgrounds / edited by Yoni Ryan and Ortrun
Zuber-Skerritt.
        p.   cm.
    Includes bibliographical references (p.   ) and index.
    ISBN 0-335-20372-8 (hb)
    ISBN 0-335-20371-X (pb)
    1. Faculty advisors.   2. Graduate students – Counseling of.
3. Students, Foreign – Counseling of.   4. Teacher-student
relationships.   5. English language – study and teaching –
Foreign speakers.   I. Ryan, Yoni.   II. Zuber Skerritt, Ortrun.
    LB2343 .S86 1999
    378.1'94046–ddc21
                                              98–45151
                                              CIP

Typeset by Graphicraft Limited, Hong Kong
Printed in Great Britain by St Edmundsbury Press, Bury St Edmunds, Suffolk

Contents

Contributors

Tania Aspland is a PhD student within the Graduate School of Education at the University of Queensland. She also teaches curriculum theory and pedagogical studies at the Queensland University of Technology. Her teaching and research interests focus on generating better practices in the areas of culturally responsive teaching, supervision and learning within the emerging culture of the 'new' university context. She has recent publications in the field of curriculum leadership, advocacy-oriented action research, postgraduate teaching and thesis supervision. (E-mail: t.aspland@qut.edu.au)

Gerald Brameld has been Director of the Physical Infrastructure Centre at Queensland University of Technology since its inception in 1980. Located within the School of Civil Engineering, the Centre is responsible for all postgraduate research training. It contains a strong ethnic mix of graduate students from Asia, India, Africa and Australia. Gerald Brameld has a particular interest in the professional development of graduate students, especially in written and verbal communication. (E-mail: g.brameld@qut.edu.au)

Christine Bruce is a Lecturer in the School of Information Systems in the Faculty of Information Technology at the Queensland University of Technology. Her research interests are in the perceptual worlds of information users. She has published various articles on the theme of information literacy in higher education, focusing on curriculum design, institutional responsibility, postgraduate study and supervision, and staff development. (E-mail: c.bruce@qut.edu.au)

Glenda Crosling is a Lecturer in Language and Learning at Monash University. She is responsible for language and learning programmes in the Faculty of Business and Economics at the Clayton campus. Glenda provides discipline-based programmes for undergraduate business students, together with support for NESB and international research students. She co-authored, with

Helen Murphy, *How to Succeed in Law*, Butterworths, 1994 (2nd edn, 1996), and has published a number of articles related to second-language learners in tertiary education.

Pat Cryer is a Senior Visiting Fellow at the University College London (UCL). Her research and development interest is in the support of postgraduate research students and supervisors, and in this connection she convenes a national Network on Postgraduate Issues for the Society for Research into Higher Education (SRHE). She is series editor for an ongoing series of guides on postgraduate issues, published jointly by SRHE and *The Times Higher Education Supplement*, has run training for various institutions in the UK and overseas, and was a member of the Engineering and Physical Sciences Research Council's Advisory Panel on good supervisory practice. She is the author of *The Research Student's Guide to Success* (Open University Press, 1996). (E-mail: p.cryer@ucl.ac.uk)

Pam Denicolo is a chartered psychologist with a practising certificate, and a Reader at the University of Reading (UK). Before 1995, she was Director of the Professional Courses Unit of the Centre for the Advancement of Teaching in Higher Education and of Postgraduate Research at Surrey University. Her teaching has been in three main areas: psychology, academic staff development topics and research methods. Her research is underpinned by Personal Construct Theory and focuses on the development of learning, particularly in the professional context, and of research approaches and techniques which enhance understanding of learning/teaching. She is Chair of the Southern PCP Group, Convener of the Guidance Panel of the European PC Association and UK representative for the International Study Association on Teacher Thinking. Under the auspices of the latter, she has co-edited two books and is an associate editor of the journal. (E-mail: P.M.Denicolo@reading.ac.uk)

Allan Ellis is a Senior Lecturer in the Faculty of Education, Work and Training at SCU. He currently teaches and supervises postgraduate students in the field of training and development. His research interests are in the areas of adult learning and educational technology, with a particular focus on electronic networks such as the Internet and the World Wide Web. He is the co-organizer of the AusWeb conferences (http://www.scu.edu.au/ ausweb98) and a member of the Organizing Committee for the 6th International WWW Conference. (E-mail: aellis@scu.edu.au)

Mary Farquhar is Deputy Dean and Head, School of Languages and Applied Linguistics, Faculty of Asian and International Studies, Griffith University. She is a China specialist with research interests in cultural studies as they impact on film, literature, popular media, language and the law. She studied Chinese at both the Beijing Languages Institute and the Beijing University in the 1970s, and has supervised a number of Masters and PhD students in China Studies. These postgraduates include NESB students. (E-mail: M.Farquhar@ais.gu.edu.au)

Alan Frost is Professor of Veterinary Microbiology, and heads Veterinary Pathology and Anatomy, in the School of Veterinary Science and Animal Production at the University of Queensland. He has supervised a large number of PhD and Masters students to successful completion, and is currently supervising four NESB and two Australian PhD students. His research interests are currently focused on eradication of Pasteurella diseases in poultry and pig populations in rural Vietnam and Sri Lanka. This is a $1,000,000 funded project in collaboration with Vietnamese and Sri Lankan scientists. (E-mail: a.frost@mailbox.uq.edu.au)

John Geake is a Senior Lecturer in the Faculty of Education, Work and Training at Southern Cross University. He teaches courses in educational psychology, gifted education and secondary practicum, and supervises postgraduate students, including several from non-English speaking backgrounds. His current research interests include non-linear psychophysical models of music and visual perception. His publications explore the educational implications of this research, particularly for academically gifted students. A recent consultancy involved the use of computer technology for NESB gifted secondary students. (E-mail: jgeake@scu.edu.au)

Nick Knight is Associate Professor in the Faculty of Asian and International Studies at Griffith University where he has been both Head of School of Modern Asian Studies and Deputy Dean (Teaching and Learning). He teaches political science, problems and methods in research, and politics and ideology in China. He has supervised many Honours, Masters and PhD students, a considerable number of whom have been NESB students. His publications include *Mao Zedong on Dialectical Materialism: Writings on Philosophy, 1937* (M.E. Sharpe, 1990), and *Li Da and Marxist Philosophy in China* (Westview Press, 1996). (E-mail: N.Knight@ais.gu.edu.au)

Christine Maingard is a Lecturer and PhD student at Southern Cross University. She teaches Japanese and instructional design/educational technology, and is researching towards her PhD in the area of technology-based Japanese language learning. She graduated in 1994 with First Class Honours and was recipient of the 1994 Southern Cross University Medal. Her background is multilingual (English, German, French and Japanese) and in teaching computing in industry and TAFE. (E-mail: cmaingar@scu.edu.au)

Yuriko Nagata is a Senior Lecturer in the Department of Asian Languages and Studies in the University of Queensland. She is active in projects about quality issues in teaching and learning. She has published book chapters and journal articles on history and Japanese language issues. She is the author of *Unwanted Aliens* (University of Queensland Press, 1996). (E-mail: y.nagata@mailbox.uq.oz.au)

Eunice Okorocha is a Nigerian with a background in teaching and learning in higher education and guidance and counselling. Her PhD from the University of Surrey was on the experience of international students, cross-cultural work and counselling, and she currently runs a consultancy in cross-cultural education and counselling. She regularly presents papers at conferences such as the Society for Research into Higher Education, and has presented at the European Conference of the Association for Student Counselling. (E-mail: eokorocha@aol.com)

Renata Phelps has studied both internally and externally through three institutions over the past nine years. She completed her BA (Library and Information Science) through Charles Sturt University in 1992, and was employed at Southern Cross University library for seven years. She is now completing her Master of Distance Education through Deakin University, in which she has addressed the information needs of external tertiary education students. She is currently employed as a research assistant with the Faculty of Education, Work and Training at Southern Cross University. (E-mail: rphelps@scu.edu.au)

Maureen Pope is a chartered psychologist, and Professor and Dean of the Faculty of Education and Community Studies, University of Reading (UK). She teaches research methods on the Community Studies Masters courses and on the faculty's Higher Degrees Research Methods Programme. She has a long-standing interest in academic staff development and an international reputation in the area of personal construct psychology as applied in education and professional development in the private and public sector. She was a founder of the International Study Association on Teacher Thinking (ISATT), a convenor of the Guidance Panel for the European Personal Construct Association, and a member of the British Educational Researchers Association (BERA) and the European Association for Research on Learning and Instruction (EARLI). Her current research interests include constructive approaches to interprofessional education and student teacher stress. (E-mail: ecspopem@reading.ac.uk)

Yoni Ryan is a Senior Lecturer, Teaching and Learning Support Services, Queensland University of Technology (QUT). She has worked in staff development at QUT, teaching postgraduates in the Graduate Certificate of Higher Education, and has also had responsibility at QUT for research development of staff. She co-edited, with Professor Ortrun Zuber-Skerritt, *Quality in Postgraduate Education* (Kogan Page, 1994). (E-mail: y.ryan@qut.edu.au)

Elizabeth Sandeman-Gay is a lecturer and study skills adviser in the Learning Development Unit at the University of Wollongong, New South Wales. She has extensive experience teaching academic discourse, language and learning development and has special responsibility for international students. She sits on the university's committee for English Language Support for

International Students and has been instrumental in the development of a new Language and Learning Resource Centre. Her research interests focus on contrastive rhetoric and the genres of postgraduate writing. She is currently enrolled in an Honours Master of Education in English as a Second Language.

Jim Sillitoe is an Associate Professor at Victoria University of Technology (VUT). Having spent the past four years seconded to the Department of Education as Coordinator of Postgraduate Research Students, he has now returned to the VUT Student Learning Unit with responsibilities for undergraduate statistics and science support in addition to providing research skills development for postgraduate students. Jim supervises a number of NESB research students. As part of his university duties, he provides workshops on Concept Development for Research Programmes for staff and research students through the Office for Research at VUT. (E-mail: jimsillitoe@vut.edu.au)

Doug Smith is a Lecturer in Learning Assistance at the Faculty of Asian and International Studies at Griffith University. His current duties include the provision of academic support for both undergraduate and postgraduate students within the faculty. Doug's own research interests concern the role of cultures, especially those influenced by Confucianism, on reading strategies and skill formation. (E-mail: D.Smith@ais.gu.edu.au)

Helen Stacy is currently a research fellow at the Faculty of Law, Queensland University of Technology, and writes on legal theory and comparative law. She is Barrister-at-Law, South Australia, Queensland and England and Wales, and Solicitor, New South Wales. After graduating from the Law School at Adelaide University, Helen worked as a barrister for eight years, the first four years as an industrial lawyer representing Shell Australia in Melbourne, Perth and Sydney, and the last four years as a Senior Crown Prosecutor representing the Director for Public Prosecutions in London and Oxford. After returning to an academic career in Australia, she was awarded a scholarship by the Deutsche Akadamisher Ausland Dienst in 1992 to undertake doctoral studies at the Max Planck Institute for Comparative and Public International Law in Heidelberg, Germany. (E-mail: h.stacy@qut.edu.au)

Ortrun Zuber-Skerritt is an Adjunct Professor in the Faculty of Education at Griffith University. She is also an Adjunct Professor and the Director of the Institute for Workplace Research, Learning and Development (WoRLD) at Southern Cross University. She has published widely and convened many conferences on action research and postgraduate supervision in Australia, New Zealand, Europe (Austria, Sweden, UK), Hong Kong and South Africa. She is the author of Professional Development in Higher Education and Action Research in Higher Education (Kogan Page, 1992) and the editor of Frameworks in Postgraduate Education (Falmer Press, 1996). (E-mail: O.Zuber-Skerritt@mailbox.uq.edu.au)

Acknowledgements

As usual, in our previous publications on supervising postgraduate students, we gratefully acknowledge the insights we have gained from our students and the colleagues who have contributed both directly and indirectly to the present volume.

Thanks are also due to WoRLD Institute, Southern Cross University, and the Queensland section of the Staff Development Consortium for their initial support of this publication. It should be noted that the following chapters benefit from being read in conjunction with the video series (Series IV) on 'Supervision of Postgraduate Students from Non-English Speaking Backgrounds' – Chapters 2 (Video 2), 3 (Video 2), 5 (Video 2), 6 (Video 1), 8 (Video 6), and 11 (Video 5). Details on obtaining the videos are available from Pam Price, GCM, Southern Cross University, Lismore NSW 2480 Australia, fax: 617 266 212 717, E-mail: pprice@scu.edu.au. Earlier print publications in this series on postgraduate supervision are *Manuals 1* (Ryan and Zuber-Skerritt 1998a), *2* (Ryan and Zuber-Skerritt 1998b), *3* (Ryan *et al.* 1998a) and *4* (Ryan *et al.* 1998b), which may be obtained from the same address.

We also thank Erica Maddock, who prepared the manuscript with her usual meticulousness and patience.

Introduction

1

Supervising Non-English Speaking Background Students in the Globalized University

Yoni Ryan and Ortrun Zuber-Skerritt

Amongst the multitude of pressures operating on and within the university sector worldwide as we enter the new millennium, the supervision of postgraduate research students from non-English speaking backgrounds (NESB) has received, thus far, only scattered attention. Concern has been expressed by a handful of academics involved with such students, and sometimes from the international offices of universities. However, we confidently predict that this collection presages a sharper focus on the complex issues involved in the supervision of non-English speaking background postgraduates. There are many factors which have contributed to the numbers of NESB students studying in English language university systems.

External pressures on English language universities

External pressures on universities have led to strong growth in the numbers of postgraduate NESB students in the major education-provider countries – the USA, UK, Canada, Australia and New Zealand. Those external pressures include:

- the universal demand for higher education in the late twentieth century, and the subsequent move from elite to mass university sectors in all developed countries at the undergraduate level, with subsequent flow-on effects to postgraduate studies;
- the reduction in public funding to universities in major Western economies, with a consequent search by universities for alternative revenue sources, one of these being non-national, full fee-paying students;
- the challenges of communication and information technologies and the incorporation of these into teaching and learning practices; and

- the growing significance of lifelong learning, leading to an increased demand for postgraduate research studies.

More general trends have also catalysed the growth in numbers of NESB students in Western countries:

- large-scale international migration, with subsequent large NESB populations in most developed economies – in the UK from Commonwealth countries, in the US from Asia and South America, especially Spanish/Portuguese-speaking countries, in Australia from South East Asia. These populations are drawn from cultures which place a high value on education;
- a globalized economy, which stresses both the exchange of goods and services, and the frequent movement of staff in organizations with world-wide representation;
- the recognition of English as a global language (Crystal 1996); and
- within globalizing tendencies, the emergence of aggressive regional blocs encouraging cross-national migration and cooperation, e.g. the European Union (EU), the North American Free Trade Association (NAFTA) and the Association of South East Asian Nations (ASEAN).

The internationalization of universities

Universities have, of course, always been international, both in their focus and in their populations, attracting travelling scholars who communicated in what was then the *lingua franca* of the educated, Latin. Even as the nature of the university changed to accommodate a greater emphasis on applied research and distinctive *national* responsibilities for higher education, universities did not lose this international focus. 'New' universities have appointed visitors and advisers to ensure their programmes are of 'university standard', implying a recognizable universal level of quality. To facilitate international standards, they have encouraged staff mobility and exchanges. The 'great' universities have always attracted research students worldwide – in the UK from Commonwealth countries and beyond; in the US from its spheres of influence. However, those students have generally been the elite of their home countries, educated in English in International Schools or other selective schools.

The international movement of students has now moved into the realm of a 'business'. Newly developed or developing countries have struggled to provide higher education facilities in their own countries, hampered by the high infrastructure costs of establishing universities, and the difficulty of meeting demands from their burgeoning middle class. For example, Malaysia, until the 1997 currency crisis, 'exported' 55,000 students and A$1 billion per year to meet its population's demands for post-secondary education and English language training. The Malaysian government's alarm at this annual outflow led it to commit to four new universities and to extensive 'twinning' arrangements with Australian and UK universities to develop 'satellite campuses' of established universities in Malaysia. Thailand too has entered such arrangements, through joint ventures such as the Asian University of Science and Technology, a private English-language university under the auspices of the Imperial College of Science, Technology and Medicine, London. Such institutions are of course, often staffed by native English speakers. In the case of the Asian University of Science and Technology, expatriate staff will constitute 70 per cent of staff numbers. Such expatriates will face a student body of second-language English speakers.

Distance learning has also expanded the number of NESB postgraduate students, the majority in coursework programmes, and an increasing number in research programmes, sometimes after a period of residence at a host institution in an English speaking country.

It is difficult as yet to extricate the numbers of research NESB students in Western universities through aggregated statistics. One reason for this is the problematic nature of the definition of 'NESB'. It is commonly assumed that all international students within a Western university are of non-English speaking background. Hence aggregated statistics in Australia, for example, detail 'overseas students by country and level of enrolment', but not home language; or 'non-overseas students by home language', but not level of enrolment. Yet international students may derive from another English speaking country (e.g. of Australia's 4000+ overseas postgraduate students, nearly 500 are from the UK). International students may have English as L1 (first home language), or may be fluent L2 English speakers. Equally, as a consequence of international migration, 'local' students may not have English as a first language, but may be well acculturated into local educational norms and practices. Such students may have markedly different problems in their research programmes, e.g. working in a family business while studying. In this book, the term NESB generally connotes international students with English as L2, but the situation of local NESB students is acknowledged as requiring fuller attention.

The magnitude of NESB research students' contribution to university income can be perceived through some broad indicative figures. Some 18,000 UK university students are EU citizens, but they represent only 42 per cent of overseas students in the UK, with 31 per cent of such students coming from Commonwealth countries (*Times Higher Education Supplement*, 16 May 1997, p. 5). Student exchange programmes like ERASMUS in the EU, and UMAP (University Mobility in the Asia Pacific) enhance these figures. Back *et al.* (1996), quoting Blight, estimate that international students studying out of country will amount to 1.78 million by 2000, up from 1.49 million in 1995, with a large proportion of these studying in English-language systems. In 1998, the UK, USA and Australia are the three dominant destinations for international students, and competition between the three is intense among less prestigious research institutions, since Oxford, Cambridge, Stanford, Harvard and Berkeley still predominate at the elite level. James and Beattie (1995) note that there has been 84 per cent growth in international Masters numbers in Australian universities between 1988 and 1994, and 117 per cent growth in PhD numbers in the same period. In Australia in 1996, overseas course completions included 851 research Masters and doctorates compared to 3548 coursework postgraduates, i.e. approximately 20 per cent of postgraduate overseas students are research students (*Selected Higher Education Student Statistics*, 1997). While not all of these students are fee-paying – Australia, like other Western countries, sponsors exchange and scholarship programmes – it is obvious that such numbers contribute heavily to the income of the university sector. Since the introduction of a full-fee regime for postgraduate overseas students in 1985 in Australia, the cost to students has grown to an average of A\$14 000 p.a., a substantial premium to the government-funded cost for citizens. The dependence of Western universities on NESB research students for income can only increase.

Main issues

Such patterns must give pause to those involved in supervision and university administration. The issues involved in supervision of NESB students can be categorized into three major areas: institutional, pedagogic and personal.

At the institutional level, universities must deal with both policies and practicalities associated with the entrance of NESB research students. These encompass the legal consequences of marketing and recruiting practices, the facilities provided to students to accommodate different religious and cultural practices, supplementary courses for English language training and other ancillary services such as computer training, as well as what universities offer, in competitive terms, regarding 'value for money'. As is evident in the present book, universities have adopted a variety of strategies to accommodate the learning and social needs of their NESB research students, ranging from integrated academic skills programmes to 'stand alone' 'pay-for-service' supplementary courses. Despite such institutional procedures and policies, there is much anecdotal evidence that international and NESB students are increasingly critical of their study experiences, particularly the discrepancies between marketing promises and the practical capacity of institutions to deliver on these (and see Stacy in this volume for the legal consequences of this).

At country level, most university-wide advisory bodies have introduced (non-enforceable) codes of conduct for international activities. For example, the Australian Vice-Chancellors' Committee has a Code of Ethical Practice. All Australian universities provide English language, academic bridging and study methods courses. However, the Back *et al.* report (1996) reveals wide variations in the quality and integration of such courses into both coursework and research programmes.

Pedagogic concerns are uppermost in the minds of supervisors. They range from possibly inadequate linguistic skills in English, culturally-based conceptualizations of knowledge and consequent learning styles, inculcation into the disciplinary discourse and poor disciplinary preparation (Felix and

Lawson 1994), to differing expectations of the roles of student and supervisor. There is for many supervisors the additional complication of a lack of understanding of the many varied cultures from which their students derive, and the effect of these on the student–supervisor relationship.

Few rigorous ethnographic studies of comparative learning styles have as yet emerged in the literature of higher education. The present volume canvasses research with African, Iranian and Chinese students. Further work obviously remains to be conducted with students of other cultures. Our experience, and the experience of our contributors, has in the main been with students from what Biggs (1996a: 46) calls 'Confucian-heritage cultures', broadly, students from East and South East Asia: China, Taiwan, Singapore, Hong Kong, Japan and Korea (*Campus Review*, 27 May–2 June 1998, p. 2). This reflects the demographics of international students in Australian universities: Australia's five major source countries for international students are Singapore, South Korea, Hong Kong, Malaysia and Indonesia. The last two are not of course Confucian, but entering students from those countries are in fact often ethnic Chinese, because of particular social and educational policies in those countries. Indeed, 40 per cent of all international students in Australia are Chinese (*Campus Review*, 24–30 September 1997). The limitations of generalizing on the basis of Confucian heritage are acknowledged, and it is of course imperative that national and individual influences on learning styles are taken into account.

At the personal level, which can never be ignored in the learning environment, there are issues for student and supervisor – ensuring students are relatively 'comfortable' in their cultural and social milieu, that 'body language' misunderstandings are minimized and do not interfere in the student–supervisor relationship, and that the personal 'match' between student and supervisor is productive. Choi (1997), for example, explains that in Korea, the formal instructor–learner relationship is expected to develop through the duration of study into a deeper mentor relationship, almost parental in its nature, partly because students and staff live in close proximity on many campuses. Yet many Western supervisors resist such a relationship as unprofessional: Channel (quoted in Choi 1997) reports supervisors complaining that NESB students are 'over-demanding and overly dependent'. Clarification of the expectations of each party in the student–supervisor relationship is clearly necessary.

About this book

The present volume arose from a staff development conference held in Ballina, New South Wales, in 1996 (Ryan *et al.* 1998b). The conference was intended to assist supervisors of NESB research students to develop personal strategies for supervision, and to exchange institutional approaches. The organizers had recognized that there was a dearth of information on supervision of NESB students, other than surveys of student perceptions of their experiences, and the few excellent books directed primarily at students, such as that by Ballard and Clanchy (1991). Hence the contributors to the present volume are largely practitioners who have grappled with the issues presented by supervising NESB students; in many cases, they have used a focused qualitative approach based on content analyses of in-depth interviews conducted at their own institutions, and drawing on a range of discipline areas: education, sociology, linguistics, organizational behaviour and cultural studies. They often take, as in the case studies and survey chapters, a 'storied' approach from which principles of practice may be derived, i.e. theirs are descriptive theories. Hence the focus is not on cross-cultural learning *per se*, as in the Watkins and Biggs (1996) collection, but on contextual issues which affect the NESB student, the supervisor and the institution. These contextual issues will differ from discipline to discipline (Becher 1989), institution to institution (research-oriented 'established' universities vs. 'new' universities), country to country, and of course for individual students and supervisors.

Nevertheless, we believe that elucidation of the issues will alert readers to question their own circumstances. The contributors offer a variety of perspectives and strategies which should prove useful to university management, international officers, individual staff involved in the postgraduate education of research students from non-English speaking backgrounds, and students themselves. Some of these issues are not confined to the supervision of NESB research students: several of our authors argue that the principles of good supervision span cultural considerations. There are some excellent studies, e.g. Zuber-Skerritt and Ryan (1994), Cryer (1996b), Phillips and Pugh (1994), which argue that mutual knowledge and respect between student and supervisor are the touchstone of good supervisory practices. However, the standard desiderata of the supervisory relationship are intensified when language and cultural differences complicate communication.

The structure of this book

Part 1, 'The NESB Student: What's the Difference?', is a sequence of case studies and personal stories which illustrate the difficulties faced by students in unfamiliar research contexts. These are presented first to direct the reader's focus onto the student both as individual and 'cultural construct'. It should not be forgotten however, that supervisors, while institutional representatives, are also individuals constructed by their cultures. McMichael's (1993) study, for example, refers to his earlier research with Scottish supervisors who displayed very different attitudes and behaviours to students destined to return to prestigious careers in their countries compared to more 'ordinary' or less ambitious students.

In Chapter 2, Japanese Yuriko Nagata compares her postgraduate research experience in two countries, the US and Australia, and demonstrates how motivation, life experience and self-confidence intertwine to contribute to student attitudes and approaches to research study. In Chapter 3, Aspland details the pedagogical alienation experienced by a Chinese PhD student paired with a supervisor who had little empathy with her learning style and her personal situation. Mei's story illuminates the personal pain student–supervisor mismatch can cause, and demonstrates that sometimes changing supervisors is the only solution. Chapter 4 by Sandeman-Gay takes us to another culture – the Middle East. It examines the pedagogic and cultural expectations of several Iranian students, and the importance of mutual respect between student and supervisor. Finally, Geake and Maingard (Chapter 5) relate the efforts of a very new, non-metropolitan Australian university to accommodate the social and language needs of its fee-paying NESB students, and those students' responses to university research in a country town. It is a salutary lesson that the diversity of NESB students is matched by the variety of institutional settings in which students are placed: regional cultures inform the research climate in which students operate. It also supports the observation by McMichael (1993) that supervisors in new universities have a high level of anxiety about the adequacy of research infrastructure in their institutions, and the time they too have available for good research.

Part 2, 'Examining the Issues', takes an international perspective, and should be of particular interest to university managers and recruitment officers. It includes an introduction to the psychological and educational difficulties experienced by students and supervisors in the British context (Chapter 6 by Denicolo and Pope), and an examination of the legal and ethical dimensions in enrolling NESB fee-paying students, drawing on Australian, UK and US legal precedents (Chapter 7 by Stacy).

Part 3, 'Establishing Some Principles for Effective Supervision', deals with principles of effective supervision in relation to NESB students. Chapter 8 by Knight examines the responsibilities and limits of supervision, particularly in relation to the editing process which is crucial to successful thesis writing in the social sciences. Chapter 9 by Frost is particularly significant since the vast majority of overseas research students are enrolled in engineering/surveying and the sciences (*Selected Higher Education Student Statistics* 1997), a reflection of the science facilities available and the more globalized career structure open to research scientists than to social science graduates. Frost argues that while NESB students have many of the same difficulties as English language students, they can benefit from the large numbers of NESB students in strong science research centres with generous funding arrangements and a recognized research programme. Becher's (1989) study, although confined to elite research institutions in the UK and US, demonstrated the importance of epistemological differences in research paradigms, and these are highlighted in the Knight and Frost chapters.

Chapter 10 by Cryer and Okorocha explores differences in styles of teaching and learning, and cultural views of time, personal space and culturally acceptable social behaviour, as well as the influence of religious practices and non-verbal communication. As argued above, institutional support structures, including the design of research programmes in academic writing and research skills, are a major component of support for the NESB student; one successful approach is the focus of Chapter 11 by Farquhar.

Part 4, 'Practical Responses', details particular strategies which have been successful with NESB research students. Although this section posits a number of strategies which institutions and individual supervisors can adopt to assist NESB students, it should not be assumed that the chapters in this and other sections originate from what has been criticized as the 'deficit model' of NESB students (Volet and Renshaw 1996; Volet and Ang 1998), the implication that non-Western models of teaching and learning are inferior and/or must be adjusted to Western modes of thinking and researching. Indeed, as the chapters in Part 1 suggest, institutions, supervisors and English speaking students can all learn from the different approaches of NESB students, to internationalize curricula. As Cryer and Okorocha argue here, 'the key . . . lies in mutual understanding'.

Ellis and Phelps, in Chapter 12, canvass the potential of information technology to assist NESB students, both in their research and their social linkages. It is often argued (e.g. Felix and Lawson 1994) that critical thinking is integral to the Western intellectual tradition, but is not a feature of many other, more traditional learning cultures, with consequent difficulties for NESB research students. Choi (1997), for example, explains that criticism in the Korean context is constrained by the necessity to maintain 'social harmony' within a formal relationship between student and supervisor, and to avoid a student 'losing face'. Smith in Chapter 13 argues that culture affects reading practices, with students from Confucian backgrounds reading for ethical and historical outcomes, while Western university research programmes expect critical and knowledge-accretion outcomes. He outlines a reading programme which can assist NESB students in adjusting to a different paradigm. Nurturing critical thinking is the subject of Chapter 14 by Bruce and Brameld.

Chapter 15 by Sillitoe and Crosling confronts the problem of unconventional discourse structures consequent on cultural patterns of thinking and academic conventions, and outlines a graphic strategy to clarify thinking in a Western discourse through concept mapping.

Conclusions

Several themes such as the robust tradition of debate in the Western research tradition, the Confucian respect for authority and problems posed by different conceptions of personal space recur throughout the chapters of this book. In our editing role, we chose not to eliminate these, since their repetition in different institutional and research settings will assist the reader to reconstruct the world of the NESB student, varied as that is. It should be noted that the identities of individuals, whether students or supervisors, have been disguised in this book, except where explicit permission was sought and given for publication.

Although it is conceded that many of our NESB students are migrant-nationals, it is increasingly the case that our institutions rely on international student fees for supplementary income. Many supervisors feel somewhat compromised by the commercial aspects of their teaching in this situation, and this issue is not ignored by our contributors. Many would argue that their primary motivations in supervising NESB students are expanding discipline knowledge as well as international tolerance. Our institutions have, nevertheless, particular responsibilities and ethical requirements in the context of the globalized market for higher education. However, our contributors are testimony to the fact that for most supervisors, non-English speaking background students provide challenges which have expanded both their own cultural understandings and those of their students, and contributed to knowledge creation – the real 'business' of universities.

Part 1

The NESB Student: What's the Difference?

Part 1

2

'Once I couldn't even spell "PhD student", but now I *are* one!': Personal Experiences of an NESB student

Yuriko Nagata

Introduction

The purpose of this chapter is to discuss my own experiences as an NESB student and to make observations and comments on issues concerning NESB postgraduate students. I have obtained two higher degrees, a Masters in Applied Linguistics in America, and a PhD in History in Australia, both English-speaking countries.

NESB postgraduate students are a diverse group. They range from overseas students who stay in the country only for the duration of their study to those who are migrants. Their motivations vary greatly. Some are sent by governments and are fully sponsored, while others are self-funded without any organizational back-up from their own country. I spent two years as a self-funded international student in the United States, while in Australia I was a permanent resident and was already employed in the university system.

This chapter is presented in two parts. First I discuss my United States experience to focus on two issues – motivation and alienation. In the second part, I discuss my PhD experience in Australia and make observations on research skills and language issues.

American experience

I was born in Japan and received all of my early education up to my first degree there. I studied English from the age of twelve, but by the time I finished my first degree, even after ten years of English language education, my English skills were still minimal. In 1973 I decided to go to America to improve my English as well as my qualifications and took an English language proficiency test called the TOEFL (Test of English as a Foreign Language) which is widely used to decide whether overseas applicants have the required level of English skills. I applied for a two-year coursework Masters in Applied Linguistics at the University of Indiana. It required a TOEFL score of 550 to enter (TOEFL scores range from 200 to 677). The TOEFL entry score varied from programme to programme and from institution to institution. One university required 600 for a similar programme to the one I was interested in. My score was just over 500 but, to my surprise, I was accepted on the condition that I would be given an oral interview by an admission officer upon arrival.

At the interview, I was trying to give a good impression to the admission officer in accordance with how I would normally behave in front of a person of authority in Japan – that is, 'Be polite, say little and accept authority.' I apologized to him for my poor language skills. His decision was that I should attend classes on campus for a term to improve my English before starting the coursework. After a month or so, I found that the classes were not helping me at all. They were for general-purpose English and had no focus. I felt I was wasting my time. I thought I needed to improve my language in the academic context and went to discuss this with the same admission officer. I was more assertive than the previous time. He said, 'You speak English all right. If you had spoken like you are now when you arrived, I would have accepted you in the programme straight away.' This incident made me realize that my approach to authority might work in my own cultural environment, but had worked against me in the American system. It was a true culture shock.

The programme I enrolled in had students of many different nationalities – one Iranian, one Turk, two Thais, two Japanese, one Indian, one Filipina, one Malaysian, one Chinese from Singapore, two Germans and one Zambian. There were only three Americans. Among the international group, the Iranian, Turk, Thais, Japanese and Germans were NESB students, while the rest were educated in English and had no language problems.

Most of the students lived in the university's postgraduate hall of residence, which some American students referred to as the 'foreign ghetto' because of the high proportion of international students. However, for many of us the place provided a feeling of being at home with students from other countries. This type of accommodation can be of great benefit during the initial settling-down period. It functioned as a place for socializing and networking, not only within national groups, but also between different groups. Most of the people in the programme stayed in this hall. After a while some found cheaper places off campus, while others remained in the residence for the entire period. Some avoided this type of accommodation out of a belief that it didn't help their language improvement.

Although I managed most subjects, in the early days I struggled with subjects which relied heavily on essay assignments. In addition to the obvious lack of general language skills, my difficulty was largely due to a lack of training in writing essays during my undergraduate studies in Japan. My first few essays were returned with comments such as 'Not acceptable', or

'Too descriptive, where is your argument?' I was unable to conceptualize what I was reading and to form arguments, therefore I relied heavily on the original text for the body of the essay. In so doing, I was plagiarizing without knowing it was wrong.

The programme had a good infrastructure for supporting overseas students. There was an adviser specially assigned to deal with overseas students who were having difficulty in their studies and life in general. He advised me to improve in two areas – referencing and paragraphing. This benefited me enormously in both the short and long terms. Along with my general language proficiency, my essay-writing skills improved over the two years and I was getting good marks for essays in some subjects towards the end of the degree. The subjects I was doing well in were the ones I had a strong interest in, and where I was able to approach the topic more critically. In the end, I was able to conceptualize what I was reading and use my own words to make more sense. In hindsight, the so-called introductory subjects are perhaps harder to handle, as they are unfocused and superficially cover a wide range of topics. They rely on a higher level of language skills – paraphrasing, decoding and synthesizing.

Another difficult area was discussion. There were no straight lectures and all classes were of the lecture/tutorial style. Among the NESB students, the Germans were very good at English and as outspoken as most Americans. In general, the Asian and African students were quiet, but the Malaysian and Filipina were very good at expressing themselves when needed. The Iranian tried hard in discussions. He was much older than the others and not so good at English. I used to feel sorry for him because the lecturer used to interrupt him, as he often didn't make much sense when he spoke. Of all the students, the quietest were Thai and Japanese.

I wanted to join in discussions like the others, but used to get so nervous that my body shook. In my mind I was fully engaged in the discussion and had something to say, but feared making a fool of myself in front of the class. 'Have I understood what's been said? Is my question too obvious? Am I on the right track? Am I going to get stuck halfway? Am I going to make a grammatical error?' Usually I missed the moment and never got around to saying a word. My Thai friends were different from me in this aspect. They weren't even interested in trying to say anything. They thought speaking up or arguing with the lecturer in class was not the right behaviour.

Discussion in a foreign language requires a high level of aural–oral skills, including good comprehension, confidence and the ability to use common expressions and a range of vocabulary. The bigger the discussion group gets, the harder it becomes. You have to know when and where to put your first words in. This is a difficult skill for anyone, regardless of whether they are NESB or not. You have to have the right personality backed by language skills. My Chinese friend used to say to me, 'Why try so hard to speak in class? You don't achieve anything by doing that. Just be yourself.'

Conversely, one lecturer used to say, 'Why don't you say anything?' Many of us thought what he said was offensive. We decided to let him know, so we sent our Filipina friend. She told him that being quiet does not mean that we were not thinking. He apologized to us.

I used to suffer from my own double perception of myself – the mature, socially functioning person in my native language and the incompetent non-communicator in the target language. Mary Farquhar (1996) expressed this well at a conference when she described how she felt when she was a student in China – 'If you don't have command of the language, you don't have a personality.'

Apart from the Indian and Japanese students, the rest were all government-sponsored and intended to go back to their countries where jobs were already arranged. Many of them were already university teachers. My Thai friends were married and often got homesick. They did everything together and were not interested in mixing with the American students. The Singaporean was the same, and was counting the days until he could go back to his job. The Malaysian student had his family with him on campus and always looked secure. He was an official of the Ministry of Education at home and was in the US for a very specific reason. The socio-linguists, Gardner and Lambert (1972), describe this type of motivation for being in a foreign country as instrumental. The purpose of study reflects more utilit-arian values, such as being primarily interested in getting a qualification from the institution. Others are more intrinsically motivated. They wish to learn more about the other community's culture because they are interested in it in an open-minded way. I was, perhaps, one of the few in the pro-gramme who was, in Gardner and Lambert's term, intrinsically motivated.

Life on campus is often very limited and isolated from the rest of the world. I was interested in getting out to the local community outside the university campus. In my second year I did some babysitting work for the parents of a two-year-old girl. My job was to give her lunch at 12 o'clock, take her for a walk and put her to bed for a nap. I enjoyed this routine and above all the responsibility. I got to know her parents well and they opened the door to ordinary American life. Through them I signed up as a volunteer with a welfare/educational programme called Headstart. It was a type of pre-school for children with learning difficulties. I was matched with a five-year-old boy called Tom, who would not speak. These off-campus activities created a sense of living, helped my confidence and, most importantly, made me feel I was not a 'nobody'.

Overall, my experiences in the United States were a success. I became confident in English and completed the course. In hindsight, the overall confidence I gained in living in a foreign country helped to improve my study performance. I was able to go home with a Masters degree which eventually opened up more opportunities in later years.

Australian experience

I migrated to Australia after marrying an Australian in 1980. My first job was as a Japanese teacher in a state high school in Adelaide. In 1982 I became a full-time tutor in Japanese at the University of Adelaide. In 1984 I decided to pursue further studies because I was supposed to be doing research and, in addition, I needed to be familiar with the research culture in order to function effectively in the university community. I decided to enrol in the Masters Qualifying course in the Department of History of the University of Adelaide. Although I already held a Masters degree, it was a coursework Masters and I was not ready for a degree based on research. Also, my research interest had shifted from linguistics to history since my last degree. Unlike my experience in the United States, my admission into the course was handled via the normal procedure applied to Australian citizens, as I was a permanent resident. There was no check on my English proficiency.

In Australian universities, English language requirements for international students are usually checked by TOEFL or IELTS (the International English Language Testing System). While TOEFL is an American test, IELTS is a British system which is widely recognized as a language requirement for entry to all courses in further and higher education. There are nine bands for the overall score and for individual modules – listening, reading, writing and speaking. TOEFL also has a writing component called TWE (Test of Written English) and a speaking test (TSE – Test of Spoken English), which did not exist when I did the test.

If I had been an international student wishing to study at the University of Queensland, for example, I would have needed Band 6.5 for the overall IELTS and Band 6 for writing, or 550 for the overall TOEFL and Band 5 for TWE. According to the *IELTS Handbook* (1996: 26), the interpretation of Band 6.5 falls somewhere between 'Good User' and 'Competent User'. For a definition of terms, refer to Table 11.1 in Chapter 11 of this volume.

TWE scores are also reported on a scale of one to six. Band 5 is explained as follows:

> Band 5: Demonstrates competence in writing on both the rhetorical and syntactic levels, though the essay will probably have occasional errors.

(Bulletin of Information for TOEFL 1996–7: 31)

It is interesting to note that the English requirements are the same for *all* applicants, regardless of whether they are undergraduates or postgraduates, and also that the requirements for research students are slightly lower. Overall, IELTS for research students is Band 6 – 0.5 lower than for coursework or undergraduate students. There seems to be more flexibility in English requirements, particularly at PhD level. Admission is normally decided at the discretion of the department concerned. If the prospective candidate has a good publication record, but has a lower level of English skills, he or she is likely to be accepted (Thwaite and Bonney 1996, personal communication, 21 August). Never at any point in the procedure for admission, nor in the application form, was I asked about English language skills. In one way I had passed the English test together with the assessment of my academic qualifications when I was interviewed for the tutor's job.

The contents of the Masters Qualifying course were arranged to suit my needs. The Department suggested that I complete one undergraduate subject in Japanese history, do two research papers on Australian history and attend a postgraduate seminar on historiography. This gave me a good orientation and introduction to research methods and further training in academic writing. After the Masters Qualifying, I progressed to a part-time thesis-based Masters. Some of my colleagues thought that it was a waste of time to do a Masters and that I should upgrade to a PhD. However, my supervisor and I felt that I was on the right course. For me, the idea of a PhD was frightening – to use Hodge's expression, an 'impossible standard of scholarly rigour' (Hodge 1995: 35).

Five years later, I completed the Masters thesis and it was examined by two examiners. It came back with two recommendations – I could be awarded a Masters or I could expand and upgrade it to a doctorate. By then I had moved to the University of Queensland as a lecturer on a tenure track. This was during the period of rapid growth in Japanese studies in Australia and obtaining a PhD degree was given high priority for academic staff. The idea of a doctorate was a realistic option and no longer a frightening one. I decided to take up the latter recommendation.

In fact, the basic research standards and expectations for both degrees – Masters or PhD – are about the same. The *Postgraduate Information Handbook* (n.d.) of the Department of Asian Languages and Studies at the University of Queensland, for example, states:

> The main criteria are the same as those for the PhD, including the originality requirement; a greater level of originality and contribution to knowledge is expected of a PhD. Whereas a PhD thesis has at least three examiners, a Masters has two, one external to the university and one internal . . .

It is extremely difficult to quantify what is 'greater'. The difference seems to be arbitrary. My Masters thesis was original enough and contributed to knowledge by new discoveries. What it lacked was that it was not substantial enough for the award of a PhD. I expanded the 57,000-word thesis to 90,000 words and two years later I completed it. In terms of research, my doctorate thesis virtually grew out of my Masters. This meant that my research topic was, perhaps, potentially doctoral. In hindsight I could have done the research for a PhD right from the start as my colleagues suggested. However, a thesis is a process as well as an end product. The process from Masters Qualifying to the PhD was one continuous progression in which I acquired skills both as a researcher and as an academic in the Australian higher education system. More rewardingly, I improved my academic writing. I appreciated this gradual process – which is, perhaps, the only way for people like myself who are NESB, work full-time and have family commitments. The pre-doctoral nature of a Masters should be considered more as a viable step for both NESB or non-NESB candidates who are not quite ready for a PhD.

There is an interesting case where one Japanese overseas student was refused permission to enrol in a PhD programme in history, even though he had obtained first-class Honours in history with the same department. His application was refused on the grounds that his English was not good enough. His supervisor was reluctant to accept him, as his English skills were assessed as inadequate and the supervisor would not be able to spend enough time in correcting his English. He also thought the student lacked skills in conceptualizing issues from wider contexts. He was accepted into the research Masters.

I retained my original supervisor right from when I started to study for my Masters until I completed my PhD. The fact that I was already teaching in the university may have affected our relationship. It was more of a colleague-to-colleague one. His role was a combination of 'adviser', 'critic', 'freedom giver' and 'supporter'. He didn't require me to have regular meetings: I went to see him when I needed his advice. In 1996 I had a conversation with him during which he made comments which I would summarize as follows:

> In recent years a lot of rules have been introduced about postgraduate supervision. It is expected these days that supervision be more regular. It seems to me that the less personal supervision becomes, the more it relies on routine and rules. I want students to think about what they want from me as a supervisor. This is important. Everyone has a different approach.
>
> (Gammage 1996, personal communication, 18 August)

I asked him what I was like to supervise:

> You always came to me with a list of questions and when you got the answers, that was the end of the session. Sometimes you didn't come back for months after that.

On reflection, my questions were often of a technical nature and perhaps I would have benefited more from discussion with him on theoretical issues. However, as a full-time teacher myself, I was always conscious of his time and mine. I was given much of the control and planning for the research and he supported my decisions. Once I got into the stage of submitting draft chapters, our communication was basically by writing. I read his corrections and suggestions on the draft, rewrote the sections of the draft and resubmitted. It was effective and, in fact, I was able to concentrate more on his comments when they were written.

When I submitted a draft chapter, I always had the English checked so that my supervisor was able to concentrate on the actual content. I consider English checking is not the job of a supervisor and also feel it is not right to ask the supervisor to do work which could be done by others. But still the chapter always came back with a lot of corrections to my English. He was strict about clarity and disliked repetition of any kind.

In the course of writing the thesis, my writing style was naturally influenced by my sources, as my thesis was based on both written records and oral interviews in English, Japanese and some Chinese. My translations from Japanese, in particular, needed a lot of rewriting. At the same time, some Australian government correspondence files had a very bad influence on my writing, as they were full of long-winded and ambiguous sentences!

Many NESB postgraduate students rely on the assistance of native speakers of English to check their English. The *Postgraduate Information Handbook* of the Department of Asian Languages and Studies at the University of Queensland states:

> Where English is the student's second language, it is the student's responsibility to see that final drafts are proofread by native speakers. Members of the Department are willing to help with this when requested.

Australian universities generally offer such services free of charge; however, such services are often not readily available when you need them. The Careers and Counselling Service of the University of Queensland has a learning assistance unit where three full-time staff are available to a student population of 25,000. Of these three, one works specifically with postgraduate students (Samuelowicz 1996, personal communication, 20 August). Some students will make personal arrangements with friends and family members who are native speakers of English, while others pay professionals for such services. I am fortunate that I have a personal resident proofreader – my husband. My supervisor commented:

> I have supervised many postgraduate research students, mostly Australians who are native speakers of English, but not necessarily native writers of English. Even being native writers of English doesn't mean they are good writers. Some of them used the university's remedial English service, not for grammar checking, but for sentence organization, clarity, etc. This kind of service is essential to have an effective postgraduate program.

The 'language problems' of NESB research students are not necessarily the kind of language skills which are assessed by English language proficiency testing. These tests tend to assess passive use of language. Test scores do not really tell whether one can do research and write a thesis on it. My supervisor further commented:

> The real test is whether one has got a research method or research skills in his/her discipline. This can be said for both groups. The so-called 'English problems' are secondary to the real problem at PhD level.

There are discourse patterns and conventions characteristic of each disciplinary field. Samuelowicz (1996, personal communication, 20 August) from the Careers and Counselling Service of the University of Queensland commented:

The so-called 'English problem' is often beyond language. We deal with students across disciplines and sometimes there is a limit to how much we can help. They have to learn themselves about conventions common to their field of study. The problem in academic writing is not unique to NESB students. Our services are used by everyone.

She stressed the importance of checking the student's writing skills at as early a stage of his or her candidature as possible.

Language skills are environmentally bound. English assistance would, perhaps, be most effective if offered at a faculty level. Students benefit more if it is given in context and is more focused. Language acquisition cannot be separated from the overall development which NESB students need to make in other areas such as research skills, social contacts and relationships with native speakers. They need time to adjust not only to the culture of Australia, but also to the culture of Australian academia.

Conclusion

Australia, like other major education-provider countries, is increasingly looking to the enrolment of fee-paying overseas students. Armitage (1996) reports that 'overseas student numbers on the whole doubled every year between 1987 and 1990, and have doubled again since, growing at 40 per cent a year, on average, for the past seven years'. There are now more than 57,000 overseas students in Australian universities comprising 10 per cent of students. Of those, more than 85 per cent are Asian.

No matter how qualified applicants are on paper, overseas students bring 'problems' with them. The host institution, in one sense, inherits the 'problems' from the students' home country – English language skills and cultural differences. However, not all overseas students are in the NESB category, or vice versa. Some are from countries such as Singapore, Malaysia and India, where English is used as the medium of education, while others, like myself, study English as a foreign language. Armitage (1996) claims that 'lecturers do not usually know which of their students are international fee-payers and which are not. On top of the overseas contingent, a further 15 per cent of students are from non-English speaking backgrounds.' Biggs (1996c: 12), Visiting Professor of Education at the University of Sydney, warns us not to stereotype Asian students. He further asserts:

Of course, many international students experience cultural adjustment and language problems, and to the extent that they do, they have a right to expect institutional help. But let these particular issues be the focus of special intervention, not interventions based on exaggerated assertions on how they are inherently different from other students.

Enhanced understanding of the issues surrounding the supervision of NESB postgraduate students in many ways improves postgraduate supervision in general. I feel my experience as an NESB student benefits me in my current role as an NESB supervisor. I endorse Moses' (1984) approach to supervision. She stresses the importance of tailoring supervision to the needs of the individual postgraduate student: 'The starting point for each individual student is different: thus the supervisory process must differ for different students. It is the outcome that counts – the independent researcher.'

When I look back over the years of effort, pain, loneliness and intermittent success I have had as an NESB student, I regret that there were relatively few of the services that are available now. I benefited from the help of some good people, but would have found the whole process much easier if there had been clearer signposts for NESB students. Vague feelings of disquiet and guilt plague students who do not feel in control of their own work. By giving targeted help to these students, they can be empowered to control their own educational progress. Legitimate and justifiable language assistance can be one such crucial service. However, there are still supervisors who have reservations about such language services because they think the work is not the student's own. As long as this perception persists, NESB students will be handicapped and discriminated against on campus. As the number and proportion of NESB students increases, we will have to take further steps to accept them as part of the mainstream of an education system which is already multicultural.

Acknowledgements

I owe special thanks to the following people who agreed to be interviewed for this article: Associate Professor Bill Gammage of the University of Adelaide; Katherine Samuelowicz, Adviser, Learning Assistance Unit of the University of Queensland; and Gail Thwaite and Jenny Bonney of the International Student Office of the University of Queensland.

3

'You learn round and I learn square': Mei's Story

Tania Aspland

Introduction

This chapter is part of a long-term study of overseas women undergoing thesis supervision across three Australian universities. One of the major purposes of the study is to theorize the ambiguities, dilemmas and contestations that evolved for each student as she engaged in the pedagogical processes of supervision. The chapter opens windows into the world of Mei, one of these students.

Mei's story has been drawn from the wider study that was shaped by a methodology drawing on phenomenology, the work of symbolic interactionists and critical ethnography, particularly the feminist work of Dorothy Smith (1990). The study required a methodology that was responsive to each woman's cultural and political positioning in the complex, changing and contradictory patterns of supervisory relations over the three-year period. What emerged was a methodological pastiche (Aspland 1995): a methodological art form whereby perceived incongruent research forms came together, seemingly in opposition, yet ultimately creating ways of living research that were cohesive and effective in generating new knowledge. This invited innovative ways of looking at supervision for a group of women, including myself.

Initially, a series of interviews were conducted in a semi-structured format directed by the key research questions. However, as the years unfolded and the research population reduced from fifteen to six, we met regularly as a focus group. By the third year of the study, we had formed a strong friendship group, offering each other support as we struggled through the final phases of PhD completion. The focus group interviews transformed into dialogical conversations based on an 'explicitly open-ended dialogical and reciprocal manner' (Roman 1992: 580) as we talked and generated stories about our own supervised lives as women.

Each of the interviews/conversations was recorded and transcribed, but this became increasingly difficult in the final year as the conversations became more interactive, and I became a more active participant within the group. In the latter weeks I felt more comfortable engaging in our conversations without the audio recorder. I would leave our meeting and write furiously about the significant moments articulated throughout our conversations, relying on memory and my perceptions of the discussion. It was imperative that I ratify these perceptions with my friends at our next meeting (and I always did so). This in fact served as a useful catalyst for picking up where we left off. My perceptions and jottings were not always accurate, but the informal nature of the group was conducive to the process of clarification and elaboration.

Initially, it was envisaged that the analysis of this database would be shaped by a grounded theory approach (Strauss and Corbin 1990), which required a 'systematic set of procedures to develop an inductively derived grounded theory' (Strauss and Corbin 1990: 24) about the phenomena of thesis supervision for women such as ourselves. As time unfolded, however, this systematic approach was continually ruptured by the significance of the need to capture the complex, and often paradoxical, qualities of supervision for each woman, rather than for all women. Whilst connections were made across the group through our conversations, it remained important to each of us that our stories captured what was peculiar to our own subjectivities and social situation. The grounded and systematic coding that Strauss and Corbin advocate failed to provide the flexibility required to do so. A far less systematic approach, albeit grounded in the data, was pursued – an iterative process of checking and rechecking the evolving database formed the agenda for our conversations as we tried to ascertain what was significant for each of us and how common the experience was within the group. More often than not, we raised more questions that generated ongoing discussion and critique. We continually failed to generate common propositions that were representative of our experiences.

Over the three years, the stories that we shared were documented as cases. Case studies in this inquiry aimed to investigate and report on the particular in its own right rather than to generalize beyond the case. Each case attempted to tell 'who I am' in a way that captured the historical, material and cultural relations that have constituted the 'self that I am reporting', while at the same time reconstituting 'myself as I speak' (Gergen, quoted in Mann 1992). As such, each case, whilst derived from the ongoing storytelling that we engaged in collectively, has been co-written by two women – myself and the subject of the case. Thus the documented cases have been authorized by each subject continually verifying the 'legitimacy' of the case as it emerged.

It was essential to pursue this process as an integral part of the research project, inviting each woman to speak for herself, as Mei does in this text, in order to reveal the differences and discontinuities that each woman experienced in supervision. The continual editing of the cases with each woman ensured that this was realized.

In exploring what was problematic about the supervisory struggles faced by Mei, excerpts from her case are reported here to illustrate a process of pedagogical alienation that became central to her supervised experiences as she struggled to re-situate herself within a discourse of education that was culturally and historically different from that which she had previously experienced. As stated above, the purpose here is not to generalize about student responses to supervisory problems and further promulgate the dogma of existing essentialist thinkers. Rather, the purpose is to exemplify the highly personal nature of the pedagogical relations found within supervision as one woman relocates herself in ways that are often incongruent with her own identity.

Mei's story

Mei is a mature age student who came to Australia from Shanghai, having completed a Masters degree in education in her own country. She aspired to complete a research-based higher degree in social sciences in an Australian university that was well respected internationally in her field. Prior to coming to Australia, Mei had made a ten-year commitment to her profession of teaching in China and had spent the last five years in her homeland as an academic in a major university. Her husband worked for the 'authorities' in China. As a high-level decision maker for the government, his disciplined nature had been his strength in his professional life, yet it had led to the demise of his relationship with Mei who, as an educated woman, was looking for greater 'freedoms than he offered' her. She left her husband through mutual agreement. Leaving her own family behind in China in order to complete her work proved to be far more difficult than she expected. Mei, due to her marital status, was dependent on her father for ongoing financial support. For this she was truly grateful to her family, who in return expected her to 'do well' in Australia. She was not awarded a scholarship at any stage to assist her financial status in Australia and lived independently while she studied. She tried to engage in part-time work within the university, although none was forthcoming through her department.

She lived in a very poor part of an inner city area, in a cramped two-roomed apartment that required a great deal of maintenance. She was surrounded by migrants from other overseas countries, but had little to do with any of her neighbours who spoke very limited English. She spent most of her time at the university library or with a small group of Chinese friends whom she had met in the local Chinatown. She did not communicate with many other higher degree students due to low enrolments in the faculty. The small number with whom she communicated were overseas students. She was particularly friendly with a woman from Africa and a Fijian Indian woman. They did not spend a great deal of their time together; rather, they generally sought out communication in times of trouble.

Mei's arrival in her Australian university – a new university set in a large provincial city – saw the beginning of a series of struggles that continued to permeate her life for the duration of her candidature. These struggles led to ongoing ill-health and emotional anxiety, despite her ultimate academic success. Each time we met, particularly in the first year of the candidature, Mei was highly agitated about her status as a student. She referred constantly to her perceived inability to cope and her difficulty with eating due to the high levels of stress that she was experiencing. She looked increasingly frail each time we met and our conversations were permeated by tearful outbursts such as the following:

> This university does not care for us overseas students. The authorities are not clear about what is expected or who can help us. I must complete on time but I cannot. I am angry. I cannot compete with other students and I am not getting the support that I expected.

These feelings became evident at the outset of the candidature with the process of appointing a supervisor.

Finding a supervisor

During the three-year candidature, Mei worked with two supervisors. The first supervisory relationship into which she entered could be characterized as problematic at a number of levels. The first difficulties were created by the cultural incongruencies that permeated the relationship; second, the differing educational expectations and visions that impacted on the relationship became an ongoing frustration for Mei; finally, the lack of a shared discourse in which to communicate effectively with her supervisor was the source of a number of pedagogical struggles endured by Mei in the early part of her candidature. These struggles began when Mei was told by the student administration to 'go and find a supervisor' for her work.

> First up, I did not know how to find a supervisor and the authorities were not useful in helping me. I spent a long time looking for one without really knowing what to look for. This is why I made a bad choice. It was a very bad choice and I wasted a lot of valuable time and money. But the authorities – they did not care, they did not care, they did not see and they did not understand what my problem was.

On entering the university context, Mei brought with her a set of historically situated and culturally embedded constructs about the roles of universities, staff and students in higher degree education. Mei believed that it was the responsibility of the university administration, 'the authorities', to appoint the most appropriate supervisor for her on arrival – 'the Chinese government does everything for the people'.

In attempting to deal with this inadequacy, Mei approached a head of department whom she characterized as 'helpful'. Following a short meeting, Mei approached the recommended supervisor to begin the proposal-writing phase of the candidature. Based on her assumption that this supervisor was the best in the field, Mei immersed herself in her work, only to find the emerging relations highly unsatisfactory.

I can judge now that he had no specialized knowledge of my topic, but we Chinese are humble and do not like to question these matters. I continued to assume that he must be the best person because of the recommendation by the authorities. But this one day I asked him about some references and he said to me 'it is not my area'. Why did he not tell me this before? Then I realized this to be the truth. The real truth! I soon realized that we did not go into any detail in our meetings. There are insufficient references here for this topic and no one with the expertise. What could I do? For a long time I just sat there like a fool.

The first of many dilemmas that permeated her candidature emerged. On the one hand, Mei felt compelled to continue with the supervisor who was appointed for her by the university, for it was disrespectful to voice her dissatisfaction. Yet, on the other hand, she struggled with her sense that the supervisor had no expertise in the research field and even less interest in her as a student.

I am very embarrassed because things with this supervisor are not right. He knows nothing about my topic but I am too frightened to challenge him or the authorities. I just say yes all the time but I am not happy. In my head I feel like a fool.

Supervisory partnerships: who is in control?

Mei began her communications with her supervisor based on her previous experiences in a Chinese university where the bureaucratic structures demanded limited roles for students as decision makers.

The Chinese authorities investigate for you, they do everything for the people and decide what is the best thing for you. You know this is so and you accept the decision as the best one.

Based on such an assumption, Mei went to meet the supervisor to 're-ceive instructions'. Her first meeting with her supervisor was one that was fraught with misunderstanding.

I wanted to get a plan and to talk about every detail of the plan so I [could] get to know what I have to do. I think it was the duty of the supervisor to do this and for me to follow that plan.

Such a plan was not forthcoming and ensuing meetings became more complex as the supervisor engaged in what Mei perceived to be non-systematic discussions 'that had no clear purpose', were 'confusing' in terms of tasks and 'contradictory' in terms of direction. This early situation was considered by Mei to be a problem requiring urgent action. Mei engaged in many attempts to complete the required tasks that, although unclear in her mind, seemed to be of significance for the supervisor. She became highly frustrated when tasks such as the writing of a questionnaire were later considered redundant by the supervisor.

After spending a great deal of time designing a questionnaire to use in my study, he said it was of no use. I tried it out on my Chinese friends and they said it was OK. When I gave it to him, he said this was of no use at this time . . . then why did he tell me to write it?

Over the initial 12 months, Mei pursued different strategies in trying to 'fix what was going very wrong', including requests for appropriate readings, and the generation of extra meetings with the supervisor.

I wanted to discuss every detail of the tasks that he asked me to do but I could not see the significance of them to my topic. I could not see the big picture and I needed a tighter picture for me.

These requests failed to elicit a response from the supervisor that Mei considered appropriate. He would schedule a 30-minute meeting once every two weeks and would not respond positively to her requests for extra meet-ings. Mei's feelings were deeply hurt and she expressed the following senti-ments on a number of occasions: 'I feel this is a business arrangement but he is not a good partner. He is not really interested in me or my work. I feel insulted by his rudeness.'

As time unfolded, so too did Mei's ill-health, as she continually struggled with a perceived lack of direction in her work and a lack of support from her supervisor. Despite advice from her Australian friends to confront the situation, Mei opted to comply with the ongoing procedures put in place by the supervisor.

The supervisor knows nothing. He has wasted so much of my time and money. I do not want to work this way but I must respect him for he is my teacher. I am very embarrassed because this situation is not correct . . . [but] I am frightened to say so. In China it is regarded very rude to challenge the teacher. No student would do that so I just say yes, yes, yes all the time.

Incongruent expectations

Mei came into this supervisory relationship, as do most students, holding preconceived images of how the supervisory partnership should function. Mei's perception of her role in the early stages of the candidature was that of listener, yet at the outset she experienced feelings of uneasiness as her supervisor expected her to be more active in constructing the pedagogical dialogue.

Because the teacher [supervisor] is the learned person I was expecting that I would listen carefully to what was required and work hard to do what was necessary. In the early days I was frightened to ask questions all the time because I think it is not polite.

The supervisor made it clear to Mei that passive participation was not expected of a postgraduate student in the university. Rather, it was expected that she 'interrupt all the time and not worry about being rude. He wanted me to be more like the Australian students.' While Mei was receptive to such advice 'to be more critical and questioning', she was unsure of exactly how to go about this new role. In attempting to respond, she followed the supervisor's examples, yet felt that, at the same time, she was condemned for doing so. He would ask her to 'go away and do something specific', yet when she completed the tasks, he would question their relevance at the next meeting.

> He would say, 'What is this?' and put it to the side and say, 'Don't worry about this for now' when I had spent many weeks working on it and spending a lot of time finishing it for our meeting. This would make me very angry.

She continued later:

> You see in China we are not fools. We remember many things and we are very smart. When someone tells you that this is not required when in fact this is what you were asked to do – you ask yourself then what is it that I am required to do?

This statement accurately captures the dilemma for Mei in positioning herself within a supervisory relationship. She was willing to acquire and develop the skills necessary for her growth as a postgraduate student, yet exactly what was required of her was never made explicit by her supervisor: 'I was to keep guessing all the time what it was that I had to do.'

It was taken for granted by her supervisor that she understood the requirements of being an autonomous learner. In dealing with this challenge, Mei attempted to pose questions in differing forms, completed work that she perceived contributed very little to her thesis, and attempted to 'do more talking' in the initial meetings – qualities that she assumed characterized what was required of her. Unfortunately, her attempts to manage this dilemma resulted in the creation of a further, more complex dilemma that ultimately contributed to plummeting self-esteem. 'I am always thinking that I have failed again. I never feel, ah this is good.'

Mei, who on the one hand considered herself a highly successful academic, soon came to believe that her supervisor considered her a highly inadequate student.

> My attempts to change my ways failed very badly. I just felt depressed all the time and it really was no good. We were not understanding each other very well. It was because we think in different ways and we could not talk. He began to think I was a fool.

When encouraged by her friends to explore the situation with her supervisor, Mei continued to argue that she felt uncomfortable in doing so – 'it is not our way'. Mei firmly believed that it was the responsibility of the supervisor not to identify personal problems within the relationship, but to set appropriate tasks for completion. Mei's image of herself as a learner was to complete those tasks, despite the ongoing difficulties associated with relevance and respect. Initially, her way of managing this dilemma was to 'work harder' with a view to eventually gaining the respect of her supervisor. The fact that this was a one-sided relationship was immaterial to Mei's academic commitment, despite her ailing health and increasing frustration with the situation.

Dealing with inadequate supervision

Mei was aware of her declining health and in discussing her situation argued:

> It is even harder for me as a woman going to university in this new country because we are faced with so much more pressure than the Chinese men. We have not learned how to speak of our dissatisfaction . . . we are not as brave as our men to say what it is that we are thinking. The supervisor is like Chinese men also. He does not stop to ask me what I think or if I can understand. He thinks that his instruction is good and that I should follow it 100 per cent. I feel very depressed about this and . . . [as a result] we are not communicating very well. I just agree with him all the time . . . but I am really not happy and I am unwell all of the day.

Some of her Chinese friends were experiencing similar situations in other universities, and in discussing their problems offered her some support. A number of solutions were put forward by others, but Mei concluded that immediate solutions were not possible due to the perceived 'bad relationship' between her supervisor and herself.

> Because we think in different ways – he thinks Western and I think Chinese – we can never communicate. He never understands me and I cannot understand him.

Herein lies the reasoning for Mei's projected solution to the problem, a solution supported by her Chinese friends, to find a new supervisor and 'to start all over again'.

> I will ask the faculty to find me another supervisor. I will not say that this teacher [is] 'no good'. I will ask for a supervisor who knows my topic and has worked in China so that he understands the culture of my topic.

It was Mei's contention that if her supervisor was more familiar with the cultural constructs underpinning her thinking about her research work, then she would have a better chance to communicate in ways that fostered a common understanding of her topic as well as her own learning needs.

The struggles that have been outlined here give new insights into the pedagogical struggles that permeated supervision for Mei during the first year of her candidature. They also portray the ways in which she strategically managed a unique set of pathways through the supervisory process as the interplay of two discrete sets of social visions and pedagogical practices (Gore 1993) – those of Mei with those of her supervisor – was realized.

While it is useful to examine the range of pedagogical dilemmas that Mei experienced, together with the ways in which they were managed, the purpose here is to deconstruct the webs of beliefs and practices that form an integral part of the dilemmas, and consequently the sites of tension, with a view to better understanding why they emerged. It is essential to raise our awareness of how such pedagogical practices and the underlying social visions (Gore 1993) are inextricably linked to the marginalization and disempowerment of students; and how these practices are covert forms of social regulation that impact in differing ways on the reconstituting pedagogies of women such as Mei.

By examining the second phase of Mei's supervision, whereby she elected to find another supervisor and begin her candidature again, new and exciting insights can be gained.

It should be noted that at no time did Mei feel encouraged to discuss what was unsatisfactory about the pedagogical relations inherent in the first phase of supervision with her supervisor – she simply walked away and started afresh. This action gives credence to the argument that for too long now the contradictions and tensions that permeate the life of overseas students' academic work have been suppressed by generalizations that focus on a deficit model. Recognizing and exploring supervision from within these contestations generates alternative ways of perceiving and understanding these experiences (Smith 1990: 20). This will be approached through the contrasting of phase two of Mei's candidature with her earlier experiences in phase one – the significant point of comparison focusing on a process of rebuilding that occurred for Mei as an integral part of the supervisory process.

Starting again

On the recommendation of a Chinese friend, Mei approached a supervisor in her faculty whom she believed would be better able to 'understand the sorts of problems Chinese students have', because of his active interests in China. Following the discussion of the problems she was having with her supervisor, Mei gained a renewed confidence when this man agreed to become her supervisor and the decision was accepted by the faculty. She felt she was able to communicate openly with him and, within a very short period of time, she was confident that he respected her 'Chinese' ways and did not think of her as 'an inferior person'.

> Everything I said, he understood . . . I laugh – he laughed. He very much understands the ways of the Chinese student. He went to teach in China and he understands the Chinese culture and education system. He is able to understand the Chinese students and the difficulties we face here. He also understands why I have come here.

More importantly, what was established in the early stages of this supervisory relationship was a mutual understanding between Mei and her new supervisor which emerged out of the incongruencies and difficulties that Mei had faced with her first supervisor.

> He says that he understands and I feel very good that truly he does understand. He knows what I am saying is true and why I am confused and depressed. He is aware of these difficulties for Chinese students like me and he suggests things for me to do.

The new supervisory relationship began by reaching a consensus that certain adjustments had to be made to Mei's existing orientations to learning in order to address her problems.

> You learn round and I learn square – I need to learn how to think round! He told me that critical thinking was the most important thing for me to develop and I agree with him. I think it is very good to be in Australia and learn new ways of thinking.

Such a process of reorientation is commonly accompanied by a number of losses as well as many gains for the student, but what was of greatest significance in this process was the element of choice that accompanied the reshaping of the pedagogical constructs and visions for Mei. In the previous phase, the processes of pedagogical relations in which Mei engaged through supervision were 'forced' in ways that served only the interests of the supervisor and the promulgation of hegemonic practices. Mei's actions were essentially 'survival strategies' as she attempted to overcome the increasing levels of pedagogical alienation while struggling to position herself within supervisory relations. In this second phase, however, the disembedding (Giddens 1991) of the alienation from her work through the construction of more responsive supervisory relations offered Mei an opportunity to reconstitute pedagogical practices by way of choice. It was she who decided what was to be changed.

> I feel as though I am making a contribution for the first time. Though he is setting the tasks and saying what is good and not so good, I know that I am learning and that my thesis is coming. I never felt this before.

As a result, the process of supervision focused not only on the substantive project, but integrated a shared process of rearticulating Mei's ways of knowing from within (Smith 1990; Shotter 1993) through a series of pedagogical processes that enabled the ongoing reshaping of her academic self more effectively in the new cultural context of a Western university. 'He taught me how to adjust my thinking to accommodate Western ways – together we built a bridge that I could cross.'

Re-situating the supervisory process

The pedagogical processes designed by Mei and her supervisor as ways of re-situating herself in a new discourse included three major strategies:

1. writing a plan;
2. generating meeting structures;
3. an ongoing review of the writing process.

Writing a grand plan

First, the formulation of a long-term plan, with specific timeframes, was put in place. It articulated each step of the candidature in terms of components of the thesis, financial resources and library resources. Key points of achievement along the way delineated when certain tasks had to be completed and how specific tasks contributed to the development of the thesis.

> First of all, we both worked out a plan together. I would tell him what I wanted to do and then he will say what he thinks. We change things until he agrees that this is the way to go. At first we are meeting three times a week until we get the plan right and then I can get on with my work. This time I know exactly what to do and am not frightened to go to him if I am having problems. This is because he understands.

Generating formal meeting structures

Formal meeting structures were put in place for the ensuing twelve-month period. Meetings were initially held once per week at least, and sometimes up to three times per week, with Mei feeling comfortable about calling extra meetings when necessary.

Each meeting had a set agenda and timeframe decided on prior to the meeting by both the supervisor and Mei. A tape recorder captured each meeting, with Mei replaying the tape a number of times after the meeting to ensure that she had 'heard things properly' and checking for details that she might have missed during the meeting.

> It is important that I meet all of the requests and understand exactly what I have been asked to do. So I listen very carefully to the tape many times. It is a very helpful thing to do.

Instigating an ongoing review of the writing process

In assisting Mei to develop 'a more critical approach to writing and thinking', a sequentially developed process of writing and rewriting exercises focusing on the generation of a more appropriate genre was developed by the supervisor in consultation with Mei.

> He told me that my writing was the most important thing to change. He said in China we are good at writing shopping lists, 1, 2, 3. You see

we can learn and write these very long shopping lists but he told me this is just like mathematics – it has no argument. It has no critical argument. You can't pass, he tells me, if you write shopping lists. You must learn . . . He said you write your shopping lists for now and I will teach you how to write in Western ways that are important in thesis writing.

The process began with Mei writing 500-word essays on topics that would ultimately contribute to the literature review of her thesis. With each statement, the supervisor and Mei would engage in discussions about the topic that were intent on developing the skill of openly questioning and reconstructing an argument put by an authority documented in the literature.

He would ask me what it was that I was thinking about in my writing. I would just know the main ideas and he would help me find the hidden meanings in the books that I am reading. One paragraph at a time he would explain things and show me the argument that he would make. I soon learned that making this argument was not easy but as I changed my ways, I could do it too. He showed me how to do this. He knew that I was not stupid because he understood the Chinese ways. I have never thought this way before and I am learning that it is a good way to think. At the moment I am not perfect but I am getting better.

The discussions and strategy development continued in very structured ways for the next twelve months of the candidature. Meetings became less frequent, although discussions took longer, sometimes up to two hours every other week. The supervisor continued to offer Mei good examples of critical, argumentative writing, helping her to reshape her own writing through ongoing discussions. As a new phase in the candidature was entered (e.g. when Mei moved into data collection and analysis), new strategies were introduced and modelled for the time necessary for Mei to feel comfortable.

Now [at completion] when I read I just notice something . . . not like before. I would just see the facts – when, where, how, what's the plot? What's the result? Now I'm finished. Now, when I am reading, I am subconsciously looking for different things – where's the argument, what do I agree with? What is good? What is not so good? And why is this so?

Throughout this process of supervision, dilemmas no longer blocked Mei's progress. Rather, they formed the heart of a supervisory process that addressed each dilemma in turn, as it emerged, with a view to enriching her learning rather than exacerbating her frustration. 'We address my problems together and I no longer feel like a fool. He respects me and I respect him.'

The contestations and tensions of trying to succeed in a university context that was problematic culturally, socially and academically were no longer considered as inadequacies. Rather, they became central to what Mei regarded as good supervision. The way in which these struggles were faced by Mei in conjunction with her supervisor is worthy of noting at this point and lends itself to the key argument offered in this paper.

Pedagogical alienation

What is significant is that students like Mei undergo a process of pedago-gical alienation when they enter postgraduate programmes of this nature. On entry, they bring with them particular orientations to learning and to university practices that are alien to the central constructs of Western aca-demics and the hegemonic practices that permeate universities. As a result, each student is required to undergo a process of transformation that is fraught with dilemmas and contestations which are difficult to resolve, par-ticularly in isolation. This concept is not new to the field. It has previously been referred to as a cultural clash (Gallois *et al.* 1995) or conflict, and in some contexts as cultural disequilibrium (Taylor 1994). However, significant differences underlie the differing conceptualizations. Implicit in such con-ceptual thinking is that the two 'clashing' orientations are incompatible – one even inferior to the other – and further, that it becomes the responsib-ility of the visiting subject to undergo adjustment (Ballard and Clanchy 1988) to succeed.

This is compounded by a commonly accepted image of overseas students held by many Australian academics that such students are passive (lazy) learners, dependent on lecturers (therefore immature) and low-level thinkers (hence poor scholars). As a result, many students like Mei engage in ped-agogical relations that marginalize them as students in ways that are op-pressive and that instigate processes of readjustment that accommodate the supervisor rather than the student. This type of 'adjustment' totally devalues the very constructs that constitute each student's unique sense of self as a learner: 'It is like selling out your homeland – suggesting that this one is superior when really I don't think that this is the case.'

Consequently, the pedagogical struggles faced by students such as Mei are permeated by feelings of worthlessness, inadequacy and lack of aca-demic success. The process of domination that she experienced in phase one through a supervisor who (knowingly or otherwise) imposed oppressive pedagogical processes of supervision upon her, continued to a point where she was forced to reshape her thinking in ways that were incongruent with her very essence of being, ways that ultimately resulted in a repositioning within supervisory relations that trivialized her own subjectivity.

The initial impact of this type of relationship upon Mei resulted in a reshaping of her ways that simply engendered further and more complex alienation as she tried to accommodate the demands of a supervisor who had little interest in her project or in herself as a person or learner. As a supervisor, he engaged in the dominant form of institutionalized supervision in a non-responsive way – shaped by a social vision (Gore 1993) that could be characterized as 'the one size fits all approach'. Inherent in this approach was a complete disrespect for Mei as a student with a unique history, culture and pedagogy, a subject who could not be easily located in his existing hegemonic supervisory practices that had limited space for diversity or ped-agogical responsivity.

Phase two of supervision for Mei, however, reflected a more responsive approach to constructing supervisory relations – that is, it was grounded in a frame of reference commonly found outside the dominant supervisory practices generated within Australian institutions. The pedagogical relations that emerged in phase two of her supervision were underpinned by a social vision (Gore 1993) that valued the rearticulation of the learning self as an integral component of the supervisory process. Mei reported that this supervisor acknowledged that supervisory relations were fraught with dilemmas and tensions that emerged with the coming together of cultures, each with a history, and social and cultural constructs that were situated in differing world views. As such, Mei, together with her supervisor, was able consciously to structure a 'both-ways' supervisory relationship that focused on the presence of difference as a central starting point. In searching for a set of shared values, tasks and directions as the basis of a supervisory plan, supervisory relations in this context celebrated the struggles within the search. These struggles were considered to be pathways towards successful learning. In this sense, the incongruencies that were experienced by Mei in phase one through the denial of difference became central to the emerging relations in phase two. The tensions did not marginalize Mei from the centrality of her work; rather, as a thinking, speaking and signifying subject (Jordan and Weedon 1995), Mei was encouraged by her supervisor to articulate the nature of such differences as sites of possibility, opening up new pathways for reconstructing supervisory and pedagogical relations.

A 'both-ways' approach to supervision

This was a complex process for both Mei and her supervisor, fraught with tensions and struggles and the continuing crossing and recrossing of cultural and historically located pedagogical boundaries. Moments of struggle such as these, however, formed the heart of a 'both-ways' supervisory process that took place in zones of uncertainty. Each supervisory partner was called on to 'voice' his or her uncertainties to the other, who could well hold a differing position. Supervision became a process of 'making sense' of such uncertainties. Supervision for Mei in phase two became a relational phenomenon that was able to overcome former experiences of pedagogical alienation through a systematic and sustained approach to addressing the incongruencies that so often stifle 'good' supervision.

Conclusion

We, as an academic community, can no longer ignore the alienation experienced by students such as Mei as an integral component of thesis supervision in our universities. If we do, overseas students may well have to continue to struggle within supervisory relations through a 'legitimate' process recognized as adjustment (DeVos 1992) which, it is argued here, can be more accurately described as pedagogical alienation. Such alienation forces each student to comply, or reject the oppressive conditions. What is required in addressing pedagogical alienation is a reconstructing of postgraduate pedagogical relations (Green and Lee 1995) in which supervision is located. Such a reconstruction enables each student consciously to re-situate his or her ways of knowing in relations that, through a parity of esteem between supervisor and student, promote successful pathways through the tensions and dilemmas of the supervisory process.

This case and others (Aspland 1995) illustrate that each woman reacts differently to the culturally embedded practices of supervision and the dialectical interplay of ways of knowing as her sociocultural and sociohistorical constructs are juxtaposed with those of her supervisor. We need to acknowledge that supervisory relations are culturally and historically embedded in personal frames of reference, of which we presently continue to have little understanding (DeVos 1992).

4

Supervising Iranian Students:
A Case Study

Elizabeth Sandeman-Gay

Introduction

This chapter is based on a wider study into Iranian postgraduates' conceptualization of written academic discourse, learning styles and the cultural contexts of their learning at the University of Wollongong in 1995 (Sandeman-Gay 1995, 1996).

This research and anecdotal evidence from Iranian postgraduate students, their supervisors and learning development advisers suggests that much tension and frustration invades professional relationships, as students strive to achieve a higher degree in an academic language unfamiliar to them, a learning style often at variance with their prior experience and an academic discourse mode which is rarely made explicit. Despite extraordinary efforts expended on writing, corrective consultations and rewriting, frustrations remain and often increase while the features of discourse itself remain implicit for supervisors and unknown for students.

This research hypothesized that, if an Iranian learning style or styles were known, it would be easier for advisers and supervisors to adapt strategies in order to clarify, for the students, the nature of Western expectations of academic discourse. With students' focus lifted from grammar to discourse, perhaps some of the tensions would ease.

Academic discourse, adapted from Fairclough (1989), is defined here as writing and speaking informed by analysis, critical and reflective thinking, speculation and synthesis of ideas and information within discipline-specific and wider social and cultural contexts.

This chapter first outlines the author's framework and method before describing the four cases briefly and then presenting the main findings and their implications for other supervisors of NESB students.

Theories of learning

Although Iranian researchers Hashemi (1992) and Mehran (1992) help explain ways that Iranian students learn English in Iran, and Baydoun and Willett (1993, in Kennedy 1995) have 'investigated the phenomena of Islamic accounting theory', no other research was located relating specifically to Iranian learning styles. Hore (1993) asserts that the sheer number of learning theories confuses academic staff; and Clarke (1994: 4) claims that, despite 'the large amount of psychological research' into learning processes, little has impacted on educational practice, particularly at the tertiary level. Ramsden (1993) maintains that teachers often operate on 'informal' and usually conservative learning theory. The assertions of Brislin *et al.* (1986), relating to cultural communication factors, shed valuable light on the current investigation and serve to reinforce what Biggs (1993) has to say about the cognitive systems approach to learning. Ballard and Clanchy's (1991b) widely accepted claim that students from Asia tend to have a more conserving attitude to knowledge than the extending attitude expected of Western students is usefully applicable beyond Asia. In a limited way, Kaplan's (1966) findings that there are five major rhetorical patterns according to the language background of the writers is also useful, but stereotypical. Clarke's (1994) use of the Perceptions of Learning Environments Questionnaire (PLEQ) to identify the way students conceptualize learning and actually go about learning, regardless of language background or nationality, confirmed the present approach.

Method

The qualitative methodology chosen for the investigation was case study. Four Iranian PhD candidates in social science disciplines, and their supervisors, were selected for study. The two women students and one of the men had spouses and children in Australia, the single man had a brother here, also studying at postgraduate level. The single man intended becoming an academic, the other three were already university lecturers in Iran. The graphic representation of the four students and their respective supervisors in Figure 4.1 links each pair visually and encapsulates their biodata. They are presented and numbered in the order in which they were interviewed.

Each of the interviewed students had had sufficient contact with the researcher through learning development consultations and previous research to have developed good rapport. A fifth student declined to be taperecorded and, despite proffering valuable data, was excluded from the study.

Data were gathered using personal interviews based on the in-depth style of Minichiello *et al.* (1995), which allows interviewees freedom to use their own words in an informal conversational situation within the framework of the research question and problem. A 'help and hinder' matrix (similar to questions on Clarke's (1994) PLEQ survey) was devised to focus and limit each interview. To avoid negativity, it was assumed that students had discourse

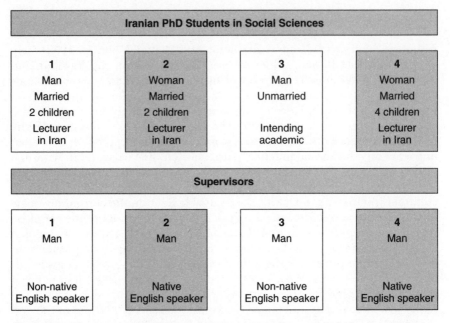

Figure 4.1 The case study subjects: four Iranian students and their supervisors

competency. However, because initial interview data showed almost no understanding of the term 'academic discourse', subsequent questioning focused simply on learning. Additional information was gathered by analysing recently written assignments of each student.

Learning theories relating to constructivism (Leder 1993), phenomenological conceptual change (Prosser 1993), holistic constructivism built on prior experience (Boud 1993), action learning (Zuber-Skerritt 1993), hermeneutics (Taylor 1993) and a cognitive systems approach (Biggs 1993) were used as essential tools of data analysis, and categories of cultural communicative behaviour (Brislin *et al.* 1986) were used to examine data for cultural contextual effects on learning.

Case description: supervision and learning approaches

The following is a brief summary of four cases discussed in Sandeman-Gay (1995) with quotations from these cases.

Student and supervisor 1

The supervisor of Student 1, a non-native speaker of English who had spent some years as an academic in the US, was very supportive but modelled two contrasting approaches to discourse tasks. On the one hand, he spent hours meticulously and patiently attending to grammatical errors and explaining his corrections of the student's writing; on the other hand, he left him to 'go ahead and do your research' (25: 14)[1] and to 'read the other articles and get the structure [of a] research report' (24: 21).

Student 1's learning approach underwent significant change in his first two years in Australia. His initial efforts fitted prior learning experience models discussed by Boud (1993), Leder (1993) and Prosser (1993). He employed a dependency approach, theoretically congruent with grammar-based, non-functional language-learning modes (Hashemi 1992). Dissatisfied and distraught after months of perseverance, trying to 'get the structure' and distinguish the differences between Australian expectations and the expectations he held from his American MBA studies, Student 1 finally took a more active problem-solving approach and sought help from other sources, which led him to a more holistic and actively constructivist approach (Leder 1993).

Student and supervisor 2

The supervisor of Student 2, a native English speaking Australian man whose data showed he had the best interests of his students at heart, nevertheless took for granted graduate initiation into the discipline-specific discourse community and, whilst many of his expectations were made explicit, the analytic nature of postgraduate discourse was not.

Student 2 was enrolled at this stage in preliminary doctoral coursework. She was absolutely self-assured about her learning style and strategies. She had been a good and natural learner since the age of six, she said, and was accustomed to high distinction grades. She told me, 'I can learn very easy . . . it is natural' (33: 150).

Student 2's learning approach in Australia, however, remained steadfastly as it had been in Iran, and despite unsatisfying results, she maintained her stance. Her data indicated a mono-dimensional memorization learning style such as is revealed in Clarke's (1994) study, and a conserving attitude to knowledge (Ballard and Clanchy 1991b). Evidence such as her statement, 'the adult learn when repeating something . . . the repeating cause more learning' (34: 116), also indicated rote learning. She seemed to use a strategic approach based on extrinsic motivation, but her subject focus was disjointed by the decision to study here and her 'Australian experience' was further diffusing her focus, thus disabling her learning.

Student 2's supervisor once unwittingly challenged her self-esteem by praising the content of her seminar presentation and paper as 'brilliant', but grading her just below a credit because analysis was lacking. Difficulties arose because of their different but unstated conceptualizations of the discourse in which they were operating.

Student and supervisor 3

The supervisor of Student 3, a non-native speaker of English, was on study leave and unavailable for interview. His absence and the student's data indicated that supervision was less intensive than Student 3 had hoped for. The student said, for example, 'Sometimes he can give me some just ten minute' (44: 191).

Student 3 employed a controlled style, using narrowed contexts and carefully selected 'experts' to help achieve his objectives. In pursuit of his goal to learn academic English to a sophisticated level, he hypothesized, questioned, discussed, made linguistic connections and challenged teaching staff. His actions suggested a constructivist approach (Leder 1993) and an action learning style (Zuber-Skerritt 1993), using the spiral of cycles, each cycle consisting of 'plan, act, observe, reflect, revise plan'. He had intrinsic motivation and an independent attitude but, perhaps because of the inaccessibility of the supervisor, seemed to develop a service dependency.

Student and supervisor 4

Student 4 also employed a learning approach similar to Zuber-Skerritt's (1993) action learning concept. Her style, however, was phenomenological (Prosser 1993), in that she was able to shift her perspective from that of student to that of lecturer. She operated in a broad contextual framework. She used analytic, problem-solving and hierarchical questioning techniques to consciously construct and extend her understandings – or, in her own words, 'When you ask me "What is this?" that is different when you ask me "Why this happens?" or "Do you have any suggestion about this?" ' (49: 83).

Students 2 and 4 shared the same supervisor. He approached his interactions with Student 4 in ostensibly the same way as with Student 2, but Student 4's action learning approach and ability to think and write more 'like me' (transcript, p. 14) seemed to provide a more culturally acceptable base from which he could supervise. He expressed admiration for her 'good progress . . . the quality of her writing is now really quite remarkable' (transcript, p. 13).

This supervisor saw no need to adapt his own or his staff's teaching strategies to account for cultural differences and he saw his role as being satisfactorily fulfilled – except for the hours he had had to spend correcting English! However, he was considering revising his overseas postgraduate selection and admission procedures.

Findings

An initial, but unsought, finding was that each student expressed an overt and assertive wish to be seen as an individual person, not as 'an Iranian'.

Despite my initial uncertainty about different learning styles, I had assumed individuality as self-evident.

Results showed that three of the four students had almost no understanding of the term 'written academic discourse', taking it to mean mere writing, grammar and vocabulary, and/or text structure. Students 1 and 3 had become relatively competent within the discourse of their discipline despite their inability to talk about it, but Student 2 thought it was 'exactly the same' (32: 112) as in Iran and was having trouble. The fourth student showed a much greater understanding and ability. She spoke of Iranians' need to 'improve our abstraction thinking and creative thinking and . . . analyse everything and give the hypothesis for something' (48: 80) and she argued that Australian academic writing was completely different: 'Structure of sentences is different and grammar, that's one thing. And another thing, not the style of writing, but about what point is important we express' (48: 82), and 'the style of our thinking is different' (48: 107).

Despite the clear differences in learning approaches and styles, the study found some common factors – three of which helped students, and seven of which hindered their learning.

Common factors which helped learning related to:

- discussing problems with native English speakers;
- receiving explanations about languages, writing and discourses;
- consulting learning development advisers, individually or in workshop classes.

(The last two factors could be biased responses, given that the researcher is a learning development adviser.)

Common factors which hindered learning related to the context or condition of learning, rather than to ways of learning.

- Time pressures, imposed externally by the Iranian Scholarship Board and internally by students' slowness in processing the English language, were an extreme hindrance.
- Language inadequacy frustrated students in their ability to express themselves, respond to queries or challenges and participate in discussions and therefore learn. These frustrations caused anxiety, which further hindered learning.
- Thinking styles that were slow to question but quick to accept and memorize – particularly accumulated detail – interfered with the kind of analytic thinking supervisors expected.
- Anxiety problems were often exacerbated by family members' illnesses or accidents. Similarly, social, political or religious restrictions and English inadequacies of family members also added to anxiety and stress.
- Support from native English-speaking Australians was limited; students suggested the reasons might be 'cultural', 'religious' and 'social'.
- Support from other Iranians was limited. Differences in discipline or field were cited as reasons.

- Supervisor support was often marred by misperceptions and misunderstandings in the relationship despite extravagant hours and effort spent on grammar and English expression.

Implications

Although this has been a very small study, some general comments can be made with clear implications for funding bodies, institutions, academics and NESB students.

Western academics and institutions need to recognize that time constraints imposed bureaucratically outside our countries are responsible for much learner anxiety and subsequent dependent and/or defensive behaviour.

Similarly, prior language learning experiences and thinking styles should be recognized as valid cultural contexts within which, and from which, students must overcome obstacles and be assisted towards learning goals. Students' need of explicit understanding of Western discourses is integral to those goals. External funding bodies, international students, supervisors and universities need to recognize the importance of adequate English language skills as the basis for those goals.

For academics, a prime implication of such disparate learning approaches and styles, not only between people of a national culture, but during the course of each individual student's progress, is the need to recognize that stereotyping creates barriers to learning. Stereotyping promotes damaging assumptions or omissions in teaching and learning behaviours, which can leave students untaught and distraught.

We should note, too, that Hore (1993) and Biggs (1993) may well be right in asserting academic staff confusion about learning theory and the lack of its impact thus far on tertiary teaching, and act accordingly.

Students themselves need to attempt greater communicative interaction with native English speakers to acculturate, identify and emulate modes of discourse that could expedite their learning development.

Finally, as Kennedy (1995: 35) argues, overseas students should not be regarded 'as the end products of a business transaction but as individuals with real needs and concerns that must be addressed'.

Conclusion

Language support for international postgraduate students whose first language is not English includes the problematic area of introducing students to Western academic discourse with its critical analysis, reflective thinking, speculation and synthesis of existing and new knowledge in spoken and written forms and social contexts. The notion that academic discourse is context-specific and is ideologically and culturally constructed, however, poses a number of linguistic, cognitive and ethical issues for supervisors.

This chapter has explored the ways in which four Iranian postgraduate students perceive academic discourse and their learning, as well as their teaching/learning relationships with their supervisors. It concludes that both students and supervisors experience problematic differences in their understandings of tasks to be performed, the nature of the discourses of their field, and the way these should be learned, taught and used. It also concludes that both parties experience difficulties in the ways they perceive each other and their respective roles. These difficulties and differences are clearly more than language based and could be minimized by developing shared understanding and mutual respect.

Acknowledgements

I would like to thank Dr Christine Fox, Soheyla Gholamshahi, the four Iranian students and their supervisors for their collaboration in this project.

Note

1. Numbers refer to thesis page followed by data transcription page, in Sandeman-Gay (1995).

5

NESB Postgraduate Students at a New University: *Plus ça change, plus c'est la même chose*

John Geake and Christine Maingard

Introduction

During the past decade, while Australian universities have increased their intake of international postgraduate students, a number of commentators have identified a wide variety of concerns that NESB postgraduate students have about their experiences in Australian higher education institutions (e.g. Ballard and Clanchy 1991a, 1991b; Aspland and O'Donoghue 1994; May and Bartlett 1995). For a new university like our own, Southern Cross University (SCU), it is important – both for the institution and for its growing international postgraduate clientele – to identify which of these concerns are relevant, and which are most pressingly in need of solution. This chapter describes two endeavours to seek answers to these questions.

The French title, *Plus ça change, plus c'est la même chose* (the more things change, the more they stay the same), was chosen as a gentle provocation for English-only speakers, to put the language boot (briefly) on the other foot. The title also, more importantly, reflects our central thesis – that the needs of NESB students are largely the same as the needs of native English speaking students. Consequently, the most effective strategy to address the many identifiable needs of NESB postgraduate students in a new university like SCU involves improving the quality of education for *all* postgraduate students.

The first part of this chapter describes an informal needs analysis by way of unstructured interviews with NESB postgraduate students about what difficulties they faced during their postgraduate studies. This approach was similar to many other studies of the problems of NESB students (e.g. Aspland and O'Donoghue 1994). In this case, however, postgraduate supervisors were also interviewed and their responses compared with those of their NESB students. This needs analysis was later formalized at a workshop with parallel sessions for NESB postgraduate students and NESB postgraduate supervisors through a nominal group technique which involves a ranking procedure to identify the most important issues. Again, the concerns of both groups were compared. These findings, and subsequent recommendations for action, are described in the second section of this chapter.

At SCU in 1996 there were 39 NESB international postgraduate students who were inducted through the International Office. Thirty of these students were undertaking a coursework MBA. The nine research students comprised 5 per cent of the total research postgraduate cohort. However, anecdotal evidence suggests that a similar number of NESB postgraduate students were enrolled, but they were not recruited specifically as international students. Altogether, the views of 14 NESB postgraduate students (research and coursework) are reported here. Thus, based on the views of up to 20 per cent of the target group, we are cautiously confident that our conclusions and recommendations are applicable to the wider NESB cohort at SCU, and are relevant to other institutions, especially the newer, smaller universities.

The interviews

Individual interviews were conducted with five NESB research students enrolled in PhD or Masters programmes across a number of faculties at SCU, and with three academic staff who were or recently had been supervising NESB students. Additional information was gained from a staff member of the university's Learning Assistance Unit. This last staff member helps students with academic writing and has some experience with postgraduate NESB students.

The student interviews are reported first. Students were selected entirely on a voluntary basis with the interviews held one-to-one to ensure confidentiality. The purpose of the interview was explained at the time volunteers were sought. Interested participants contacted the interviewer, who then determined their suitability as 'genuine' NESB students. In this instance, students who grew up with English as a second but constant language during their school and university years were not included.

The interview was deliberately unstructured. Apart from the major leading question, 'What are the difficulties you face, or have faced in the past, in your postgraduate research, because you come from a non-English speaking background?', there were no other pre-set questions. The interviewer encouraged each student to volunteer as much information as possible with additional questions whenever appropriate. Following Aspland and O'Donoghue (1994), who also conducted unstructured interviews with NESB postgraduate students, the interviewer herself was an NESB postgraduate student at SCU. Aspland and O'Donoghue suggested that the selection of an interviewer with whom NESB students could readily identify should increase the likelihood of soliciting candid responses from interviewees, rather than responses aimed to 'please' the researcher, as previously reported in similar situations.

Student A, working towards his PhD in the Faculty of Resource Science, spoke excellent English, which he attributed to the fact that he had already been in Australia for three years. According to A, 'the research here is more problematic than it was in Bangkok'. The major concern for A seemed to be that his expectations of his supervisor did not match the supervisor's expectations of him. In particular, A felt that his writing was 'OK', but that his supervisor did not think so. His supervisor had told him that his writing needed considerable improvement in terms of literature and structure. However, A expected his supervisor to do 'all the serious editing'. The other issue that A identified as being somewhat problematic was that the 'Australian social structure is different to the one back home and this makes it a bit difficult to return home, even just for a holiday, and to fit in again'. However, he saw Australia as an 'extremely friendly country' and he 'loves being here', even though initially he 'found it difficult to settle down in Lismore. There were problems with accommodation and too much money had to be spent on motels after arriving here.' Overall, A found that his expectations were met and that Lismore was 'a great place to study because there are not many distractions'.

Student B, another Resource Science PhD student, also spoke good English. He had previously studied towards his Masters degree in another English speaking country. There he found that he faced numerous problems initially, due to his poor English. He mentioned that there were some 'cultural obstacles' upon his arrival in Australia which made it difficult for him to engage in 'dialectics' with his supervisor. He felt that perhaps the supervisor misinterpreted this as being inactive. However, this appeared to have changed. Despite Australia not being his first English speaking country of residence, B found the first two weeks in Lismore were his most difficult time, mainly because his wife had stayed behind in Indonesia. B stated that he received and continues to receive lots of support from his supervisor at SCU. Descriptions of his first overseas experience, when he had a female supervisor, revealed many cultural undertones. The supervisor was 'very pushy and hard to deal with . . . I realized that she was in a higher position . . . but she underestimated my capabilities . . . that was too much.' When asked by the interviewer if there could perhaps have been some cultural issues making him feel that way, he vehemently denied it. B still found reading in English troublesome. He often had to use a dictionary. He still occasionally faced misunderstandings due to the Australian accent and idioms. However, overall, he saw Australians as being very helpful.

Student C, a Masters student in education, came from Germany but had been in Australia for about five years before commencing her research. She mentioned that anyone, even with rather good English skills, would face some difficulties trying to understand the Australian accent. During the early stages of her research, she found it problematic to change her internal thought processes from German into English. She stressed that, while this was not a major issue any more, it still occasionally slowed down her writing. C found that there was a general lack of feedback from Australians with regard to her inaccuracies in speaking English. Being an NESB student, in her opinion, did not present any other particular problems or concerns.

Student D arrived in Australia from China in 1994 to do his Masters at SCU and is now continuing with his PhD in Computing. Like C, he also mentioned that his initial problems were largely due to his inability to comprehend the Australian accent. Other than that, he found no particular language problems. However, he did face a number of difficulties during his 'settling in' period, such as not understanding the general university system, the library, etc. He was aware, however, that the lack of awareness in the university to the orientation needs of overseas NESB students had changed since his arrival, and now overseas students receive a more thorough introduction to the facilities at SCU. D loved living in Lismore and found its quiet environment rather conducive to study. He also emphasized that, because his supervisor at SCU came from the same cultural background (Chinese), 'this might have helped enormously'.

Student E, also Chinese, a recently completed Masters student, had been in Australia for two years prior to commencing her Masters degree. Unlike D, she still found great difficulties with the English language, particularly with reading and writing. E hinted at a number of negative experiences, which were mainly related to language and isolation, and included cultural issues.

From these few student interviews, several themes emerged. Whilst many of the issues the students identified generally fitted into the categories described by Ballard and Clanchy (1991b) as 'predictable problems' – language difficulties, homesickness, culture shock, housing problems and difficulties in fitting into Australian student life – these did not appear to be the dominating factors in the difficulties reported by the students. Rather, many of the perceived difficulties – for example, difficulties with written English at postgraduate level – were not much different from some of the difficulties experienced by native English speaking postgraduate students. On this issue, Aspland and O'Donoghue (1994: 71) note that 'even for first-language speakers of English, academic terminology is a potential source of alienation'.

This, of course, was not apparent to the interviewed students. The majority of problems mentioned were seen as unique to them, and perceived by them as problems which would not have happened had they been born in Australia. Nonetheless, these 'unique' problems typically included such issues as lack of library resources and supervisor–student relationships – problems for postgraduates which are far from being NESB-specific. It could be noted here that, whereas Ballard and Clanchy (1991b) list another 'predictable problem' as 'gaps in background knowledge and training', there was no indication that this issue was of any relevance to these students.

The views of the supervisors were also ascertained via unstructured interviews. During these interviews, two distinct groups of issues emerged, one group concerning difficulties a supervisor faces when dealing with NESB students, and the second concerning issues which a supervisor recognizes as difficulties NESB students might experience.

Four issues were included in the first group.

1. *Economic background:* This included the absence of formal research training. In a discipline such as computing, the rapid pace of technological change can be problematic for those who come from less developed countries.
2. *Language:* The semantic, idiomatic and construction aspects of the English language are always seen as problematic, and whilst the supervisors showed a high degree of understanding towards problems in these areas, they did not see teaching English as part of their role.
3. *Academic culture:* This often related to the supervisors' unrealistic expectations of their students. For instance, Asian students are typically regarded as being reluctant to engage in critical discussion with their supervisors. These students take everything their supervisor says as 'gospel' (which was seen as both positive and negative). Asian students, in particular, are often seen as 'too' polite, trying to please their supervisors too much.
4. *Motivation:* On the other hand, difficulties in the above areas seemed to be somewhat offset by the high degree of determination, single-mindedness in achieving their goals, and general academic motivation which the NESB students appeared to show.

There were five main issues which contributed to the second major theme of supervisor-perceived student problems.

1. *Family:* Overseas NESB students are generally older than native postgraduate students. Whereas there is a great willingness to sacrifice on the part of NESB students, this often creates tensions. For example, leaving their family behind is problematic, but so is bringing their family along.
2. *Financial:* Some NESB students were suddenly thrust into a socioeconomic level of relative poverty.
3. *Language:* The demands for academic writing were not reinforced with everyday spoken English, particularly with slang words and general speech in an Australian accent.
4. *Isolation:* At a relatively small university, an NESB student might be the only national from his or her home country.
5. *Student expectations of supervisor:* Students from many countries expect great contributions from their supervisor towards the research and/or the thesis.

In addition, there were a number of issues which were seen by supervisors to be compounded and/or related to the fact that a student is non-English speaking. However, we suggest that several of these issues are independent of NESB status, such as writing in an academic genre and, more specifically, writing for particular discipline genres.

Comparing the views of the NESB students with those of the supervisors, a number of issues emerge. First, negotiation is often recommended as a means of establishing satisfactory supervisor–postgraduate student relationships (e.g. Zuber-Skerritt 1992a). In fact, one supervisor argued that 'the need to negotiate is "doubly" important for NESB students'. However, we suggest it might be twice as difficult to do so, particularly if the notion of negotiation with a superior is itself one of the issues of concern. In general, it might be unreasonable to expect NESB students to negotiate issues which are often extremely sensitive, even for non-NESB students.

A more pervasive issue was that of English language proficiency. Generally, students did not perceive this issue to be as problematic as supervisors did. However, when challenged, some supervisors did acknowledge that, whereas an NESB student may require a longer reading time to reach understanding, such understanding is often achieved at a higher level in the end. In other words, a slower but more careful reading may in fact result in a higher degree of comprehension. We suggest that, even where levels of English language proficiency are modest, the high general cognitive abilities of most NESB postgraduates more than compensate in the reading typically required in directed research. We acknowledge that such compensations may not be so readily applied to coursework.

That said, there is both the general problem of cultural stereotyping – for example, 'Asian culture' – and of stereotyping of NESB students as a homogeneous group. This becomes more explicit for individual NESB students when one poses the question, Is it feasible to expect our supervisors to change to suit another culture? We suggest that all that realistically can be expected is cultural sensitivity and awareness. At the same time, we argue that it is reasonable to expect an overseas NESB student to be similarly aware of our culture, and to make a reasonable attempt to adapt as much as possible. Otherwise we, as agents of the university, could receive complaints like, 'There is no mosque in Lismore, I am therefore dissatisfied'. One of us recently spent some time in Japan as a foreign student, trying to assimilate as much as possible to their culture. It would have been very impolite not to do so! Why, then, are we overly concerned about the cultural isolation of our international students? Perhaps we should be promoting such intercultural experiences with the many positive values which underpin the very notion of international study.

Finally, a seemingly provocative question: Is a true definition of NESB possible? There are students who come from overseas non-English speaking countries but who have studied English at school or university. There are students born in Australia to non-English speaking parents, who do not speak English as a first language at home. We suggest caution in the application of labels. We prefer to focus on the needs of the individual as much as is institutionally possible. In psychometric parlance, we argue that there are more individual differences within NESB postgraduates as a group than between the groups of NESB and native English speaking students. Aspland and O'Donoghue (1994) similarly argue that different students require different relationships with their supervisors, ranging from high dependency to complete autonomy, and that this is often overlooked in analyses of postgraduate education. Moses (quoted in Zuber-Skerritt and Knight 1986: 92) states: 'The starting point for each individual student is different; thus the supervisory process must differ for different students.' We concur, with NESB students included.

The workshops

This section outlines a workshop conducted at SCU for NESB postgraduate students and staff who were currently supervising, potentially supervising or interested in supervising NESB students. For a complete report of this workshop, see Shevellar and Heywood (1996). The following section is taken largely from that report.

The aims of the workshop were to:

- identify the unique needs of both NESB students and their supervisors;
- recommend changes to programmes and services to address these needs better.

Nine NESB PhD, Masters and Honours degree students attended. Some had only recently arrived in Australia to undertake study, whilst others were longer term residents of Australia. They were 'matched' by nine staff members, including the Director of the International Office, the Dean of the Graduate College and a member of the Learning Assistance Centre specializing in support for international students.

The workshop was held in two stages and facilitated by the two authors. In the first stage, the group was split into parallel sessions, one with supervisors and the other with students, for a structured needs analysis. This first stage aimed to encourage peer-support mechanisms for participants in each group (both students and staff), and to allow students and staff to raise issues without fear of offence or retribution. Given the cultural issues of status, deference and respect, this was seen as a particularly important feature of the workshop design. The second stage consisted of a combined session for exchange of findings, and discussion of problem-solving strategies.

The process for the needs analysis employed within both groups was a tightly structured discussion technique called Nominal Group Technique (NGT) (Zuber-Skerritt 1992b). This technique consists of brainstorming, clarifying, discussing and prioritizing items or statements in response to a focal question or questions. The process is advantageous in that it permits every opinion to be solicited before issues are ranked and prioritized. It also encourages people to divorce themselves from their own agendas and to examine issues within a wider context.

Each group had a double-barrelled focal question:

1. For you personally, what are the major issues/problems/concerns in postgraduate NESB supervision?

For the student group:

2. From the point of view of your supervisor, what are the major issues/problems/concerns in postgraduate NESB supervision?

For the supervisor group:

3. From the point of view of your NESB postgraduate students, what are the major issues/problems/concerns in postgraduate NESB supervision?

Thus, in the first stage, each group was asked to consider the issue from both their own perspective, and the perspective of the other party.

The purpose of the second stage, then, was to compare these responses and note concerns of high priority. The workshop facilitators conducted an open forum in which possible strategies were suggested for addressing high-ranking issues and needs. Finally, those strategies which seemed to be realistic and which could be immediately implemented were noted and delegated to interested participants of the workshop.

Student issues

In responding to the focal question, 'For you personally, what are the major issues/problems/concerns in postgraduate NESB supervision?', student issues fell into six main categories: resourcing, supervisors, accommodation, language, being away from home and cultural differences. Resourcing issues were mentioned most often and referred mainly to using the library in the Learning and Information Centre (LIC) to access information. Students felt that they faced an inability to access both home-country literature and other external sources, and that slow turnaround time for inter-library loans had a negative impact on their ability to research. They also felt that computer facilities were inadequate and that there was a lack of computer training and support, particularly for the Internet. Some students also felt that their research was hindered by the lack of availability of communication equipment for research purposes, specifically phone and fax. Whilst some students had access to these, it was felt that there was a lack of uniformity across the university. Students also perceived a need for more communication with experts at other institutions.

Relationships with supervisors were also often mentioned. Students felt that the university should pay more attention to the selection of culturally sensitive supervisors, and many students were surprised by what they perceived as their supervisor's limited expertise. The majority of students felt that expectations from supervisors were unclear and that there was a problem with matching student and supervisor expectations. There was consensus about their dissatisfaction with the quantity of allocated supervisor time. Some students felt that their supervisors were 'slack' or lazy. Others felt that supervisors often did not understand their students' cultural and educational backgrounds. Other concerns included:

- *accommodation* – the major concern being the lack of suitable on-campus accommodation;
- *language* – this problem was felt across the board when students first arrived and later consisted mainly of difficulties related to understanding lectures and to writing;

- *financial hardship*, and feelings of frustration, helplessness and homesickness;
- *cultural issues* – including the difficulty in integrating different religious and cultural backgrounds and the impact this has on social occasions.

Students' perceptions of issues and concerns for their supervisors included:

- time is scarce, supervisors' time is taken up in administration;
- lack of understanding of student backgrounds; supervisors assume that students are ignorant;
- matching expectations, language and cross-cultural communication issues;
- supervisors' inability to comprehend student needs; supervisors think that students are not working.

Supervisor issues

In responding to the focal question, 'For you personally, what are the major issues/problems/concerns in postgraduate NESB supervision?', supervisors' issues fell into five main categories: language, academic, social, financial and cultural issues. Language issues consisted of problems with written language, interpersonal language (e.g. the ability to understand humour and slang), spoken language, the required language standard for students entering tertiary institutions, and language interpretation.

Academic issues included the problem of having students thrust upon supervisors, the need for shared expectations of supervisors and students, the Western philosophy underpinning academic thought and methodologies, and the quality of students entering tertiary institutions. There were also problems with differences in academic culture, the thesis process, thesis content, the mechanics of writing (e.g. cultural differences in referencing and understandings of plagiarism), general academic skills, timeframe pressures, and the availability of English language training courses. Also, supervisors expressed concerns over the student–supervisor relationship, the time and resources required by and available for the student ('How much help should I provide?') and the ethics and mechanics of editing students' work.

In response to the 'mirrored' focal question, 'For you personally, what are the major issues/problems/concerns for your postgraduate NESB students?', supervisors perceived NESB students as having social problems including peer relationships and isolation within the student body. Supervisors felt concern for students' welfare, family issues, integration into the host society, students' health, students' recreation, availability of counselling and overstaying ('What happens when the student finishes the research and wants to stay in Australia?').

Supervisors also considered that NESB students were concerned with financial issues such as time pressures on funding, available research and personal finances, and cultural issues such as culture shock, cultural habits and taboos (e.g. activities that NESB students were unable to participate in due to cultural taboos about diet, alcohol, etc.), integration of students into

Table 5.1 Prioritized issues for students and supervisors

	Issues for students	Issues for supervisors
	I	**II**
Perceived and ranked by students	A. Library resources, accessing external resources, time lag B. Lack of communication facilities (e.g. phone, fax) C. Supervisors' limited expertise	A. Supervisors' time is scarce B. Supervisors' understanding of students' background (both cultural and education) C. Matching expectations
	III	**IV**
Perceived and ranked by supervisors	A. Written language B. Social isolation C. Language standards, academic mechanisms and culture shock	A. Written language B. Language standards C. Academic quality

the host culture, the applicability of the students' research to their home culture, associated loss of status when a highly regarded professional from overseas becomes a 'mere student' in Australia, and being ready for the 'unexpected' (e.g. restriction on aliens to certain research areas, supervisor assumptions about 'basic skills' such as driving).

Comparison of students' and supervisors' views

Table 5.1 shows the highest ranked (A, B, C: high to low) student and supervisor concerns. A number of differences, and some similarities, are readily apparent. The main issue for students identified by students (cell I) was one of resources (I-A). This was followed by lack of communication facilities (I-B) and limited supervisor expertise (I-C). None of these issues is necessarily NESB-specific. Neither are what students perceived as issues for supervisors (cell II): lack of time (II-A) and expectations (II-C). Only matching of culture (II-B) is exclusively an NESB student issue.

The main concern for supervisors identified by supervisors (cell IV) was to do with language (IV-A, IV-B), as was the main concern for students by supervisors (III-A). The supervisors' concerns were about both written language and the language standards required to enter university. By being accepted into a university, NESB students assume their language is appropriate, whereas the experience of supervisors suggests that this is not the case. However, the process of acquiring the necessary academic language skills is a learning experience for all students, and this process is simply exacerbated for NESB students. Although NESB students may meet the requirements of the English entry tests such as TOEFL (Test of English as a Foreign Language) and IELTS (International English Language Testing

Systems), it is only in the process of applying written language skills to the research thesis that areas of need are identified. As such, it was suggested, a much higher score may be more indicative of the language skills required by postgraduate research students. However, May and Bartlett (1995) argue that the evidence is quite inconclusive that students' levels of English proficiency are determinants of academic success. May and Bartlett argue that, rather than English language skills, academic skills development is needed. This may be true for domestic as well as NESB students. The authors cite a case in a postgraduate course where three Australians and seventeen international students were given the task of writing a critical essay. 'When the essay was graded the three Australian students received the three lowest marks and began attending [academic skills] classes thereafter!' (May and Bartlett 1995: 146).

Interestingly, and perhaps not surprisingly, both students and supervisors had concerns over the 'quality' of the other party. One of the students' major concerns was their supervisors' limited expertise (I-C), which was linked to students having a set of expectations prior to pursuing their course of research. Supervisors had an equal concern over the quality of students being accepted into the university (IV-C). This suggests that there could be a major discrepancy between the expected standards of the students and those of their supervisors, an important contributor to the general issue of matching expectations (II-C). Again, it is not clear to what extent this can be attributed purely to the students' non-English speaking background. As Ballard and Clanchy (1991a: 99) note: 'Nearly all research students, whether local or from overseas, experience difficulties with their supervisors at some stage of their course.'

Nevertheless, the issue of supervisors' limited expertise – characteristic of new universities with a small academic staff with limited supervision experience – has implications at the institutional level. Enthusiastic international marketing of postgraduate courses by Australian universities, particularly in Asia, may not necessarily match academic reality. This creates unmet expectations which are no fault of the supervisor, or the student. The responsibilities of university marketing in international forums are emphasized by Aspland and O'Donoghue (1994). Four of the five international students interviewed by these authors suffered a serious decline in motivation because supervisors did not convey the impression that they were experts in their field.

On a more positive note, issues concerned with induction mentioned in the unstructured interviews – for example, that newcomers need both practical 'know-how' and some briefing about underlying cultural systems (Aspland and O'Donoghue 1994) – were not reported in the workshop. This suggests that the International Office at SCU is satisfactorily meeting these needs with its present personalized induction programmes.

At the conclusion of the workshop, participants indicated that the experience had been extremely worthwhile. Both staff and students were appreciative of the opportunity to raise problems in such a collaborative forum, and to begin to find ways of addressing both staff and student concerns. The workshop was a learning experience for all involved, highlighting the importance of addressing student and supervisor expectations together.

Recommended strategies

To address the highest ranked issues (I-A, I-B, II-A, III-A, IV-A), the combined group suggested many strategies (Shevellar and Heywood 1996). Most of these strategies and recommended future actions will be of benefit to all postgraduate students at SCU, not just NESB postgraduates. The strategies include:

- *improving library resources* – enhancing support for inter-library loans;
- *supervisors' workload* – reducing administrative responsibilities, giving more formal recognition of supervisors' additional supervisory workloads within faculties, and recognizing the additional time NESB students may require;
- *regular commitment to meetings with students* – organizing regular times to meet for those students on campus, or 'dates to report in by' for distance students, and making both parties responsible for keeping these appointments;
- *allocation of culturally sensitive supervisors and co-supervisors* – whilst it was suggested that this practice could be problematic where staff are specialists in particular research areas, the provision of training for supervisors might be beneficial;
- *research skills courses* – to be conducted by the Learning Assistance Centre and the LIC;
- *employing an editor/reviewer* to examine first drafts of theses;
- *establishing an NESB student advisory group* – preferably with a member from each faculty;
- *encouraging completion of student–supervisor expectations reports*;
- *holding a second workshop for NESB research students and staff* who are currently supervising, potentially supervising or interested in supervising NESB students in six months' time.

Conclusion

The concerns of NESB postgraduate students and their supervisors at SCU were ascertained through a series of unstructured interviews and a structured workshop employing the Nominal Group Technique to prioritize articulated concerns. In both situations, the 'realities' of students and supervisors were compared. In terms of the highest ranked concerns, these 'realities' had more differences than similarities. But, taking all of the issues raised by students and supervisors into account, there was considerable overlap and agreement about areas which were in need of immediate improvement. The main concern of students was about the limited university support for postgraduate research, especially the LIC provision for inter-library loans. Quality time with supervisors was also sometimes problematic; regular access was sometimes difficult when supervisors had heavy work-loads, while cultural insensitivities sometimes compromised clear two-way communication between supervisors and their students.

In particular, the English language issues for the students in the work-shop were much the same as in the unstructured interviews. Many of the students had English well established as a second language. Supervisors' concerns about English were mostly in the context of thesis writing. How-ever, such concerns were not held by the NESB students. Given that there is a recognized range of thesis writing abilities, wherein some native English speakers do well, while others have considerable problems, we support an approach for NESB postgraduate supervision which, building on high levels of general cognitive ability and high levels of motivation, aims to individual-ize rather than stereotype.

Although different students were involved, the issues which were raised in the workshop were quite similar to those raised during the interviews. This suggests that the issues are of general concern. To sum up, most of the issues were more related to general problems encountered by postgraduate students and supervisors at a new and small university than to NESB status *per se*. To this end, many of the recommended strategies for improvement, such as improving LIC services and implementing supervision contracts, are applicable to all postgraduate students and supervisors.

Supervision of postgraduate NESB students is a relatively new phenom-enon at our university. The interviews and workshop sessions described here represented an opportunity for staff and students to lay the founda-tions for culturally sensitive and constructive supervisory practices, to pro-vide support for both staff and students involved in NESB postgraduate supervision, and to enable the university to meet more readily the needs of a growing clientele of culturally diverse students.

Part 2

Examining the Issues

Part 2

Examining the issues

6

Supervision and the Overseas Student

Pam Denicolo and Maureen Pope

The absolute height of panic culminated in a course presentation which required
me to give a short explanation of my research project to student colleagues
and the course tutors . . . Asking to be first to present, in order to relieve the
unbearable stress I was experiencing, I nervously rambled through my presentation,
at times actually physically shaking and feeling out of breath . . . I couldn't help
thinking that I was now not only a private failure, but a public one as well.

(A PhD student from overseas)

Introduction

The above quotation haunts us. It was written by a student for whom one of
us (Denicolo) had some responsibility, not as a supervisor but as the departmental Postgraduate Studies Director and the leader of the mandated Research Methods course. The student, at that point six months into his studies,
was a mature person who had given up a relatively senior academic post in
his home country to embark on PhD studies in the United Kingdom. What
had we done to reduce such a person to this state? Had all our years of
developing a research course and a research community intended to be
supportive and person-centred, as well as academically rigorous, been in
vain? His other comments suggest not, but the incident itself, its anteced-
ents and aftermath, which we will return to later, were salutary experiences
warning us never to become complacent.

We clearly still have much to learn from our students, though we have
between us over 30 successfully completed doctoral supervisions, a further
ten for which we acted as consultant supervisors for other departments and
other institutions, and many more making good progress. Nevertheless,
experiential learning is only one facet; we also value learning from our
peers and so have attended and run several training courses for supervisors.

We are reminded of Elton's (1994: 26) words: 'At the level of research
supervision, where there is usually a unique student experience . . . learning
from experience can hardly ever be an adequate preparation.'

In that paper, Elton recommended a form of staff development programme for supervisors, while in a previous one (Elton and Pope 1992) he
advocated a collegial relationship between all involved in research in a
department – that is, academic and support staff with postgraduate students.
We endeavour to implement both of these recommendations. However, we
would go further and say that even the three together are insufficient if
alertness to the diversity of our students is lacking. Sweeping generalizations
about research students are as inappropriate as any others about a nominal
group.

In this chapter, we refer to work which suggests that students from
particular backgrounds may have specific problems but we emphasize that
these are guidelines only, given the present diversity of our students. We
suggest that successful supervision, though requiring many skills and a reasonable knowledge of the academic field and research methods, rests on
sensitivity to the uniqueness of each student's experience and on a professional flexibility which allows us to respond appropriately to it.

Let us first address the context of both the students' and the supervisors'
experience.

The British scene

When describing management education in the United Kingdom, one of
our students (Tjok-a-Tam 1994) used the evocative metaphor of a circus
ring in which academics attempt to build themselves into a pyramid on the
backs of cantering ponies. Much the same can be said of all academics in
the British higher education system, whose role now encompasses striving
for high levels of quality in teaching, in their own research and in supervising the research of others, at the same time incorporating an entrepre-
neurial aspect in attracting students and consultancy work, all in the face of
diminishing resources. Lecturers from other national contexts of higher
education may empathize.

One of those diminishing resources is funding for research, especially
that from the various research councils. The latter are seeking increased
value for the money they expend in supporting research students, being
particularly concerned with both attrition and slow completion rates. Their
attempts to counteract these problems in the 1990s have included conferences on research training and workshops on the supervision of research
students. These have provided academics with hitherto rare opportunities
to discuss with a wide range of colleagues their perspectives on what constitutes 'an adequate standard' for those activities, and what factors influence
the achievement of such standards.

For attendees at the first round of these conferences/workshops, once
the professional masks of composed competence were discarded, common
concerns emerged. Most revealed that they had embarked on the supervisory aspect of their professional role with little or no training for it. Those

who had higher degrees themselves had personal experience of the com-
plementary role to draw on – practices they were concerned either to emulate
or to avoid – while most participants had experience of a form of 'buddy'
system, an apprenticeship as co-supervisor with an experienced colleague.
They reported finding little in the literature to guide them other than:

- codes of practice, such as that produced in 1991 by the Economic and
  Social Research Council (ESRC), which contain checklists in question
  form on good supervisory practice – for example, 'Does the student see
  the supervisor often enough?' (there is no indication of what constitutes
  enough and for whom);
- their institutions' regulations for the award of a higher degree which deal
  with particular requirements, such as the presentation format; practical
  generalities, such as the boundaries on periods of registration; and guidelines on content – a contribution to knowledge which could be achieved
  in the equivalent of three years' full-time study;
- sporadic articles in the academic press, such as 'Left to their own devices'
  by Wright (1991) in *The Times Higher Education Supplement,* which are
  critical of supervisory practices;
- occasional journal articles which catalogue experience and demand improvement, such as 'Doing a thesis: the loneliness of the long distance
  runner' by McGarry (1990: 15), who makes the following point:

    Acceptable supervisors are as scarce as gold dust . . . compilers of
    databases please note: how marvellous would be a file on specialist
    supervisors who were ready, willing and able to supervise.

Discussions at these early conference workshops revealed enormous vari-
ation between departments and institutions on the amount and kind of
research training provided for the students and undue variance, even within
departments, on what constituted the process of supervision. When elaborating on the guidelines about supervision roles and responsibilities and
their practice, novice and experienced supervisors alike found it hard to
distinguish between those they had invented themselves, those derived from
institutional regulations and those with their roots in tradition, usually that
of the discipline area. What did become apparent was that practice was, to
a large extent, dependent on belief and value systems, traditions – and,
dare we say, myths – which had seldom been articulated, far less disseminated within and between institutions.

Those workshops and similar ones provide valuable opportunities for
articulation and dissemination so that the bounding parameters of good
practice can be recognized. The urgency for this in the United Kingdom is
exacerbated not just by external pressures for quality – from government
agencies – but also by internal pressures from academics, who seek the
satisfaction of knowing they are doing a reasonable job, and from students,
whose studentships are hard won or who are self-funding.

In 1996, a consultative document entitled *Review of Postgraduate Education,*
produced by a HEFCE/CVCP/SCOP1[1] group chaired by Harris (1996),

made strong recommendations about the support and training of postgraduate research students. It recommends, among other things, that what may be expected of and by students should be clearly spelled out and that a code of practice be adopted which would require institutions to have in place 'appropriate facilities and supervisory arrangements'. Further, it was the group's view that such students should only be eligible for HEFCE research grants to study subject areas within institutions which have a 'pervasive research culture, and can deliver excellence in research education' (1996: 8, 9). Referring particularly to overseas students, the document (1996: 37, 38) recommended a directory, modelled on the Australian listing provision, which should include full specification of prices and sources of support for students. It is clear from this reference, and several like it, that cognisance had been taken of the practice of other, sometimes competitive, countries.

The international context

Although it is no consolation to British academics, the universality of the problem is evidenced by an increasing number of articles in the academic press, at conferences and in journals dealing with related issues. A sample is provided here as an illustration.

A recent and continuing polemic in *The Times Higher Education Supplement* about joint European Union projects and exchanges with Italian universities, where student:staff ratios suggest that individual supervision must be negligible (e.g. Davies 1996) points to a European dimension. A poignant paper (Mullen and Dalton 1995) given at a Canadian conference, reflecting on the tension between promise and myth in postgraduate studies, was received with empathy by other recent participants in the postgraduate experience in North American universities.

McMichael (1993) reported on workshops in Australia and Sri Lanka developed in the context of establishing criteria to reduce student and staff uncertainty over requirements and standards in postgraduate degrees. She reported that, while some national differences in anxieties and aims emerged, these were a matter of degree rather than content.

Noting that many staff in the newer Australian technological universities, in common with those in British former polytechnics, have previously devoted their energies to teaching courses and do not necessarily have postgraduate experience of their own to draw on (Smith 1989), McMichael proposes that they are in genuine need of help in considering the range of their responsibilities and how these might be undertaken.

Aspland and O'Donoghue (1994) confirm the paucity of research reports concerned with enhancing postgraduate study of overseas students, while suggesting that all is not well – not just in the case of supervision of overseas students, but in the supervision of higher degrees in general in the English speaking world.

The next section briefly addresses that general context, the difficulties faced by most postgraduate students and the consequences for supervision, before focusing on the special problems of those from overseas.

The 'average' doctoral student

In a recent publication (Denicolo and Pope 1994), we wrote of some research we had conducted with a group of postgraduate students which was intended to give them voice about their life roles, including that of 'student', while ensuring confidentiality and anonymity of source. One of several other motives was to give supervisors some understanding of the personal models used by students to impose meaning on their worlds.

In that work we noted (1994: 121–2) that, in many disciplines, a large number of research students are mature and hence have many roles and responsibilities which compete with the research student role. Like Salmon (1992), our experience contradicted the oft-portrayed stereotype of the full-time, funded and typically young student. Instead, the majority of those we worked with were part-time, self-funded mature people who were ful-filling simultaneously professional, kinship and social roles alongside their student one.

In spite of our extensive research training programme and departmental efforts, and their own, to establish interest and support groups, each one of the 70 responding in the research identified a range of difficulties encoun-tered in the course of their studies. Each led a complex life in which some facets were harmonious while others caused dissonance.

Although each emphasized a range of personal, developmental benefits related to their student role, many noted costs which included: the neglect or loss of previous roles, particularly social ones, with consequent feelings of guilt; the pressures of conflicting duties with consequent anger at the imposition or disappointment in self for not being able to cope; and per-sonal relationships put at risk as partners and friends react to neglect – or, indeed, to the developmental changes in someone they once thought they knew.

Okorocha (1996b) observed that, in our institutions, counselling is con-ducted in the Western mode of empowering student self-help. This can be disorientating and counter-cultural for students used to different modes of support, seeking wisdom from experts, especially when they would, in their own countries, only seek advice from close family and friends. When these networks are distant, or experiencing trauma themselves, then the prob-lems are exacerbated.

We have had experience of supporting students in both of those stressful situations – for example, a mother who left four young children back home in Malaysia and a father who brought his wife and young children with him from Pakistan. Both succeeded in their studies but would have had more difficulty in doing so, we would suggest, had the institution not been tolerant of frequent visits home or of campus work being undertaken well within school hours to allow for school runs, or had it not introduced the students to Muslim support networks and provided a small space for religious observance, and so on.

Again, Harris (1996: 45) made the point that both social and working environments conducive to postgraduate study should be provided as a matter of course in all institutions undertaking such work. He was – as we are – clearly aware that, for many institutions, the social welfare of postgraduate students comes low in the list of priorities.

We review in the next section some of the points made in the literature about the additional responsibilities which arise for supervisors when the particular problems of overseas students demand a special duty of care.

The dilemmas inherent in studying abroad

First, lest we forget our caveat about not jumping too readily to stereotypes about overseas students, let us return to the student given voice at the beginning of this paper. He had arrived in England after giving his research proposal a lot of thought. His research questions were clear and his research design, based on his Masters training in research methods, almost complete. Let him provide the essence of his dilemma, after six months.

> One consideration that never crossed my mind while developing my ideas . . . was the paradigm, or world view, with which I was approaching this important task . . . What I soon discovered after my arrival in England was that a concept of 'the', or a single, research paradigm did not exist . . . I was overwhelmed by the discovery of literally an entire other world of perspectives on the research process . . . As the new information filtered in, I began to feel my proposal start to unravel little by little. I had doubts about my original ideas, my original proposal, as well as my place in this new system. I felt incredibly vulnerable and naive.

From the evocative way in which he described his predicament, it is clear that his command of English is good, so from what exotic context did he come? . . . His home base is a prestigious university in the southern States of America. As his PhD story is still in progress, we cannot provide readers with a 'happy ending'. With the support of his supervisor and peer students, he has come to enjoy reconstruing research and its approaches and methods, but still faces the challenge of ensuring the credibility of his own work in his own context.

Such first-hand experience supports points made in the literature referred to in this paper and highlights for us that, although supervisors-as-teachers should be change agents, they must also be sensitive to the point of departure of the students and to the context to which they must return on completion of their studies. However, we do them a disservice if we do not respect their need to produce work which both meets our exacting standards and is politically acceptable in their own national higher education context.

Though it is important that students are helped to adapt to our respective cultures, it is not enough for us to expect, as Ginsburg (1992: 6) advocated, that 'students need to modify the world-view of their native culture and the academic culture in which they were educated if they are to gain acceptance in this new academic context'.

Modification with understanding is required by *both* parties if we are not to risk our educational values being perceived as a dangerous threat to the national cultures of others. Recognition of the diversity of academic styles that exist in other countries, including European partners, can be an enriching experience for supervisors and fellow students. However, we are aware that some differences pose particular problems. We have considerable experience of working in South East Asia and in welcoming Asian students within our university. We have focused on these in this chapter.

Two dimensions of our shared academic culture should be set in relief against the background of Asian, particularly South East Asian, education norms. One is the concept of argument/debate, while the other is the notion of originality. In the United Kingdom, we expect to hone our ideas by subjecting them to challenge. Debating societies are a common feature of secondary schooling – we are taught to plan our propositions carefully, to be alert to potentially contradictory views and to marshall our arguments accordingly. It is interesting to reflect on Lakoff and Johnson's (1980) observation that, in English, the 'war' metaphor pervades our language concerned with argument – for instance, we 'shoot' arguments down – while in some Eastern languages the parallel metaphor is a dance of equals in which steps are matched. It is Lakoff and Johnson's contention that such predominant metaphors reflect the culture and values from which they emerge, so it comes as no surprise that in many Eastern cultures it is considered inappropriate to query the wisdom of experts, of those in authority, that is the teachers (see also Smith, Chapter 13 in this book, on this). Further, such cultures may place a high value on compromise as a survival technique. Divergence is thus viewed as a social evil with unanimity regarded as a social good to be aspired to. For example, strong religious traditions in Thailand condemn any expression of displeasure or avowal of conflict (Tambiah 1990). The resultant attitudes can frustrate attempts at intended intellectual development by setting opposing views in counterpoint.

It has been our experience in working in a variety of Thai universities that energies are devoted to remarking and elaborating the similarities in counterposed examples; even though we may see differences to be of interest and to contain potential for creativity, to emphasize them would be considered very bad manners indeed. It would be helpful if we took time to reflect on the possibility of adopting some Eastern values in our postgraduate provision. The PhD viva may be a case in point. We suggest that the 'war' metaphor which prevails when we require our students to defend their thesis could be replaced by the metaphor of the dance. The viva should be seen as an opportunity for the candidates to display their interests and engage in a conversation which allows all participants to benefit from the engagement of minds rather than adopting an adversarial stance. The dance metaphor can be adopted without any diminution of standards.

Innovation, creativity and originality are key parameters by which we judge the quality of MPhil and PhD theses. Nevertheless, we expect initial contentions to be justified by reference to preceding literature, while new ones require the support of data collected with expertise and integrity. It is surely not surprising that students whose main education has been in societies in which conformity is valued above individuality, in which social replication is the norm, experience a degree of confusion. Indeed, we are frequently asked even by our British-bred students why they need express things in a novel way when some revered expert has already expressed them both pithily and cogently.

Our conventions, too, are derived from tradition and it is incumbent on us to make them explicit to others. A case in point is where we draw the boundary on the continuum between authenticity and plagiarism, since for us acknowledgement of sources is an ethical issue while for others it is a latent assumption that all that we say is derived, in some way, from the work of others.

Just as we need to challenge the suppositions of others, so too we need to confront the premises to which we are heir. Jones (1979: viii) made the following point which is still salient today:

> The assumption underlying much practice in adult learning, in Higher Education at any rate, is that the students are vocal, articulate and well-read in English. Consequently, when teachers meet college students who are silent and who, in addition, lack a background in English, they may get the impression that they are instructing inferior students. The students' silence may breed suspicion of apathy.
>
> Of course, reticence does not imply resistance to learning, much less stupidity. Reluctance to speak may be a cultural value, a norm picked up from society.

The norm of reticence frequently accompanies that of avoidance of contention and may also be accompanied by forms of non-verbal communication which we may not always recognize between cultures. This is a huge topic[2] which we encourage supervisors to explore in relation to the cultural origins and customs of their own students. On a light note, readers may be amused to contemplate some of the following: the contortions to which we subject our ageing English bones while trying to sit decorously on low stools while avoiding the insulting behaviour of pointing our feet at Thai colleagues; the inelegant way in which we try to incorporate a Western handshake while not giving or receiving gifts with the left hand, deemed 'unclean' in many Asian cultures; the deliberate suppression of feelings of panic and consequent flinching when our Middle Eastern students invade the rather large personal space that we British people find it comfortable to inhabit. Even though we are aware that in some cultures an averted gaze is a mark of respect, our own culturally ordained need to look a speaker in the eyes has led to many a cricked neck when working with, for instance, our Malaysian students.

On a more serious note, this reminds us that, though we may intend to make the students' interpersonal transactions more comfortable and fruitful during their stay with us by alerting them to our habits – for instance, of eye contact – it would be unfortunate if they took those habits home with them, thereby earning for our respective education systems the reputation that they produce arrogant and ill-mannered academics.

In addition to behavioural disparity, Jones (1979) also raises the issue of an incomplete command of English. Perhaps this is the most prolific source of potential disaster in our work with overseas students. NESB students must cope with understanding both our spoken and written words and must reciprocate by demonstrating that understanding, in an oral and written form, themselves. This is a difficult enough task at degree level without combining it with the intellectual rigour and original research required of higher degree students.

The order of magnitude of the problem with which NESB students must wrestle is difficult to contemplate for those of us for whom English is our main language. If it were only differences in spelling and grammar, information technology and common sense would come to our rescue. However, in addition, there are complications such as the nuances of meaning of words which appear to be synonyms, the social, cultural and literary referents of our metaphors and the subtle shifts in language register which denote a move from informal to formal communication, to name but a few. These are compounded by the use of professional jargon, not to mention the complication of dialect and accent. Recent research (Chincotta and Underwood 1996) on the link between working memory span and native language indicates that the structure of some languages, such as Arabic, limits the amount of information which can typically be held in working memory. This results in both slower reading speeds and limits on comprehension of strings of spoken words, no matter in which language the person is subsequently working.

To illustrate some of the language barriers that supervisors might face when working with NESB students, we will focus on one potential source of students, Papua New Guinea (PNG), drawing on the work of two authors: McLaughlin (1996), writing about improving the quality of education in PNG as a developing country, and Speier (1990), one of our own students resident and working in PNG, who investigated the development of preparation courses for overseas studies for indigenous academic staff, most of whom were Australia-bound.

Both remarked that, in many instances, levels of spoken colloquial Australian English were deceptively good – deceptively because this disguised poor comprehension of academic lectures, limited reading ability and very limited formal writing skills. They noted the predominance of ritual in learning, just as ritual predominates in other aspects of traditional society – 'the essence of ritual is on the correct utterance of a spell or secret name' (McLaughlin 1996: 110). Speier suggested that many of those who do well in PNG secondary and tertiary education do so because they have conformed to the rote learning process demanded by their home society and are thus unprepared for individual study initiatives and for critical thinking. McLaughlin illustrated this vividly:

> *Teacher:* A gibob is a zingut and is used for willoting things together. Alfred, what is a gibob?
> *Alfred:* Sir, a gibob is a zingut and is used for willoting things together.
> *Teacher:* Excellent answer.

He used this as an example of a survival tactic rather than a learning strategy, adopted when individuals are unwilling to admit to, or demonstrate, a lack of understanding.

The survival of his colleagues when they do study abroad is the focus of Speier's concern. Whether or not they achieved success in their studies, most cited isolation from their extended families – particularly their spouses – as being most traumatic. This arose from guilt about those remaining in PNG who were considered to have been left vulnerable to gossip and even sorcery threats, worry exacerbated by not being able to judge the seriousness of typically alarmist media reports, as much as from the loneliness experienced by the students themselves.

In Speier's programme devised to prepare his colleagues appropriately for study abroad, there is preparation of the family as well as the prospective student for a new form of life. Although it would be ideal if his suggestions were implemented by the country/institution of origin of all such students, some of the information he discovered could be supplied by host institutions as a matter of form. On reading his list, most points seem obvious. However, his recommendations for information to be supplied to students far exceed what we typically supply. Some examples are:

- relative costs of living – important for those on a fixed income;
- a city plan with special aspects noted, such as suburbs to avoid;
- special habits and customs so that inadvertent transgression might be avoided;
- the position of women in the respective culture; and
- how to deal with racial problems.

Speier (1990: 67) illustrated the importance of helping students find adequate accommodation by reflecting back to his own distant experience as a student when African colleagues spent the whole winter in bed (not conducive to academic study!) because they had failed to check the heating provisions properly (the first thing a German student would do, he assured us).

There are many other dimensions of threat to successful completion of study of our students from the Pacific Rim: the family's economic sacrifice for many students from South East Asia, and the fear of being wrong – thereby losing face – which inhibits some Japanese students are but two examples. What can we do, given our limited resources? And where do our responsibilities end?

Further dilemmas for supervisors

If resources were unlimited, including our own time, energy and patience, the problems above would be less critical, but academic roles and duties are now complex and demanding. Dedicated people must daily choose to do some things less well than they would wish and to omit doing some things altogether. Other experts need to be called upon, such as those who can provide courses and guidance on English language problems or counsellors for personal problems. As Harris (1996: 38) highlights, the full cost of this additional support should be overtly noted in the fee structure, for institutions have budgets to meet and support systems cannot be stretched indefinitely to cope.

Harris (1996: 47) also suggests that particular regard be paid to student feedback. Home students will become disaffected and vocal if their resources, including supervision time, are reduced to meet the needs of overseas students. They may also question the justice of being required to write elegantly themselves while others have support for their writing, and it is to their supervisors in the first instance that they will address these apparent injustices, so we need to feel comfortable with the answers we provide. Supervisors have a duty to society, as well as to their students, to ensure that standards are maintained, that funds are expended on useful original research, and that all students, whatever their origin, develop new expertise and learning styles appropriate for lifelong learning in ever-changing contexts. In order to do this, they too need support.

Main conclusions

Three particular points seem worth distilling from the foregoing. First, just as it is a mis-assumption that academic staff can supervise by instinct, so it is wrong to assume that students have an inbuilt potential to respond appropriately to any individual form of supervision. It is only just and productive that we make our respective roles and limited responsibilities clear.

Second, although there are some good arguments for and strong advocates of the cultural melting pot notion, it may be more appropriate to value diversity and help NESB students to preserve some of their cultural differences, especially when they have to return home when their studies are complete.

Finally, we could do well to heed the advice given by Little (1988: 19) to potential consultants selling their educational advice to developing countries:

> Only when prepared to spend time doing our homework to learn and understand more about the situation on which advice is sought, and only when prepared to share responsibility when things go badly wrong, should we erect our 'for sale' sign.

As supervisors we must note that each student brings a unique combination of:

- needs, desires and expectations – personal, academic and social;
- skills and abilities – cognitive, conative and affective, embryonic, partially developed or well-honed;
- experience and style.

Each case has political, economic and legal connotations and ramifications. Supervisors respond to this complexity in their own unique ways, often supported by inadequate organizational structures and vague guidance on *modus operandi*.

Viewing overseas students as desirable in principle but generating problems in practice is no recent dilemma. Elsey and Kinnell (1990) quote:

> Unless you conduct yourselves with more restraint and moderation towards them [overseas students], they will be driven into abandoning their studies and leaving the country, which we by no means desire.

This statement, addressed to the inhabitants of Cambridge, England, is attributed to Henry III in 1231!

As the diversity of our postgraduate students increases, so will our needs for ingenuity and peer group support. Our needs often parallel theirs. And they are not all insensitive to the demands they make on us as supervisors. Let us leave the final words to a student (Harwood 1994: 37):

> The personal characteristics and talents required ... call for a super-being (being human, most of us can only do some of the things some of the time). For most research students the most they can expect from a supervisor is the ability to apply the right degree of pressure at the right moment in order to keep their momentum rolling towards completion. For my part, I want a supervisor to be a kind, considerate friend whilst at the same time operating as a devil's advocate. This is probably asking the impossible of any human relationship, but I ask it nonetheless.

Notes

1. Higher Education Funding Council for England, HEFCE; Committee of Vice-Chancellors and Principals, CVCP; Standing Conference of Principals, SCOP.
2. For a very readable and detailed account of differences in non-verbal communication, readers might like to refer to Morris (1978).

7

The Law, Policies and Ethics: Supervising Postgraduate NESB Students in an Era of Internationalization

Helen Stacy

Introduction

This chapter looks at the legal and policy effects of internationalization of higher education in English speaking universities, and the ethical consequences of increasing internationalization for NESB students. It describes the guidelines for postgraduate supervision in various universities in Australia, the United Kingdom and the United States of America, demonstrating that, although there are similar policies for postgraduate supervisory practices across universities and across countries, there is little access to fora external to individual universities to which NESB students may take their perceived or actual grievances. There is a description of the slowly growing legal field of 'educational negligence'. Educational negligence as a head of legal redress has arisen from the sense of frustration that students experience when their educational institution manifestly fails to attain the appropriate standards.

These legal benchmarks will to some extent influence universities and 'peak' higher education bodies to standardize and enforce good postgraduate supervision as part of a greater recognition of 'value for money'. This is especially important to the NESB student whose educational costs are increased through living abroad. In conclusion, a checklist for good supervisory practice of NESB students is offered as a means of avoiding legal difficulties in the supervision of NESB international students.

The standard for good postgraduate supervision in the English speaking world is an accumulation of historical and pedagogical factors. In most cases, universities in the United Kingdom, Australia, and, by extension, other countries that work off the Oxbridge model of postgraduate education, as well as in the US, have articulated these traditions in explicit postgraduate policies that set out the respective rights and responsibilities of the university, the academic supervisor(s) and the postgraduate student.

In some universities, there has been recognition of the more acute supervisory dilemmas that arise when the postgraduate student is studying in a foreign culture and, for the student, the foreign tongue of English. More generally however, the NESB student is reliant upon each university's policies and guidelines on postgraduate supervision. These policies and standards are not uniform across the higher education sector; they are internal to each university. Even where there is a 'peak' university body (as is the case in the United Kingdom and Australia) the self-regulatory nature of postgraduate supervisory practices within universities underscores the unique position of the NESB student.

In the relationship between the NESB postgraduate student, the supervisor and the university, the balance of power clearly resides in the university. Just as for the English speaking student, it is often imprudent for a postgraduate student to complain about the standard of his or her supervision because the dynamics of the student–supervisor relationship depend to a large extent upon mutual goodwill. This aspect is emphasized when the dynamics include either cultural difference or difficulties of language and communication. Additionally, NESB students frequently have the imperative of completing their degrees within the strict timeframe of a scholarship. The time pressures exerted by limited-term funding mean that these NESB students are even more reliant upon their universities observing practices of good supervision. When educational practices are challenged in the courts, universities may find that changes to their practices and procedures will be forced upon them by the legal system.

'Internationalization': the global student

Internationalization has become a banner for universities to wave, a claim to quality and relevance. Terms such as international education, multicultural education, comparative education, cross-cultural education and global education all describe the new global setting of higher education. The increasing interdependence of the world's economies has generated a market for internationally oriented graduates in the globalizing world economy. The shrinking of time and distance, compounded by the rapid growth in the economies of the 'Asian Tigers' in the 1980s and early 1990s, generated a significant market for universities.

For these reasons, universities have been urged to transform their curricula to

> prepare(s) the community for successful participation in an increasingly interdependent world . . . (internationalization) should infuse all facets of the post-secondary education system, fostering global understanding and developing skills for effective living and working in a diverse world.
>
> (Francis 1993)

However, the literature on internationalization of higher education suggests that in practice, the presence of international students and the development of internationally oriented curricula have not been tightly coupled (cf. Berchem (1991) for German universities, Altbach (1991) for US universities). This criticism is true also of postgraduate supervision – it is not necessarily adapted to the increasing diversity of populations in an era of large-scale global migration and student exchange.

We have a responsibility to provide the international students we have recruited with an education adapted to their needs. Internationalization is not merely a matter of recruiting international students, though the presence of international students is an enormous resource for the university. The aim of internationalization is to produce graduates capable of solving problems with cultural and environmental sensitivity in a variety of cultural and geographical locations.

There are three distinct dimensions of internationalization: cross-cultural awareness and communicative competence; professional environments; and professional discourse. With all three, there is need to develop comfortable strategies for mutual understanding and communication. As universities promote internationalization through increasing numbers of international students, student research and study exchanges, and the employment of academic staff from overseas universities, they must recognize the need to support the experiences, interests and expectations of people from culturally diverse backgrounds.

Some universities have developed policies which reflect their commitment to cultural diversity. For example, one Australian university (Monash) has published the following recommendations.

- The university should affirm and encourage through its policies and priorities an equal right of all students and staff to experiences within the university that enable them to feel supported and respected, regardless of their cultural background.
- In order to achieve awareness throughout the university of the importance of all aspects of student background for supervision practices, formal and compulsory training programmes, which encourage an awareness of equity questions and issues relating to cultural diversity, must be put into place.
- Encouragement and support should be given to programmes which already train and educate supervisors in the need for flexibility to meet the needs of a range of students, including those from culturally diverse backgrounds.
- The university should support student interactions, orientations, and educational programmes which alert students to the culturally produced expectations of them which supervisors and departments may operate with. For example, training in communication and assertiveness skills may be necessary for some students.

In considering the range of university policies on postgraduate supervision in Australia, the UK and the US, certain assumptions have been made:

first, that the NESB student (whether full fee-paying or not) has selected a particular university in which to undertake her/his research because that university has held out to the student that he or she will receive a postgraduate degree provided the student achieves the requisite academic standards. The information contained within a university, faculty or department handbook on postgraduate research degree rules and procedures can be deemed to convey this part of the university's 'bargain'.

Second, it is assumed that the NESB student has passed the test for English proficiency utilized by the university. In other words, the formalities of student enrolment have established a reasonable expectation on the part of the student and the university/faculty/department that the student is, on the face of it, properly enrolled in research degree study at the postgraduate level. The student's reasonable assumption is that, by virtue of that correct placement in the course, diligent work on the part of the student, and good supervision on the part of the university, there is a reasonable likelihood of the student satisfactorily completing the degree. (The 'reasonable expectation' here would be akin to the percentage statistics of students normally obtaining the research degree in that particular faculty or department.) Let us now consider the policies, legal and ethical issues in UK, US and Australia, in turn.

United Kingdom

The UK's higher education system is changing rapidly and energetic overseas competitors are making inroads into its traditional markets. Even so, the UK is one of the major destinations for postgraduate students from around the world. The programmes range from taught Masters and professional training through to research training (MRes), research qualifications (PhDs) and postdoctoral research. The latest statistics (1995/96) show that 34 per cent of full-time postgraduates are from overseas. Around 40 per cent of full-time international students come from the EU and 30 per cent from Asian countries. The top sending country in 1995/96 was Malaysia with 16,000 students. Their contribution to the UK economy has been estimated at over £1 billion per year (Greenaway and Tuck 1995).

What measures are undertaken by UK universities to ensure that the student experience at postgraduate level is a good one? Postgraduate research study in UK universities is traditionally based on independent learning with access to academics with a good track record in research. Good practice is encouraged through the Code of Practice on the management of higher degrees undertaken by overseas students, institutional guidance on supervision, facilities and progress reports. The CVCP Code of Practice on the *Recruitment and Support of International Students in UK Higher Education* (1996) includes the recommendation that supervisors take account of the needs of international postgraduate research students, such as provision of clear information on equipment, bench fees or additional charges required for study and details of supervision arrangements. A CVCP working group has been established to take forward the Review's recommendations.

The 1996 guidelines include the following recommendations:

1. Establishment of English language competence before entry (7 or 7.5 in British Council test).
2. Clarification of any increase in course length as a result of being required to take preparatory courses.
3. Information to students and sponsors of course length, fees and nature and frequency of reports. No supplementary fees should be charged during the course under any circumstances.
4. Annual progress reports to the sponsoring authority.
5. Students should be encouraged to bring problems to the attention of the university as soon as possible.
6. Supervisors should be sensitive to the needs of overseas students who may require more supervision. The university should offer guidance to supervisors on this.
7. Students should be supplied with detailed and accurate information on access to laboratories, equipment and library facilities prior to starting the course.
8. Universities should have a clear procedure for transfer to a different course or institution.

United States of America

The structure of higher education in the US is a massive and heterogeneous mixture of publicly and privately funded universities, and four-year colleges. There is no 'peak' national higher education body such as in the UK (above) and Australia (below). For example, only 173 universities of a total of 3,638 institutions of higher education in the US are represented by NASULGA, the National Association of State Universities and Land-Grant Colleges. Single institutions tend to form their own policies and approaches to postgraduate supervision. It is a measure of these differences that most of the litigation on educational negligence described below has occurred in the United States.

As higher education is a major income earner for the US, it is clear that a more concentrated effort will emerge to standardize NESB postgraduate supervisory practices. The present approaches tend not to identify NESB students as a sub-group of the postgraduate student population. This means that the general university policies are applied. A sense of these can be gained by a brief extract from policies at Yale and Harvard University.

Yale University Advisors and Advisory Committees
A temporary advisory committee is appointed for first year students on their admission to the graduate programme. The members of the committee will be chosen according to the particular interest or interests of

the student. The first year advisory committee, in conjunction with the Director of Graduate Studies (the 'DGS'), serves primarily to help the student start graduate work.

Students will be expected to select a thesis advisor and an advisory committee by the beginning of the third term. Before making the choice of an advisor, the student is encouraged to become acquainted with the various research programmes in the department. The advisor will supervise the student's General Examination at the end of the third term . . . If it is appropriate, a student may have more than one primary advisor. Advisors and/or advisory committees may be changed at any time to meet the needs or best interests of the students; such changes are initiated by the student in consultation with the DGS. Each spring the DGS reviews advisor assignments with all students.

All aspects of the course of study and of independent work and other activities outside the classroom that relate to study toward the doctorate and a student's particular field of interest should be discussed and planned with the advisor and/or advisory committee. It is the student's responsibility to keep in contact with his or her advisor and/or advisory committee throughout the year; the only formally scheduled conferences are those in September and May.

Harvard Graduate School of Arts and Science
The Harvard International Office (HIO) serves the foreign national at Harvard by providing programmes and services for foreign students, scholars, and their families. These programmes and services include: orientation meetings, arrival booklets, and printed information to assist with the adjustment to Harvard and living in the Boston/Cambridge area; advising and counseling on immigration regulations, social and cultural differences, financial matters, and personal concerns; referrals to other offices when appropriate; assistance in locating housing in August and early September; the Friends of International Students programme for new graduate students; English language classes, discussion groups, and activities for accompanying spouses; and information on a wide variety of topics disseminated through printed material, newsletter, a web site, and group information sessions. The International Office hosts a reception each fall for newly-arrived foreign students, scholars, and their families. In late February/early March the HIO organizes tax seminars for foreign students and scholars.

A foreign student advisor is always available during working hours to address problems or concerns.

Australia

The advent of postgraduate research degrees since 1989 in universities that were once teacher-training colleges has meant a recognition that supervision of research degrees is frequently undertaken by academics who are engaged at the same time in writing their own theses. This is occurring at a time of new measures of funding tertiary institutions through actively marketing Australian educational 'products' to neighbours in the Asia–Pacific region. The full fee-paying overseas student is a 'market' that Australian universities are consciously tapping in order to meet the gap between their operating costs and decreasing financial assistance from government. For example, *Campus Review*, September 4–10, 1996 ran a story entitled 'Battle commences for overseas students' on its front page. This has led to a 'user-pays' approach in the Australian tertiary sector, creating a contractarian view[1] of the university–student relationship wherein postgraduate students demand value for money. Australia's capture of a market share of the lucrative higher education market is quickening the recognition of the importance of servicing student needs.

Each Australian university has its own rules and procedures in relation to research postgraduate student enrolment, supervision and examination. Even within the same university, supervisory practices and postgraduate research facilities can differ markedly. The only global provisions that apply to all universities are the Australian Vice-Chancellors' Committee's (AVCC) *Generic Guidelines on Universities and their Students' Expectations and Responsibilities* (December 1994). This is a broadly worded document that simply sets out equitable goals to which universities should aspire in their dealings with students. The guidelines that are most likely to apply specifically to NESB postgraduate students and their supervisors read as follows.

Australian Vice-Chancellors' Committee Guidelines
- The university will endeavor to address the reasonable needs of all its students regardless of gender, ethnicity, age, disability or background.
- The university will endeavor to provide an environment for students which is free from harassment and discrimination as set out by relevant university policy and State and Federal anti-discrimination legislation. Where alleged harassment or discrimination occurs, procedures will be available to students to facilitate expeditious and just resolution of grievances. The relationships that university staff develop with their students should not provide any basis for the abuse of the power that staff have over students in the university environment nor of the trust that students may legitimately expect to place in staff.
- The university will endeavor to provide a suitable environment for teaching and learning and research supervision in which students will be stimulated to reach a high level of intellectual attainment.
- The teaching–learning environment should be a positive and co-operative one where students will have reasonable access to staff to discuss issues and problems and can expect fair, critical and helpful assessment and feedback on their academic work in a timely manner.

- The university will produce a clearly outlined appeal mechanism, which will provide students with an opportunity to review and to question formally their results.
- The university will endeavor to provide a harmonious work and study environment in which concerns and complaints will be addressed and resolved as quickly as possible. Student grievances that relate to academic standing and progress will be dealt with quickly and satisfactorily through a clear set of procedures provided by the university.
- Students enrolled in a particular course can normally expect to complete that course in the format as described in official university publications, providing they make satisfactory progress. Where changes to courses are made during the normal period of candidacy, these should not disadvantage students.

Conversely, the document states that students also have responsibilities.

- Students are responsible for making themselves aware of all university rules and regulations pertaining to their rights and responsibilities as students. They can expect that the university will make such rules and regulations readily available to them to access and, where appropriate, to acquire.
- Students are expected to be aware of all unit or subject information made available to them and to raise any questions or concerns with the appropriate academic staff member in a timely manner.
- Students have a responsibility to participate actively and positively in the teaching–learning environment. It is expected students will attend classes as required, maintain steady progress within the unit or subject framework, comply with workload expectations and submit required work on time.
- The university is entitled to expect honest work at all levels from students. Cheating, plagiarism, fabrication or falsification of data, are not acceptable. Students are also expected to be aware of their individual rights and responsibilities regarding the proper use of copyright material.
- Students are responsible for monitoring their own progress within the teaching–learning environment and the academic programme. They will have reasonable access to academic staff for assistance and to the various academic support services.
- Students have a responsibility to participate in the functioning of the university and to provide feedback on the teaching–learning environment. Student participation is important as students represent a key constituency within the university and provide useful perspectives on its operations.
- Students are expected to act at all times in a way that respects the rights and privileges of others and shows commitment to the ideals of a university with special reference to excellence in performance and freedom of expression.

- Students are expected to be aware of their responsibilities under the statutes of the university and to abide by these statutes.
- Student Representative Organizations have played a traditional and significant role in the life of Australian universities. It is expected that these organizations will continue to act responsibly and in the best interests of all students attending universities and that they will be supported, as the university deems appropriate, within the legislative framework of the university and its administration.

These guidelines are exemplary. However, they cannot be said to place a contractual obligation upon universities to carry out these standards of best practice in relation to NESB students, since they do not create a contractual relationship between the university and the student that a court could enforce. Nor are they sufficiently precise to be of practical use to most students. In most cases of supervisory difficulty, students and supervisors must turn to the rules and procedures of their own department and university. If there is no rule to guide a particular instance, students and academics are on their own to find an approach to their particular circumstances that is amenable to both. The power imbalance (which favours the institution over the student) means that any approach is more likely to be amenable to the academic than the student. Joo Cheong Tham has recently written (Joo 1996) that the notion that 'user-pays empowers users' is clearly erroneous in view of the 'fundamental power imbalance between the university administration and overseas students'. Indeed, the AVCC was recently reported as considering that a dispute between the university and the postgraduate student was a matter for the university to resolve; the Guidelines were nothing more than that.[2]

Legal rules about good supervision

What are the legal obligations of universities to their students in providing appropriate educational standards? If a university has a certain standard of legal liability to a NESB postgraduate research student, does this liability flow also to the university department in which the student studies? Does legal liability extend to the individual academic who supervises the NESB student in her/his thesis? If there is a legal obligation upon the university in its many functions, how might the NESB student seek to enforce that liability, and to what effect? There are five different legal actions that a student might pursue: educational negligence; educational contract; misrepresentation; estoppel; and vicarious responsibility of the university for an individual academic's poor supervision.

All of these legal avenues are available to an aggrieved student who feels unable to achieve a satisfactory outcome via the university's internal policy, processes or appeal procedures. However, the capacity of a postgraduate student to seek legal redress for below-standard supervision is affected by the dynamics of the student–university relationship. Legal action could be fatal to the interpersonal relationship between student and supervisor which is a crucial aspect of good postgraduate supervision. These factors are exacerbated in relation to NESB students. Litigation is costly – beyond the means of most postgraduate students and certainly beyond the means of an NESB student on a modest scholarship. In addition, litigation is slow – and therefore likely to extend well beyond the time that NESB students have allocated to their overseas studies. Nevertheless, legal cases brought by students will have a 'backwards' effect, in that they will force universities to have regard to good supervisory practices so as to avoid litigation and bad publicity.

Educational negligence

Negligence is an area of law which requires that a person ('A') make good to another person ('B') if A causes B to suffer loss. There are many types of behaviour that will attract the protection of the law of negligence, and these categories are not closed (*Anns v London Merton Borough Council* 1978 AC 728). All of them have in common a requirement that B show that A could have reasonably foreseen the damage which occurred as a result of A's action. In the educational context, if a student can show that she or he suffered loss from a university's incompetent or negligent teaching, then the university must be responsible for the student's loss. This is called 'educational negligence'.

In a case of educational negligence brought against a university by a student, the court asks: 'Does the university owe a duty of care to the student?' As stated above, most of the litigation has occurred in the US. In 1979, the New York Court of Appeals stated that a duty of care may exist between school teacher and student (*Donohue v Coppiagne* 391 NEZd 1352 (1979)). The 1979 court refused to let the action succeed for public policy reasons, including a reluctance to involve itself in the implementation of public policy and the fear that similar suits would place an intolerable financial burden on educational institutions. This approach was overturned in 1997 in a case before the US District Court, sitting in Pennsylvania (*Dillon and Dougherty v Ultrasound Diagnostic Schools* (1997) US Dist reported on LEXIS 20795). In the context of higher education, it is likely that the same considerations of public policy would make it conceivable for an aggrieved NESB postgraduate to sue a university in negligence. In the Australian legal context, *Introveigne v Cth* (1980) 3C ALR 351 is authority for the proposition that no duty of care to educate students is owed by a school or government. However, the case is now 18 years old, and it is not a precedent that other courts are strictly bound to follow. The 1998 US case stands as an indication of what may occur in the UK and Australia.

To hold a university liable for breach of their educational duty, a court would look at standard practices for supervision of NESB postgraduates. The student would have to show that she or he sustained hardship through the university's negligence. This loss could be in the nature of emotional and intellectual harm in the case of students who return empty-handed to cultures where emphasis is placed on public standing and where 'failure' may lead to a loss of face. Economic harm would also be established where funding bodies require repayment if a student does not complete the work, as evidenced through obtaining the postgraduate degree. It must also be established that the university caused the student's loss. The Australian judgment argues:

> [causation] is difficult to establish because the learning and knowledge accumulated by a student is not limited to the classroom . . . [T]he learning process is such a complex matrix of variables which include the background and motivation of the student that it would be difficult to conclude that a student's failure to learn would not have occurred but for the negligent teaching (Vol. 11 (1988) *UNSW Law Journal* 184–219, at 206).

Educational negligence can be expected to be a growing aspect of legal enforcement of postgraduate supervisory standards.

Educational contract

Contract law allows a remedy where B has given A something of value (usually money) and A has breached her or his promise to do something in return. Assuming a contract where B, the NESB postgraduate, gives A, the academic institution, a fee, B has an entitlement to performance by A of A's contractual obligations.

Students seeking a remedy in contract must show that a contract exists between them and their supervisors.[3] The specific terms of that contract will depend on the representations made by both parties before the contract is struck. This raises the question of whether by advertising their postgraduate courses, the university will be considered to have made a pre-contractual statement which ought to be considered part of a contract. Contract law makes a distinction on the one hand between 'puffery' or 'sales talk' (which are seen as unguaranteed statements of fact) and 'terms of the contract'. Only statements that amount to 'contractual terms' are considered part of a contract and therefore legally actionable where there is a breach of those terms.

A decisive consideration is the relative position of the parties, and their knowledge of the facts (Carter and Harland 1996). Where a student is relying on a university to provide information needed on a subject for which there is no source other than the university, it follows that the duty of the university is onerous. Whether this duty will amount to a fiduciary duty, or whether the duty has the effect of converting advertising material into contractual terms, will depend upon the circumstances of each case. It is unlikely that statements made in advertising material to induce entry into a contract will form part of the contract itself such that an action for breach would lie. However, *misrepresentations* by the university will form a basis for action by the student against the university for misrepresentation. Indeed, the AVCC has issued a code of practice for recruiting overseas students, which specifically forbids 'misleading promotion' (reported in *The Australian Higher Education Supplement* 1998: 33), but the penalties for institutional misdemeanour are unclear.

Advertising material circulated overseas by universities may thus be seen in terms of pre-contractual representations. If the student can show that these representations formed the reasonable basis of her or his entry into the contract (the court would ask: 'Did the advertising cause the student to seek enrolment at the university?'), then university advertising may be considered by a court to be terms or conditions of the contract. If the student can establish that the university has breached these terms or conditions, the student has a legal remedy of financial restitution.

Additionally, the payment of higher fees by overseas NESB postgraduate students may create a higher obligation on the university in the context in which fees are lower to domestic students. The provision of greater 'consideration', the legal term for something of value which is the price of A's promise to educate B, is a factor which may imbue the NESB student–supervisor relationship with a stricter contractual flavour.[4] It is clear that some legal obligation should fall on the shoulders of institutions who misrepresent themselves overseas in order to compete for government funding and student fees.

Misrepresentation of the educational facts

This area, like educational negligence, requires that the student show that the university owed the student a 'duty of care'. The nature of that duty differs in this context, however. In *Shaddock & Associates v Parramatta City Council* (1981 150 CLR 225, 225–6), the High Court of Australia held that a duty of care arises when a person provides information in circumstances where the speaker realizes, or ought to realize, that he or she is being reasonably relied upon and where the recipient ('B', here the student) believes the speaker ('A', the university) to possess a capacity for judgment. If a 'duty of care' can be established, the student must show a loss occasioned by a breach of that duty. The close relationship of the postgraduate student with her or his supervisor will assist the student in establishing that the supervisor caused the loss. If the student were part of a class of 30, it would be harder to establish a causal connection between the academic's conduct and the student's loss.

Estoppel

Estoppel is a legal device which prevents a person from saying something (usually making a denial). Its main thrust is to protect a person from the negative consequences of relying on the words or actions of somebody else. Estoppel may operate when someone seems about to renege upon a promise they have made, and that would lead to circumstances that are unjust. At this point, a court will step in to prevent the harm. In other words, where a university makes a promise about the research and support facilities that will be available to postgraduate students, courts may issue an order saying that it is unjust to allow the university to renege on the promise. In legal jargon, estoppel allows the postgraduate student to whom the promise has been made to 'raise' an estoppel against the university. This would prevent the university from denying its liability towards the postgraduate for the loss which flows from the breach of the promise. The university would need either to make good its undertaking and supply the promised facilities, or to financially compensate the student for its inability to carry through the promise.

To raise an estoppel against a university, a student must show that there is a promise (which can also be an *implied* promise) that the student relied upon to her or his detriment. The student would need to show that the university was at fault (or, in legal language, had acted 'unconscionably'), and that the university's promises related to representations of present (not future) fact(s). A recent Australian case casts doubt on this last requirement so that it may not be fatal to an action in estoppel if representations are made as to postgraduate facilities or supervision which were not in existence at the time the representations were made (*Verwayen* (1990) 170 CLR 394). As to the element of detriment, the problems encountered by NESB postgraduate students will not have difficulty in falling within the legal definition. The sort of outcome that might be expected if a postgraduate student succeeded in a claim would be a court ordering a university to meet the costs of financing a student for a further period until completion of the thesis work. It is unclear whether opportunity costs would be compensatable. 'Opportunity costs' are the costs to the student of being able to avail herself or himself of the employment outcomes had the postgraduate study been completed on time. These types of costs are notoriously difficult to calculate, as they involve an element of conjecture about future performance.

Vicarious liability

Vicarious liability is the legal term given to the liability of employers for the actions of their employees. It is relevant in the context of NESB students, as it refers to the liability of the university for the performance of the academics supervising NESB students. There are two forms:

1. *Tort*: This is potentially an area of concern for universities that have haphazard appointment of supervisors, unclear processes, or where supervisors have not yet completed their own theses. Employers are liable for any acts they have authorized or ratified. It follows then that a university will be liable for the conduct of academics where the university has

made representations about academic competence, and those representations do not match the postgraduate student's experience of supervision. The vicarious liability of the employer university for harm caused to NESB postgraduates because of supervision problems will be clearest where the academic supervisor is hindered in the provision of the advertised service to the student. An example would be circumstances where the university has failed properly to appoint, train or resource the supervisor.

2. *Contract*: On balance, there is probably not a sufficient connection between a postgraduate's university fees and the academic's salary to show that the academic was acting as the *agent* of the university when carrying out supervisory activities. 'Privity of contract' in law demands that only the parties to the contract are legally bound by and entitled to enforce it (*Dunlop Pneumatic Tyre v Selfridge* (1915) AC 847). This would mean that where a student pays a fee to the university, an academic supervisor would not be individually liable for breach of the terms of the contract because she or he was not a party to it. There has not yet been a case in any country canvassed in this paper as to whether the academic supervisor or the university is the agent or principal respectively.

Tertiary administrators should therefore be aware: when universities venture offshore to entice foreign students and their fees, it would be reasonable for a court to consider that the university should have an accurate conception of the different and special needs of NESB students.

The ethical dilemma for universities supervising NESB students

If university policy and legal liability are imperfect tools in setting educational standards of supervision of NESB students, what are some further issues that merit consideration? In the absence of easily enforceable standards of legal liability likely to be actionable by a dissatisfied NESB research student who must nevertheless return home within the allotted time and somehow make the best of things, and university postgraduate policies that probably have no more than an exhortative effect, the question must be asked: 'What ethical standards might universities generally adopt in relation to NESB students?'

There is little in the literature on ethics and applied ethics that deals with education, and even less that deals with higher education, although at least in Australia, some professional associations such as the National Tertiary Education Union have published a *Code of Ethics* (1998). Reynolds and Smith (1990) argue for an ethic of responsibility for higher education professionals: to be mindful of the consequences of their actions as a means of providing ethical guidance, drawing on Max Weber's argument that good intentions alone could not ensure ethical outcomes in complex modern society.

Reynolds and Smith (1990: 39) argue for 'a statement of principles of responsibility that can guide the choices of individuals and institutions in higher education'. In practice this ethic considers, like law, the reasonably foreseeable consequences of its actions in formulating rules to guide behaviour. Under this model, offshore advertising which overstates a university's capabilities in supervising NESB postgraduates would be unethical. Perhaps higher education bodies should consider formalizing a code of practice in the manner of some individual universities, such as the University of Adelaide. Indeed, there is some move in this direction by the AVCC in Australia (see 'Code for higher degrees', *The Australian Higher Education Supplement*, 1 October, 1996: 32).

There is a growing awareness of the need for universities to follow up their marketing of courses overseas with close attention to the way in which overseas students actually manage when studying abroad. If the costs of particular university courses continue to rise, it is not unreasonable to foresee a rise in NESB students' expectations in relation to the conduct and completion of their research postgraduate degrees. At the same time, heightened levels of legal responsibility of individual academics means that supervisors are likely to bring their own pressure to bear on their institution to provide the resources and ensure the availability of time for academics to supervise their postgraduates properly.

The following points are suggested as a 'checklist' on supervision of NESB students, adapted from the guidelines produced by the British Science and Engineering Research Council (SERC 1989: 18–19).

A checklist on good NESB supervisory practice

1. Is there a departmental document available to NESB students and their supervisors, laying out the department's view on good supervisory practice?
2. What steps are taken to try to make a good match between a supervisor and the prospective NESB student?
3. Does the NESB student present a report in the first year which is assessed by people other than the supervisor who are familiar with the NESB student's cultural background?
4. Does the NESB student see the supervisor often enough in the light of the student's English reading and writing capabilities?
5. Are there regular occasions when the NESB student's progress and background knowledge of the subject are both assessed?

And some general points . . .

1. Is the first year assessment procedure seen as satisfactory by both supervisor and student?
2. Are there occasions when the student has to make a public presentation and are these presentations satisfactory?

3. How is the topic of research refined in the first year?
4. When is a long-term programme of research laid out and has a critical path been defined?
5. Is there a point where the supervisor checks the student's record keeping to see whether it is systematic?
6. Is it clear by half-way into the second year that it is possible to finish the project in the determined time?
7. Does the student get a mock viva between six and twelve months before he/she is due to submit?

The above questions are largely aimed at the supervisor and department, though some of them apply equally to the student. There are several questions specifically directed to the student, as follows.

1. Have you identified the major difficulties?
2. Do you understand the relevant references?
3. Do other people find your written English difficult to understand?
4. Have you tried to plan your work satisfactorily?
5. Are your records in good order and could you answer a question on something you did six months ago?
6. Have you drafted the first version of any portion of the work that has been completed?
7. Are there any tables, figures and other matter which could usefully be prepared at an early stage?

The problems and solutions described here are just as relevant to the native English speaking student body as they are to NESB postgraduate students. One point needs to be emphasized in conclusion. Universities have a uniquely powerful capacity in relation to their students' futures. This is particularly so in the case of NESB and/or international students.

Notes

1. For a critique of this view of the concept of students as customers or consumers, see Terry (1995).
2. 'Student's bitter row with Bond rages on', *Campus Review* 31 July–6 August, 1996, p. 2. This case involves the university's refusal to refund a Master's programme fee where it could not provide the student with a supervisor in the second year of the student's course.
3. The retiring Chair of the Australian Vice-Chancellors' Committee, in his farewell address, described the relationship between students and the Vice-Chancellor (representing the university) as 'like a doctor–patient relationship' (*Campus Review*, April 24–30, 1996, p. 7). This remark was made in the context of a scenario which arose in the early 1970s, where the Vice-Chancellors' Committee indicated that its members would be prepared to risk imprisonment rather than divulge information over 'draft-dodging' students to the federal government. This kind of description clearly has more moral than legal force.
4. With the demise of free tertiary education in Australia it will be interesting to observe the development of the law in this area for domestic students.

Part 3

Establishing Some Principles for
Effective Supervision

8

Responsibilities and Limits in the Supervision of NESB Research Students in the Social Sciences and Humanities

Nick Knight

The revolution in Australian higher education over the last decade has seen a rapid rise in the enrolment of postgraduate students, particularly at doctoral level.[1] Accompanying this expansion in student numbers has been the increasing commercialization of the university system as universities have responded to increasingly stringent resourcing constraints by diversifying their sources of revenue. The marketing of higher educational services has adopted a number of strategies, but internationalization has been a common response as universities have sought to attract full fee-paying overseas students, most of whom have been from non-English speaking backgrounds (NESB), particularly from Asian countries.[2] The student body on the Australian university campus is now much more diverse than in earlier periods, with this diversity particularly marked along the dimensions of ethnicity, native language and academic competency (Ballard and Clanchy 1988; Ballard 1995).

The rapidly changing character of the student population at Australian universities poses a very significant challenge to university teachers, for modes of teaching which were successful in the past need to be evaluated in the light of the changed competencies and backgrounds of students, as well as the growth in class sizes. Nowhere is the challenge more acute than at the postgraduate level, for many of the premises of good supervision are being tested – and in some cases found wanting – by the increasing numbers and particular characteristics of NESB research students. In the face of this challenge, a number of critical questions about supervision need to be posed.

- Are the conventional tenets of good supervision adequate for the supervision of NESB research students?
- What additional strategies are required to assist NESB students to complete their research?

- What ethical problems are created by the particular characteristics and needs of NESB research students?
- What are the limits to supervision of NESB research students?

In this chapter, I will respond to these questions and argue that, while the essential character of good supervision should not change to accommodate the different needs and problems of NESB research students, the role of the supervisor needs to be extended in a number of important areas, particularly the socialization of these students into the expectations and standards which prevail at a Western university (see also Aspland and O'Donaghue 1994). I will also argue that the limits to their supervision need to be considered carefully, particularly in the area of responding to and correcting drafts of the thesis.

Before turning to these issues, a cautionary word is in order about the generalizations which figure in this chapter. NESB research students are a diverse category – they come from different cultural backgrounds, have different levels of academic and English competence, have different capacities to respond to the rigours of postgraduate research, and of course have different personalities. Ultimately, they are all individuals. Supervisors must consequently be sensitive to difference; they must be flexible in responding to the individual characteristics and needs of their NESB students. However, while sensitivity to difference is important, it is essential at this stage of consideration of what is a fairly new area – the study of the supervision of NESB research students – to develop first some workable generalizations about NESB research students as a category on which to base both the formulation of institutional policy and good pedagogical practice. Without these generalizations, we have no basis on which to found discussion and further research; we have no basis for specific calculations of difference within this category. We must therefore commence by formulating some useful generalizations about NESB research students, and use these as a premise for more specific calculations of the characteristics and needs of these students.

For the purposes of this chapter, I am largely concerned with non-Australian NESB students, and more specifically with NESB students who come to Australia from East and South East Asia. Statistically, this is the largest group in Australia (Illing 1996a). Moreover, my own experience with NESB postgraduate research students has largely – although not exclusively – been with students from these regions. Nevertheless, some of the analysis and suggestions offered below are undoubtedly valid for NESB students from other regions, for their experiences of research in a foreign country employing a language other than their native tongue undoubtedly parallel those of students from East and South East Asia. My observations and recommendations do not extend to the natural sciences, for the nature of postgraduate research and the functions of supervision in the sciences are in some important respects different from those in the social sciences and humanities.

The core functions of good supervision

It is a mistake, in my view, to suggest that the concept of good supervision needs drastic reconsideration in light of the particular needs and characteristics of NESB postgraduate research students. Rather, the core functions of supervision should remain intact, regardless of the linguistic and cultural background of the student, although these functions may require some modification (Moses 1985; Hockey 1994; King and Margetson 1995; Leder 1995). Let us briefly consider these core functions of good supervision, and then consider what modification they may require in the case of NESB students.

First, and at a general level, the supervisor must be prepared to engage the research student in a sustained dialogue, one lasting several years, about the research project and the student's progress. A long-term commitment to the student is therefore obviously required on the part of the supervisor.

Second, the supervisor needs to encourage and assist the student to work towards an ever-clearer understanding of the nature and limits of the research problem. The supervisor should require the student to respond, at regular intervals throughout the student's candidature, to the three fundamental questions which all researchers in the social sciences and humanities must answer (Zuber-Skerritt and Knight 1992):

1. What is my research problem?
2. Why is it a problem?
3. What is my argument?

Third, the supervisor needs to provide guidance to the student on issues of theory and method (Knight 1995). This includes guiding the student to an understanding of how to research and write an effective literature review (Bruce 1994, 1995).

Fourth, the supervisor should provide detailed and effective feedback on drafts of the student's thesis (Nightingale 1992).

Finally, the supervisor almost invariably needs to provide moral encouragement and support to sustain the student's confidence and to lessen feelings of isolation that can impair the student's ability to complete the thesis on time or at all.

Each of these functions of good supervision is as important in the supervision of NESB students as for students whose native language is English. Nevertheless, NESB research students almost certainly will have a number of needs and characteristics, not all linguistic, which require modification of the supervisor's role.

The cultural background of NESB research students

The cultural contexts from which NESB students derive vary widely. This can have a significant influence on the values and expectations – some quite inappropriate – which NESB students bring to the research process in a university. This is particularly the case with the large number of students from Asian societies in which the interests of the individual are subordinated to those of the group or collective and submission to authority and respect for tradition are emphasized. These cultural values are reflected in the pedagogical practices and teacher–student relationships in their university systems, and students are socialized into a way of thinking about the creation and acquisition of knowledge that can prepare them poorly for the experience of research at a Western university.

First, the emphasis on the group or collective means that little emphasis is placed on the desirability of the individual articulating a personal position contrary to widely held and conventional viewpoints.[3] Indeed, this may be actively discouraged, and students are encouraged rather to reiterate those forms of knowledge acceptable to the group or society. The emphasis is on consensus and harmony, rather than the right of the individual student to challenge knowledge which has the status of conventional wisdom. Second, respect for and deference to authority can discourage students from challenging their university teachers' interpretations of the truth. The teacher's role is not so much to problematize socially accepted knowledge and recognize the possibility of diverse interpretations of the truth, as to inform students of what they need to know (Ballard 1995).

This intellectual tradition, with its stress on conformity and the collective, stands in stark contrast to the liberal–humanist intellectual tradition, with its emphasis on the individual and the right of the individual to hold and express a personal point of view at odds with prevailing wisdom. Indeed, in Western universities, the teaching of humanities and the social sciences is premised on the possibility of diverse interpretations of the truth, and on the importance of encouraging the student to develop a personal response to intellectual problems. Moreover, effective university teachers in this tradition are respected, not as guardians and transmitters of the truth, but for their capacity to engender critical thinking in their students and to develop in them the skills of the autonomous learner. The basis for student respect for the teacher is consequently very different.

What are the implications of these different cultural and intellectual traditions for supervision of NESB students? Most importantly, the supervisor cannot assume that the NESB research student understands the concept of originality which is the hallmark of successful research – particularly at doctoral level, which requires an original contribution to knowledge. The supervisor must attempt, in the process of sustained dialogue, to resocialize the student, to engender in him or her an understanding of the need to formulate an argument which goes beyond mere reiteration of widely held or dominant perspectives. If the student is to be successful, he or she must gain a genuine appreciation of the need to formulate a personal response to the research problem, a response which is distinctive, forceful, challenging and, above all, original.

For some students from other societies, and in particular Asian societies, this requires a fundamental shift in their understanding of the nature of academic work, the role of the researcher and the purpose of research. Some students, indeed, are bemused by the supervisor's expectations that they formulate an original and personal response to the research problem; some have expectations that the supervisor will provide them with an appropriate argument, their task being only to find the evidence to support this argument. Some students, initially at least, may lose respect for the supervisor who problematizes the concept of 'knowledge' and who insists that the student have a distinctive, individualized argument in response to the research problem, for they may well believe that it is the supervisor's role to tell the student what to argue.

However, the onus of responsibility lies not only with the supervisor, but with the institution in which the student will research. It is important that the NESB research student not be left either in isolation or reliant on other NESB research students for company and academic stimulation; to do so will impede the effective integration of the NESB student into the academic life of the institution, and retard this process of academic resocialization. The institution, be it the university, the faculty or the department, can accelerate this process by developing a thriving postgraduate culture in which students from all backgrounds meet and mingle, whether informally and socially, or in workshops and work-in-progress seminars (Zuber-Skerritt and Knight 1992; King and Margetson 1995). In such a positive institutional context, the values and norms of the Western university will more readily be absorbed by the NESB research student who comes from a very different cultural and intellectual tradition. To achieve this outcome, the institution must be prepared to invest the necessary resources, both physical and human, in postgraduate education. However, if the institution wishes to attract NESB research students who are also full fee-paying overseas students, this investment will generate sound long-term dividends.

Writing the thesis: the problem of language

The extent of the responsibility of the supervisor for editing the research student's thesis is a professional and ethical problem, whether or not the student is an NESB student. However, the dilemma is accentuated in the case of NESB students, for it is almost invariably the case that the final drafts of their theses will require significantly more editing and revision than those of students from English speaking backgrounds, in some cases very substantial editing and revision. It is often the case that the NESB student may not be capable of editing and polishing the text of the final draft to bring it to submission standard. Who then is responsible for this task? And in performing it, is an ethical boundary crossed which signifies that the final product is no longer solely the student's own work? This is a contentious issue. If the supervisor assumes this responsibility, not only is he or she taking on a very onerous and time-consuming task, normally one well beyond that required with research students from English speaking backgrounds, but the supervisor may be guilty, at least in part, of writing the thesis for the student.

There can be no definitive answer to this problem, and the response is likely to vary from one supervisor to the next, with their different standards of judgment. However, it is legitimate, in my view, for the supervisor to edit lightly the final draft of the thesis, revising the more egregious errors of grammar and expression. Where the problems of written expression require more fundamental revision of the draft thesis, the supervisor might do this for a short section or sections. The purpose here is to model for the NESB student how to identify and correct frequently appearing problems of grammar and expression. In some severe cases, it may be necessary for the NESB student to seek the assistance of a professional editor, and some universities or their postgraduate associations are now providing this facility. But again, the dilemma is how far the editor can go in revising the draft thesis before the work ceases to be the student's own.

It is important that this issue of the extent of the supervisor's responsibility to edit the thesis be negotiated and agreed between supervisor and NESB research student early in the student's candidature. This is particularly the case if the NESB student regards editing the thesis as a dimension of good supervision (Ballard 1995). It is highly desirable that the student be under no illusion that final responsibility for production of a thesis of submissible standard rests with the student; but the student should also be confident of the nature and extent of the assistance that the supervisor will provide.

Another problem which may arise for the NESB research student in the writing of the thesis is plagiarism (Ballard 1995). It is obviously impermissible for any part of a thesis to be plagiarized, and it is part of the supervisor's responsibility to identify if plagiarism is occurring, whether wittingly or unwittingly. What constitutes plagiarism is, however, not always apparent, and there is an element of judgment involved. For an academic of a Western university, this judgment is informed by an understanding, born of experience, of the norms and proprieties of appropriate academic conduct. However, for the NESB research student, the capacity to make this judgment may be poorly developed; what might appear to the student as legitimate summary or copying of another's words or ideas can cross the threshold into plagiarism. This may result from the student's cultural and academic background. In some Asian countries, for example, the convention of indicating through citations the source of an idea or quote is a relatively new importation, and only a weakly developed one. Many students from this background have not had instilled in them the necessity to indicate faithfully through citations the source of ideas or quotes.

Another reason for plagiarism may be the NESB student's poor command of English and the consequent temptation to rely excessively on his or her sources. After all, from the student's point of view, authors of English-language sources have said what the student wished to say, but so much more clearly and fluently. The supervisor of the NESB research student will need, both in the process of the academic resocialization of the student and in checking early drafts of the thesis, to ensure that the student understands the concept of plagiarism and conventions on citations. The supervisor can set the NESB research student the exercise of reading a number of exemplary doctoral theses by English speaking students, looking particularly at the way in which such students use the ideas and words of other scholars, and cite sources. It would also be useful for workshops on this theme to be made available by institutions in which NESB research students are represented.

The NESB research student: a stranger in a foreign land

A normal but somewhat intangible dimension of supervision in all cases is the personal support which the supervisor needs to extend to his or her students. One of the great burdens which the research student must carry throughout the candidature is isolation, for research in the humanities and social sciences is, by its very nature, something that has to be done individually. A common manifestation of this sense of isolation is a dwindling confidence by students in their capacity to do the research and write the thesis. Students may also lose confidence in the significance of the research problem and their argument. For many research students, the supervisor may be the main or even the sole contact with the academic community, and in this context the relationship between the supervisor and student assumes added significance. While the relationship must, of necessity, be a professional one in which emotional involvement of an intimate nature is avoided, it is very important for the student's morale to have the support and encouragement of the supervisor, particularly during the bad patches which all research students experience (Hockey 1991; Elton and Pope 1992).

If isolation is a problem for many research students, it is a problem which is accentuated for NESB research students, many of whom are strangers in a foreign land. Many NESB students have previously neither lived nor studied abroad and, in addition to the demands of study at a high level in an unfamiliar educational context, the problems of adjusting to life in an alien culture and environment may deepen students' sense of isolation and impact negatively on their capacity to devote attention to their research. In this context, the role of the supervisor may be critical. However, to what extent can or should the supervisor extend the role of supervision to support the student through the psychological and personal transition required to adjust to life and study in a foreign land? Again, this is a matter of judgment, although in the final analysis the supervisor's relationship with the student must remain on a professional basis, and if additional encouragement and support are required, these must have as their goal the enhancement of the capacity of the NESB research student to function as an effective and independent researcher. In this regard, the responsibility should not be solely the supervisor's, and universities and faculties which are the beneficiaries of the growth in numbers of NESB research students should provide the necessary facilities and infrastructure to support the difficult transition to life and study in a foreign land experienced by many NESB students.

Conclusion

In this chapter, I have suggested that the rapid increase of NESB postgraduate research students at Western universities raises critical questions about the responsibilities and limits of supervision. I have argued that the core dimensions of good supervision need not alter in the light of the particular needs and characteristics of NESB research students. However, in a number of areas, the role of the supervisor may need to be extended and modified. The first is the academic resocialization of NESB research students to inculcate in them values and norms appropriate to postgraduate study at a Western university. The second is the editing and revision of the thesis prior to submission. Here there arise ethical and practical questions concerning the limits to supervision, but it is important for the supervisor to communicate to the student his or her perception of those limits early in the student's candidature. Finally, the supervisor may need to provide more extensive personal and psychological support to NESB research students than is normally the case, although here again, the limits to this support will need to be considered by the supervisor and communicated to the student.

The supervision of NESB postgraduate research students represents a challenge. It is a challenge for individual supervisors, many of whom may not previously have been confronted by NESB research students with their particular needs and characteristics. It is a challenge too at an institutional level, for it is incumbent on universities and faculties, which will gain materially from the increased presence of NESB research students, to ensure that there are in place both appropriate guidelines for the enrolment of such students, and the infrastructure to support them throughout their candidature. However, it is the supervisor who will assume the greater share of responsibility in ensuring that the NESB research student's experience of research at a Western university is a positive and ultimately rewarding one.

Notes

1. The number of students enrolled in PhD studies increased from 7035 in 1983 to 13,623 in 1992 (Leder 1995, quoting Australian Bureau of Statistics sources).
2. In 1995, Asian students studying at Australian universities constituted 85.8 per cent of all overseas students in Australia. Hong Kong, Malaysia, Singapore and Indonesia were the top four source nations (Illing 1996a, quoting Professor Lee Ngok, Pro-Vice Chancellor (Development) at University of Southern Queensland).
3. For a useful discussion of the process of socialization and the role of the individual in Confucian societies, see Solomon (1971), Wilson (1970) and Smith in this volume (Chapter 13).

9

Supervision of NESB Postgraduate Students in Science-based Disciplines

Alan Frost

Introduction

Postgraduate education in science-based disciplines is a broad descriptor for a number of discipline areas, each characterized by different motivations and aspirations on the part of the student, and different objectives and standards in examination demanded by the supervisors. Before any discussion of the issues involved in supervision of science NESB research students can commence, the nature of postgraduate education in these disciplines must be considered.

Research studies in the sciences

In the sciences, postgraduate education falls into the following general groupings:

- coursework programmes;
- research-based programmes leading to the Masters degree;
- research-based programmes leading to the PhD degree.

Coursework programmes are usually of one to two years' duration, leading to either a Diploma or a Masters degree. Some involve a project, which may take the form of a written review, including also some experimental laboratory study. In the US, some universities have Masters or PhD programmes based largely on coursework, with a project in which the student carries out a small study involving experimental, laboratory or other investigative methods. Masters programmes, if research-based, are usually a minimum of two years' duration, while a PhD programme, if research-based, is usually a minimum of three years.

The objectives of these programmes differ, as must be obvious from their nature. Coursework is usually an extension of undergraduate study, building on a pyramid of knowledge, so that the broad objectives should be clearer to the student, and will usually represent the reason for enrolment in these studies. We would expect a precise focus on an aspect of science in which we would assume the student has a special interest; in this respect it is unlike the lack of interest shown by many students in their undergraduate courses. The number of students is usually small in these classes, with a consequent low staff:student ratio. The supervisor/teacher can identify rapidly those students with problems. The course will consist of related subject areas, in which we would expect a precise reading list, with similarly precise objectives. These objectives are achieved and assessed by a series of assignments or examinations. The overall objective would be to ensure that the student has reached a high level of understanding in the field chosen, is familiar with the literature, and can write and debate cogently at the cutting edge of the chosen area of science. Unless substantial laboratory work were involved, no special laboratory skills would be expected; indeed they could not be expected in a short degree programme. In such an experimental study, the student would be encouraged to undertake and perhaps be involved in the design of a small experiment, to carry it through, record and analyse the results, and to discuss them in context. We would hope that the evaluation would focus on the experimental design, ensuring that the student includes appropriate controls in the experiments, and understands their significance.

Research-based programmes, whether Masters or doctoral studies, are different, and in terms of objectives they can be considered together. Broadly, these objectives are that the student should demonstrate competence in reading, reviewing and analysing literature in the chosen field, leading to a definition of at least some of the problems remaining to be understood; should be able to design and carry out experiments to answer some of these problems; should analyse results and write a cogent discussion of these results, integrating the conclusions with the current knowledge in the field. The Masters programme requires less in every way compared with a PhD programme. We would expect one to two publications to result from the former; four to six from the latter.

The assessment of these postgraduate degrees differs from university to university. Any coursework is usually assessed internally, as indicated above, sometimes with assessment of the project component by an external examiner. The outcome of the research degree programme is presented in the form of a thesis, usually assessed by both internal and external examiners; the supervisor is rarely an examiner. In many European universities the student must also defend the thesis orally. In Australia, the tyranny of distance has in general precluded this, and assessment is based solely on the thesis, which will include papers published from the work, by contrast with theses in the social sciences, where publication may be encouraged but is not mandatory.

These represent the rather altruistic expectations of a supervisor on behalf of the university, but what should the award of the degree mean to an employer of our successful graduate? The employer would expect that a successful PhD graduate would have developed the self-confidence to move outside the specific field studied; have the confidence to master successfully other new techniques; and in general be able tackle at a research or investigative level any reasonable problem in the broad field, in for example medicine, physics, etc. In contrast, the successful student in coursework programmes will convince the employer that he or she has knowledge in advance of their graduate peers for employment in a specific area. The Masters is somewhere in-between.

The background or preparedness for postgraduate studies of a student can vary enormously over the range of disciplines in science. For example, an internal graduate in the biological or physical sciences would have graduated in a three-year programme, successfully have completed an Honours year, and probably a Masters qualifying course. This student will be skilled in many techniques and will easily slot into a research programme. In professional faculties, however, it is unlikely that the student will be at a level anything like that achieved by a similar student in a pure science discipline. These aspects of research, their nature and objectives, are understood well by supervisors or teachers of coursework programmes, but often only vaguely by supervisors of PhD programmes. They are understood not at all or only very vaguely indeed by candidates entering a programme, and success then depends on how quickly they gain this understanding. In the past the student's understanding of requirements was gained largely by intuition. The growth of postgraduate education in recent years has led, at least in Australian universities, to documents defining the role and responsibilities of the supervisor together with those of the student. Given the disparity in programmes at all levels across all disciplines, such edicts have, I would contend, little effect in changing the nature of the relationship between the supervisor and the student.

In the following discussion, the problems that may ensue in carrying out a PhD research programme in the biological sciences will be considered, because (a) from the above outline it will be apparent that it is at the PhD level that the expectations and complications will be greatest, and (b) it is my own area of experience.

Skills and expectations of the student

Domestic students are likely to have sought out the department, supervisor and likely project before considering enrolment. The project will be in an area in which they are interested, and if they are science graduates, most of the skills required may already have been mastered, or at least attempted and understood at the undergraduate level.

Overseas students, for our purposes NESB students, are likely to have defined only the general discipline in which they wish to work. This will reflect their background and general interest. They may have a scholarship to study in an overseas country, and may be desperate to find a suitable university, department, and supervisor. The project comes last in their consideration, and is usually only vaguely understood before the student arrives in the new country. It must involve an enormous effort for many such people to move to a new country, a new language, and a new culture. They have generally given little thought to the project on which they will work and what it will require to succeed; the supervisor will 'fix everything'.

Supervisory skills and expectations

There is probably as large a range of skills among supervisors as there is in the range of students whom they nurture. This should not be the case, given attempts by universities to improve in this regard via professional development training in supervision, and internal booklets on good practice in supervision. But supervisors are human: some have better skills, both in communication and in research; some have more grant money. A successful researcher will be likely to have a group of postgraduate students working in similar or allied fields. A postgraduate student, whatever his or her nationality and communication skills, will find research in such a group environment easier than the student who is 'blessed' with a supervisor who has little grant money, and who is probably busy with other activities. Such a supervisor may give students a little direction, then leave them to their own devices.

Problems suffered by overseas NESB students are, in the main, the same as those suffered by domestic students. However, language and especially cultural difficulties may markedly exacerbate the situation. Some of the most common and important problems have been considered in other parts of this book – see 'Mei's story' for an example. For this discussion the procedures involved in a PhD programme and the likely difficulties that will ensue are divided into three phases of the programme which obviously overlap:

- the introductory phase;
- the experimental or research phase; and
- the writing-up phase.

Some of the comments are general and will apply to students in any discipline, and these will be noted, but not elaborated upon.

Introductory phase

The NESB student usually arrives without family and will be given assistance in finding accommodation. The supervisor will try to assess the level of skills and interest of the student and a likely project will be developed. All students newly arrived at the university, regardless of background, require around three months to settle in and adjust to the new environment, to locate suitable accommodation, to find and understand the workings of the library, to understand the running of a laboratory, to adjust to and interact with other postgraduate students, and to begin to appreciate the nature and stage of their project. NESB people require even more time to adjust to these difficulties. In this phase, the objective is to read the literature with some initial assistance from the supervisor; various written assignments as an outcome of this reading and assessment should be required to focus the student on an early tangible achievement. Often this will form the basis for the review section of the final thesis. It will give the supervisor an indication of the student's skills in reading, writing and evaluation of the literature.

In my experience, personal problems of students who have moved long distances to a new institute or university have disrupted their lives. They have lost their friends' and families' emotional support systems, and must adapt to a new environment. Such problems for science-based students are, we can assume, no different from those in other disciplines, as has been discussed in Parts I and II. In Australian universities, the science disciplines attract the largest group of NESB students, as documented in Chapter 1 of the present volume. This gives NESB science students a big advantage over students in the social sciences because of their 'critical mass' in the department or school. A large postgraduate group which contains students from a range of countries will usually provide a focus to lift the confidence of a new overseas student. In our department, a small group of staff keep rough track of a range of furniture, bedding, kitchen utensils etc. which are passed on from postgraduate to postgraduate as one leaves and another arrives. Such assistance, even if minor, helps to bridge the culture gap, and improve communication. For a married student, if it is practicable, the presence of a spouse and family can transform the effectiveness of an otherwise sad student. Inevitably this depends on funds, which will usually be provided from a granting or other aid body, e.g. in Australia, AusAID. In our experience, private funds are usually exhausted quickly, unless the partner can obtain work. This can create an additional pressure on students.

Experimental phase

The approach of supervisors to the research phase varies as greatly as do their skills in generating research funds. An ongoing, integrated, well-funded programme into which a new student can fit in harmony obviously contrasts significantly with one where the student will be alone in the area and entirely at the direction – or lack thereof – of the supervisor; the programme proposed may represent a new area requiring the development of new techniques or the adaptation of old. If we go back to the objectives, it is clear that the plan of the supervisor must allow completion of the experimental work in about two years, leaving time for writing and presentation of the thesis. If the experimental skills required are part of an integrated research programme, there should be little difficulty in any student learning and adapting, whatever their background. The major problems arise when the programme devised is not focused sufficiently and the student is abandoned to flounder. It is here that the NESB student is most at risk, for many reasons. Two predominate.

1. Cultural mores often prevent NESB students from 'pestering' the supervisor on experiments which are not working or where the design is not understood. Such discussion as does occur almost invariably concludes with the supervisor asking whether the student understands the problem and its solution. The answer is always 'yes'. In fact the student, equally invariably, means 'no, it is not understood'. He or she departs, still very insecure and not knowing the next step. It is essential for the supervisor to understand this and either to keep close personal watch on the activities of the student and gently redirect and improve his/her understanding, or to request others to observe the activities of the student as she or he tries to solve the problem, and to advise his/her progress in overcoming the problem.
2. The approach may require the student to seek materials, equipment or assistance from another laboratory or department. Supervisors will usually assume that a domestic student will have the persistence and self-confidence to do this, but an NESB student may not. The student may flounder and make little or no progress simply because she/he has been unable to seek the right people or equipment, and is inhibited in confessing his or her 'failure' to the supervisor.

An effective method of ensuring progress is to hold regular meetings with graduate students, either collectively or individually. Regularity creates a non-threatening environment in which ongoing problems can be identified and their solutions sought. Progress is monitored at subsequent meetings.

The writing phase

The basic writing skills of students who have chosen science as a career are generally poor, and over the last three decades have, I believe, shown signs of further decline rather than improvement.

Learning in science involves the learning of a new language – of vocabulary and concepts – then the ability to reason in this new language. The undergraduate focuses mainly on learning the language of science, and the methods of assessment largely measure this. Skills in reasoning require writing skills that are taught and assessed poorly at undergraduate level. Many students who arrive at postgraduate studies are scientifically illiterate. Most recognize this, are inhibited and fear writing; their weaknesses are then exposed to all.

The importance of the introductory phase in reading and writing reviews or assignments must be emphasized as essential to make students aware of their weaknesses at an early stage and to encourage them to improve their skills. Indeed, it is a big advance to make a science student recognize that writing *is* a skill and it is one that they can and *must* master. Too many excuse themselves by pretending that they cannot write well, and this is why they did science. To explain that writing is hard work and requires effort from all, and that efforts to improve will be rewarded, will pay great dividends. NESB students often have a better grasp of basic English grammar than do

English system students – they have studied and understood it more recently. Nevertheless, the problems in writing are greater with NESB students. They are often initially terrified of criticism. It can assist if they are shown the work of another student that has been criticized constructively but severely, together with the satisfactory outcome. It is essential that whatever their background, the editing and criticism of their writing must always be constructive and never destructive. It is surprising to supervisors that while we often encourage students to read published papers, students rarely try to model their writing on these. It is a simple but effective strategy for improving writing skills.

There is no doubt that to write a PhD thesis is a formidable task, the very magnitude of which inhibits and demoralizes many students. It is worth paraphrasing the objectives as I have outlined them above, and to explain these as 'the rules of the game'. For the PhD degree the thesis is written only for the examiners: it is highly unlikely that anyone apart from the examiners will ever read it from cover to cover. The rule is that the examiners must be convinced from reading this thesis that the student can read, can constructively criticize the literature, and can design experiments; that he/she has mastered appropriate techniques, can evaluate and assess the work, and discuss it in the context of current work. Any student who can do this must be able easily to defend the work to examiners in any oral examination, as occurs in many countries and universities. However, like a scientific paper, a PhD thesis may be considered a 'confidence trick', in that while it may be presented as a flowing, logical story, the key experiments or observations on which the work depends may be discussed last. Yet the need for this critical experiment may only emerge after the discussions are written. Such is the 'unnatural nature of science' (Wolpert 1993).

In the efficient writing of a thesis, planning is essential. At an early stage, the supervisor should assist the student in this. The formidable task is thus broken down into smaller and smaller components until the student can see that each such component can be achieved in a finite time – a day or two and not months. In this way the pattern laid out in the plan can evolve as it is built up, and because of this, the endless repetition of a 'bad' thesis is seen and avoided. There are many variations on this theme that can be devised to suit the range of research programmes in science that are outside the scope of this chapter.

Writing in science

By contrast to some areas in the humanities, individual style and flowing language are not encouraged in the sciences. The discourse required is precise and concise, leaving no doubt as to meaning. There are various publications on scientific writing and the preparation of papers, such as Brown (1992), to which students can usefully be directed. Some assist by defining words to be used, which can help avoid ambiguity. The point is to make students aware that writing in the sciences is a skill to be learned which does not come naturally except to a privileged few.

There is a wide disparity in the skills of students, whether domestic or NESB, in writing about science. What then is the role of the supervisor in assisting the student in the final preparation of the PhD thesis? The supervisor must advise on the presentation of the data as an outcome of the research, encourage the student to try different ways of presenting the same material and to seek what appears to be the best way. Then the data must be analysed and interpreted, and the supervisor must advise on this. The review, which has already been mentioned, can be edited on its own. The remainder, however, is best seen as a whole before detailed editing is contemplated, because this is the only way in which repetition and the sequence of material or experiments can be considered as part of the whole, rather than considering each section or chapter as an entity in itself. The big question is, how much editing should the supervisor do? Some complain that they have to 'completely write the thesis', though in most cases this is a gross exaggeration. Perhaps we should be more ruthless with our domestic students in ensuring that they attain an appropriate level of writing skills before the final draft. NESB students, however, may need much more help and assistance.

This does not mean, however, that the thesis is completely written by the supervisor. The student *must* have demonstrated that he or she has done the work and interpreted it correctly, but there is no irregularity or ethical dilemma if the student receives more than the usual assistance to present it in good English. Most theses will require a general or final discussion and conclusion, where the student brings the studies together, is constructively self-critical, and points a way for the future. Most students unduly fear this section and procrastinate, yet it is the easiest to write, since the content should flow automatically from the experimental studies. This should be pointed out to the student as he/she is preparing the thesis. Regardless of the origin of the student, the need for this editing ranges from minor corrections and advice, to total major revisions, sometimes requiring many drafts. Usually this is the result of poor planning, when the writing is done out of context to preceding and succeeding sections.

Supervisors vary in the extent to which they will 'correct' English. Some go to great lengths. Others give examples of major faults and expect the student then to edit the work by example. The former converts the thesis to one written by the supervisor; the latter will be too slow to allow timely completion; it is inefficient of both student and supervisor time. The resultant thesis will almost invariably be rejected by the examiner, and require endless correction. Obviously, this second course should be avoided.

Conclusion

Provided NESB students are able to settle in the new environment, are assessed at an early stage and are placed in a project that they are competent to undertake, their problems are similar to those of English language students. The cultural background of these NESB students may modify their approach to their difficulties, especially early in the programme. Astute observation of a student's hesitancy as he or she answers 'yes' to a question regarding understanding will identify a cultural difficulty. The supervisor's response should avoid making the student lose dignity in the eyes of the supervisor and others in the laboratory.

It is salutory for the supervisor to reflect on the final outcome of research for a student. The acquisition of a higher degree in a foreign university gives the new NESB graduate great status in his or her own country, and the self-confidence to develop further. Many graduates go on to senior positions in their country, in science, in administration, or in politics. The writer and colleagues have often experienced the reward of visiting other countries to find that our graduate students are highly successful and attribute their success to the training they received under our direction. Privately, we may feel guilty for doing too little too late for them. Some academics naively and arrogantly prefer to believe that success of their students is due only to the specific skills they demand of their students. The truth is that we merely help them along the way.

A sage of the medical profession in Australia, during a heated discussion of the content of the undergraduate curriculum in another faculty of my own university, pointed out that two years after graduation, it was rarely possible to distinguish medical graduates in terms of the institutions from which they had graduated. Indeed, many post-doctoral graduates never do another experiment and do no work in the field of their specific research training, yet they may be supremely successful in their careers. The confidence gained in *themselves* is the essential acquisition of their research study. To assist NESB research students in science to gain that confidence is one of the greatest achievements and rewards of good supervision.

10

Avoiding Potential Pitfalls in the Supervision of NESB Students

Pat Cryer and Eunice Okorocha

Introduction

There are potential pitfalls for research student–supervisor partnerships where the research student comes from a non-English speaking background (NESB) and the supervisor is a Western academic. This much is well known. Less well known are the causes of the pitfalls and ways of avoiding them. Our own understanding of these issues has arisen from our separate research. One of us, Pat Cryer, has conducted studies in a range of institutions in the United Kingdom and elsewhere on difficulties experienced by research students generally (Cryer 1996a, 1996b) and has identified specific difficulties and possible solutions for NESB students (Cryer 1996b: 21–2). The other, Eunice Okorocha, has conducted research on the experience of NESB students, including NESB research students, in twelve institutions of higher education across the United Kingdom, and has identified and structured the major emerging issues (Okorocha 1996a, 1996b, 1997a, 1998). Pat Cryer has additionally conducted research with supervisors on general issues which cause them concern and in so doing has identified those which occur more frequently with NESB students (Cryer 1997, 1998). Unless otherwise referenced, the observations in this chapter are based on these research activities.

The problems which have the highest profile with academic staff supervising NESB students relate to: excessive expectations of what supervisors should be providing in the way of guidance, support and actual participation in the research; excessive demands for clerical and technical support; disproportionate and unthinking quotation from the works of others; and difficulties in forming relationships as colleagues and equals (Cryer 1997, 1998). This is not to imply that all supervisors experience all these problems with all NESB students. Our emphasis in this chapter is on NESB students from those countries where it is common practice to study outside the home country in an English speaking environment. Even these NESB students are not of course a homogeneous group: they are individuals in their own right; and they come from a variety of cultural, linguistic and religious backgrounds.

In this chapter we argue that the experience of NESB research students and their supervisors can be improved and that the resulting research training and research output can be made more productive and effective. The key, we argue, lies in mutual understanding. We therefore start by presenting and discussing underlying causes of potential problems, as seen from the perspectives of many NESB students (Okorocha 1996a, 1996b, 1997a, 1997b). We then use these to elicit recommendations for supervisors, heads of department and senior institutional managers.

Differences in styles of teaching and learning

Many NESB students come from higher education systems where academics are venerated as all-knowing. Consequently, it is difficult for them, when removed to a Western system, to enter into debate with supervisors. Many feel it arrogant to assert their own opinions – Japanese students, for example, even go as far as to keep expressions like 'I don't think so' and 'I don't agree' for fights.

It is deference to authority that can cause the major complaint that NESB students quote excessively and unthinkingly. Elton (1985: 12) puts it well:

> Deference to teaching staff which [can] inhibit the debate and discussion [is] often coupled with an expectation that lengthy passages of text should be committed to memory and reproduced at an appropriate time, which could be interpreted as 'plagiarism'.

By quoting excessively, many NESB students believe that they are honouring the author. Supervisors need to be aware of this and point out calmly and gently that this is not so in a Western culture. Sometimes all that is necessary is for the supervisor to give a form of 'permission' that the independent thought is acceptable and valued.

In cultures which venerate age and experience, staff do all the talking in classroom situations. So NESB students from these cultures lack experience in interacting and expressing opinions. They need the help of supervisors to make an opening for them in group discussion and to allow time for them to express themselves.

Cultural differences

The term 'culture' embraces a range of meanings which take into account linguistic, political, economic, social, psychological, religious, national and other differences (Hesselgrave 1979). Culture shock rates high as one of the difficulties experienced by NESB students. This term was first attributed to Oberg (1958), who suggested that it was a condition precipitated by the anxiety that resulted from losing one's familiar signs and symbols of social interaction – that is, losing the sense of when and how to do the right things. The experience of culture shock often leads NESB students to feel helpless and confused.

The fact that NESB students come from a variety of cultural backgrounds means that they see and value many things differently from people in the host country. Aspects which are of particular relevance to the research student–supervisor interaction are time, space and socially acceptable behaviours.

Time

There are many aspects relating to the cultural perception of time. They include the meeting time for appointments; the duration of time designated for discussion; the duration of time necessary for people to feel acquainted; times appropriate for unannounced visiting; and time schedules. Western culture is dominated by the 24-hour day in which only that time system ('monochromic') exists. Certain non-Western cultures, especially African and Asian, do not have this rigid concept of time. To them time is flexible or 'polychromic'.

The monochromic and polychromic ways of viewing time create difficulties in intercultural contacts. For example, when NESB research students do not come on time for appointments with supervisors, they may not see it as a grave offence (especially if genuinely delayed by unforeseen circumstances). Lateness, however, invariably angers supervisors because it wastes their time and disrupts their schedules. The result is often a negative feeling towards the NESB student, which is undeserved, if understandable. It calls for open discussion, or if this is deemed likely to cause offence or embarrassment, gentle exploration.

Space

Space, too, has a number of aspects, which vary not only from culture to culture but sometimes too for different sexes within the same culture. Aspects of space include interpersonal space, olfactory space, thermal space and visual space. The most important of these from the point of view of the research student–supervisor relationship is interpersonal space.

Different cultures have different conventions about the space between individuals in social situations. People from some cultures stand and converse at a much closer distance than do people from other cultures, and as a result, feelings of discomfort can soon be generated in anyone who feels their space invaded. With Western supervisors, this tends to lead to some embarrassment: they try to move backwards to maintain their interpersonal space only to have the NESB student draw closer. Again, the solution lies in open discussion or gentle exploration.

Socially acceptable behaviours

Culturally related and socially acceptable behaviour issues include: respect for age and authority figures; whether a 'present' is regarded as a bribe or a show of appreciation; whether to open or not to open gifts in the presence of the giver; the individualistic and collectivist mode of problem-solving; greeting norms such as the form of any spoken greeting, the handshake, the faint smile or cursory nod. The list is endless.

Of particular relevance to the supervisor–student relationship is the way most African and Asian cultures esteem age and respect authorities – a situation which they do not find in the Western culture. This is why such students find it difficult to address members of staff by their first names and prefer to use titles like Dr, Professor, Mrs or Mr, Madam or Sir. Academics, on the other hand, can find this either embarrassing or too formal. However, insistence on first-name informality can be confusing to NESB students. To them it signals a form of friendship that permits them, for example, to stop a supervisor in a corridor to chat, as they would a friend – something which most supervisors are under far too much pressure to find acceptable.

Communication issues

Klineberg and Hull (1979) conducted a study of NESB students of all levels in universities in 11 countries and identified language difficulties as one of the major problems. For most students of Asian, African and Latin American origin, English is often a second, third or fourth language and consequently communication can be misinterpreted.

According to Elton (1985), language problems experienced by NESB students vary considerably, and it is necessary to distinguish between those students for whom English is a 'foreign' language and those for whom it is a 'second' language. He points out that foreign language users – for example, students from the Middle East, Latin America and Europe – learn English as an academic subject, whereas second-language users like most students from Commonwealth countries have used English as the medium of education. Elton further observes that reading presents the least difficulty, but that adequate and suitable style is often a problem in written English. Students who have not studied in English before are at a particular disadvantage, both in verbal and non-verbal communication.

Verbal communication

NESB students have varying levels of competency in English. Even those who are fluent in written English can have problems with spoken English because of the unfamiliar patterns of pronunciation. Some NESB students struggle so much that they are unable to communicate basic information and facts. Inappropriate use of language may be due to being unaware of social conventions, which may create barriers and cause alienation. Supervisors tend to respond negatively to students whom they perceive as aggressive, especially when they 'demand' things rather than make a request politely.

Some supervisors may react positively to students – like the Japanese, for example – whose language and culture are rich in polite expressions like bowing. Other supervisors may dismiss continuous smiles by such students as frivolity or snobbery, instead of seeing them as a mark of respect. Misinterpretations and misunderstandings can create prejudices. Supervisors should be aware that students' manners of making requests are linked to their cultural norms and are not a deliberate attempt to 'demand' or be rude or blunt. They should give NESB students the benefit of the doubt in such situations and gently point out an acceptable way of making a request. Most NESB students will appreciate this.

Some NESB students (especially Asians and Africans) have no difficulties when asked to list facts but, because of the problems inherent in articulating their thoughts and feelings in a foreign language, are not able to participate fully in situations where communication extends to discussion and the defence of points. This invariably degrades them because supervisors do not understand what they want to say and assess them on what they think they are saying.

Supervisors should encourage their research NESB students to ask people to speak more slowly if necessary; and they should avoid slang, jargon, acronyms and complex verbs.

Written communication is less of a problem for NESB research students, but supervisors should give them clear guidelines and should encourage them to ask for clarification, where needed.

Non-verbal communication

Non-verbal communication or body language occurs in all cultures, but the meanings associated with various gestures can vary considerably from one culture to another. Across cultures, gestures can easily communicate the opposite to what is intended. Examples include the use or avoidance of eye contact, the nodding or shaking of the head and the acceptability or otherwise of touch.

Different cultures have their own implicit understandings of the meanings of variations in speech, facial expression and other non-verbal cues. So non-verbal communication patterns of NESB students can be grossly misinterpreted. For example, in the West, the use of eye contact is a sign of attentive behaviour. Yet Africans 'listen' with their ears and may or may not look at the speaker. For them, the avoidance of eye contact is a culturally essential indication of politeness and respect for the older or professionally superior person. Yet supervisors tend to regard it as indicating sullenness, shiftiness or boredom bordering on rudeness.

To reduce the barriers caused by non-verbal behaviour, supervisors should again give NESB students the benefit of the doubt in the first instance. They should then find out what a particular action or gesture means to the NESB student and not assume that it is part of a universal language.

Religious practices

Higher education institutions are multi-faith environments. Yet students' religious beliefs inevitably have a bearing on their behaviours and their values. In particular, some religions have a different status for males and females, which has implications for assigning supervisors of the opposite sex; and some religions do not allow their females to shake hands with males. Some religions have dietary regulations such as separation of pork products and ingredients, which may have implications for departmental social activities.

NESB students come from various religious backgrounds and even within a particular background may have varying degrees of commitment. So taking account of religious beliefs can be very difficult. Awareness, sensitivity and discussion can prevent embarrassment and misunderstanding. NESB students are normally happy to discuss religious matters, and often find it difficult to understand the taboo nature of religion as a topic of social interaction in the West.

Miscellaneous issues

There are other issues which impact on the ease with which NESB research students can settle to study in a Western culture. These include finding familiar or religiously acceptable food items; finding suitable accommodation; and having to work under the omnipresent burden of knowing that they have to leave the host country after a prescribed period, irrespective of whether the work is complete – and that if it is not, they go home as failures.

Another issue is that many NESB research students can experience status shock because they were used to prestigious professional jobs in their home countries. A related issue is unfamiliarity with commonplace computing, office and technical equipment, because at home its use was left to clerical and technical staff. This explains why NESB students may make excessive demands on departmental clerical and technical staff. NESB students should be told, politely and calmly, that in a Western higher education system, research students normally do their own photocopying, typing, etc. Then the use of the equipment should be explained to them.

Last but not least are the negative effects of prejudice and discrimination. Moving to a foreign country suddenly deprives NESB students of the support system provided by family and friends in the home country. They naturally feel vulnerable, anxious and sometimes disorientated. Isolation, loneliness and stress may affect their health and subsequently their academic performance. This is considered at some length in Zwingmann and Gunn (1983).

Recommendations

We have shown the origins of the problems which supervisors raise most frequently in connection with supervising NESB students and we have indicated that causes lie in the huge range of adjustments that NESB students have to make upon being uprooted from their home country to a Western higher education system. The causes do not lie in the characters or abilities of the NESB students. In fact, if they can be helped through the transition, they can become valuable members of their new academic communities.

So NESB research students need help and support. This is best given by more experienced members of the culture and by professional counsellors (Pedersen 1991). However, supervisors, heads of department and senior managers can make the transition easier. We now suggest guidelines for these groups.

For supervisors

Essentially, supervisors need to be understanding and sympathetic to the problems of their NESB research students; to give them the benefits of any doubts in the first instance; and to work with them to help them to assimilate. Table 10.1, which is adapted from Okorocha (1997b: 13–14), gives specific recommendations. Some are as valid for domestic research students as for NESB research students, but have been included because they are likely to be particularly important for NESB students.

In many areas of responsibility, supervising NESB students is no different from supervising more generally. For a full list of recommendations, see National Postgraduate Committee (1995).

For heads of department and senior institutional managers

Essentially, departments and institutions should be seen to be giving NESB research students value for money. This not only satisfies the NESB students, but also pays dividends in the long run because a satisfied customer is the best possible marketing agent for acquiring new students.

In Table 10.2, adapted from Okorocha (1997b: 14–15), we do not distinguish between recommendations to heads of departments and recommendations to senior institutional managers. As each institution has its own norms

Table 10.1   Improving the experience of NESB students: recommendations for supervisors

---

- Orientate yourself to pick up information about other cultures. This can simply be a matter of keeping your eyes and ears open and does not necessarily involve a great outlay of time. Or, should you so wish, it can involve reading books and attending social events run by or for NESB students.
- Be aware of cultural issues and of how they can lead to misunderstandings between supervisors and NESB students.
- Examine your implicit assumptions about NESB students; try to make them explicit and then question their validity.
- Initiate exploration with your NESB research students to clarify the meanings behind any verbal or non-verbal communication which makes you uncomfortable.
- Show an interest in the welfare of your NESB research students, but find out about appropriate support services so that you can refer to them should that become necessary.
- At the outset of each NESB student's research programme, devote specific attention to negotiating the respective roles of the supervisor and student and your mutual expectations.
- Explain the professional etiquette for seeking help from other academics.
- Pay particular attention to helping NESB students to work within their time schedules and keep to their deadlines.
- Monitor the progress of your students and give them regular feedback.
- Act before potential problems escalate and get out of hand.
- Where appropriate, lobby management to improve the provision for NESB students (see Table 10.2).

---

about what responsibilities are delegated from central control down to departments, some of the following recommendations are for heads of department, or their nominees as departmental postgraduate tutors or equivalent officers, and some are for senior institutional managers. Responsibilities which are most likely to fall on the institution are at the beginning and those which are most likely to fall on the department are at the end.

See the National Postgraduate Committee (1995) for more general recommendations.

Concluding remarks

In this chapter we have argued that the key to improving the experience of NESB research students and their supervisors, and hence to improving the resulting research training and research output, lies in mutual understanding – and we have considered a range of examples to illustrate how easily misunderstandings can occur. We went on to offer recommendations for supervisors, heads of department (or their nominees) and senior institutional managers, which we phrased in general terms, since the form and style of

Table 10.2   Improving the experience of NESB students: recommendations for institutional management

---

Institutions should provide:
- a member of academic or administrative staff with special responsibility for NESB students;
- encouragement, and where possible also modest funds, to operate NESB and/or national student societies;
- ways to increase awareness among staff and students generally of the experiences and potential difficulties of NESB students, e.g. talks organized by the NESB/national student societies;
- the circulation of relevant codes of practice;
- institutional facilities available during vacations, since postgraduates on research programmes, particularly NESB students, work through vacations;
- full and regularly updated publicity on services and facilities in simple and clear English;
- a channel whereby NESB students can give feedback to supervisors, departments and institutions without fear of repercussions;
- a face-to-face pre-admission interview or some other means by which all parties can check that the student, the department and supervisor are suitably matched;
- realistic pre-admission information including information on such services and facilities as the student union, computing, print, counselling, banking, services to help with language problems, chaplaincies; accommodation; nurseries; careers; shops; eating places, etc. Pre-admission information should also include information about the host department and the academic interests of potential supervisors;
- cultural orientation on arrival;
- institutional and departmental induction including access to facilities;
- some form of repeat induction to accommodate research students who arrive at non-standard points in the academic year;
- a protected and adequate workplace;
- departmental facilities available during vacations.

---

implementation must depend on personal and institutional choice. Many of our recommendations, we know, are already being implemented in various forms – but there is always room for more widespread implementation and for new ways of customizing that implementation to the needs of individual departments and institutions. This book describes some. We hope that our chapter will stimulate the development of more.

11

'Third Places' and Teaching English for Research Purposes

Mary Farquhar

Manipulating contextual frames and perspectives through language can give people power and control, as they try to make themselves at home in a culture 'of a third kind'.

(Kramsch 1993: 235)

Introduction

In this chapter, I argue that NESB postgraduate students who have problems with language proficiency, research skills, or both, require systematic support programme. While most Australian, UK and US universities offer preparatory English language courses so that students may attain language proficiency levels for entry, these levels may be inadequate for postgraduate research or coursework purposes. At the undergraduate level, there is a trend towards combining adjunct learning assistance programmes with systematic support through core skills, study skills and language (ESL) subjects at the first-year level. Such subjects may be for credit. However, postgraduate study programmes, in Australia at least, appear to lack a similar support structure.

At present, most postgraduate support is supplementary and focuses on research culture and skills rather than on communication through the required language: English. Theoretically, however, it has long been recognized that language and culture are inseparable in a communicative context (Hymes 1972). For nearly all tertiary students in the UK, USA and Australia, English is the language of communication and the context is both the local university and the wider, but still specific, culture of Western academe. NESB postgraduates who come from a non-Western culture are therefore doubly disadvantaged within this system.

The disadvantages and difficulties for such students are both linguistic and cultural. First, entry-level English language proficiency requirements are virtually identical for undergraduates and postgraduates in many universities. However, postgraduate study is presumed to build on an undergraduate foundation in an academic discipline, almost always in the English language.

Yet, for some NESB postgraduates, both may be completely lacking. It is therefore necessary to sketch the requirements and supports for NESB undergraduates – who may become postgraduates – before moving to postgraduate supervision itself.

Second, cultural differences for non-Western postgraduates are usually profound as, it is believed, Western research traditions emphasize independence and analytical approaches to knowledge (Ballard and Clanchy 1991b: 12). Hence many of the problems associated with supervising postgraduate NESB students are framed within 'a deficit model' (Gardner 1994: 10). Yet international students in particular already have a rich linguistic and cultural background of their own. Kramsch (1993: 238) argues that learning to operate in a different cultural context through another language involves students finding a space between native and target cultures, articulating 'their new experience within their old one, making it relevant to their own lives'. This is particularly true for international students, who will return to their home culture. Kramsch calls this acculturation process 'looking for third places'.

Both aspects – linguistic and cultural knowledge and skills – can be taught as part of a learning process. This learning process, it is argued, should inform curriculum development at the postgraduate level in line with recent trends at the undergraduate level. But it should also be influenced by a communicative framework which recognizes, first, the powerful potential for intercultural communication from informed students and, second, the difficulties they may encounter in 'leaving behind the naive paradise of native-tongue socialization' (Kramsch 1993: 238). Within this 'third place' framework, which sees language, context and culture as inseparable, this chapter discusses:

- the nature of NESB students and entry-level language proficiency requirements;
- debates in the field of support strategies;
- undergraduate support strategies; and
- postgraduate support strategies.

While many of the examples in the discussion are taken from my own institution's documents and teaching experience, anecdotal evidence suggests the issues are common to many, if not all, English speaking universities.

Who are NESB students?

It is often forgotten that NESB students are defined only by lack of a particular linguistic background. Their language backgrounds are not primarily English. Apart from this single characteristic, there are no other essential similarities. In an English speaking university context, however, the single similarity is that NESB students are required to study in a language and culture which for them may range from the very foreign to the very familiar, depending on their educational and cultural backgrounds.

Thus NESB students are a diverse group. Recent research by Dobson, Birrell and Rapson (in Illing 1996b: 35) demonstrates that they include those who are well equipped as well as those needing infrastructural support to study successfully. This support may involve development of skills for communication, numeracy, computing, information and general study skills (Gardner 1994: 21). One of the first management tasks is, therefore, to identify more precisely those students who need support without imposing 'remedial' requirements on an entire group. Indeed, a few NESB students have regarded staff attempts to 'remedy' or comment on perceived problems in assignments as both discriminatory and patronizing.

Identifying NESB students requiring assistance

At Griffith University, my own institution, concern was first expressed in 1988 about the English language needs of international students (Parra 1995: 2). In 1992, this concern extended to general academic support for all Griffith students. In this context, the university's *Report on Learning Assistance Provision* (Gardner 1994: 32) identified NESB students as a group requiring assistance by analysing student progress rates in 1992 and 1993 according to equity target group measures. This was followed by a student opinion survey of support services in which a significant number of respondents indicated uncertainty or dissatisfaction.

Concerns of international students, in particular, were highlighted in the review process:

> Faculty reports on learning assistance identified language proficiency, academic and cultural adjustment issues and the time involved in supporting this group of students as major concerns. Several international students interviewed expressed frustration at the difficulty experienced in negotiating adequate support in a system that is perceived as both confusing and sometimes unsympathetic.
>
> (Parra 1995: 27)

This report process, by a Pro-Vice-Chancellor, is to be applauded. It identified both learning assistance components and student concerns within a model informed by lifelong learning and equity goals. It was noted, however, that learning assistance was frequently associated with 'a deficit model' – that is, as adjunct and remedial (Gardner 1994: 10). This is in line with many Australian universities, which offer a range of options, such as preparatory English courses, foundation or first-year core skills subjects, adjunct workshops, individual tutorials and editorial assistance and, only sometimes, limited subjects for credit (Todhunter 1996). However, except for individual tutorials and editorial assistance, such options are usually for undergraduates, not postgraduates, and cluster at the first-year level.

The report identified a further problem which is central to the provision of effective support services and called for further studies (Gardner 1994:

22). This involved uneven and decentralized approaches to support services across the university.

> While there is a plethora of services provided, there is no *mechanism for coordination of these services* to ensure coverage is effective. Moreover, there is no university policy set for support services for learning assistance, *nor ways of monitoring demand for and provision of services for various groups and locations* (author's emphasis).

This finding was confirmed in our research. We asked an international student seeking tertiary enrolment to 'sweep' Australian universities asking about language and academic support *after* entry. Thirty-five universities were contacted. Compared with most of these, Griffith lacked a central coordinated response. This was especially so by comparison with the four universities – Bond, UTS, Macquarie and Melbourne – that offer courses for credit in their degree programmes. Despite the range of support services available (especially in the Commerce faculty, 'home' of most of our international students), the student was literally 'passed down the line', ending up with only a telephone contact for a voluntary Saturday morning class! At a time when international students provide essential operating income to our universities, it is essential that support services are not only offered but are also easily accessible.

The problem of English language proficiency

This is a major problem for the supervision of some NESB postgraduates. In most universities, the simple fact is that English language proficiency requirements for postgraduate coursework and research students are *almost exactly the same* as those for undergraduates. Postgraduate study assumes an undergraduate foundation which familiarizes students not only with the concepts and language of their chosen disciplines, but also with local university procedures, academic protocols and Western research culture. The postgraduate entry requirements, however, ignore this assumption and therefore ignore the consequent need for universities to provide postgraduates with the growing infrastructure support available to undergraduates.

Using the IELTS (International English Language Testing System – see Table 11.1) as a basis for discussion, all Queensland universities require an approximate score of 6.5 for admission. Some universities have a lower entry score while others, such as Griffith, have scores ranging from 6.0 (Commerce) to 7.0 (Humanities). The proficiency requirements for entry into postgraduate coursework and research degrees are virtually the same, with perhaps only a 0.5 difference. The Commerce faculty, which has most international students, is the exception with graded entry requirements across all three levels (6.0 – undergraduate; 6.5 – postgraduate coursework; 7.0 – postgraduate research). It is not surprising that some students, particularly those at the 'competent user' level (6.0), have problems with

Table 11.1 Description of relevant English proficiency (IELTS) bands

6. *Competent user:* Has generally effective command of the language despite some inaccuracies, inappropriacies and misunderstandings. Can use and understand fairly complex language, particularly in familiar situations.
7. *Good user:* Has operational command of the language, though with occasional inaccuracies, inappropriacies and misunderstandings in some situations. Generally handles complex language well and understands detailed reasoning.
8. *Very good user:* Has fully operational command of the language with only occasional unsystematic inaccuracies and inappropriacies. Misunderstandings may occur in unfamiliar situations. Handles complex detailed argumentation well.
9. *Expert user:* Has fully operational command of the language: appropriate, accurate and fluent with complete understanding.

English and that this has been the earliest recorded problem at Griffith University. But it is surprising that most postgraduate entry requirements ignore the substantial cognitive skills involved in manipulating the English language during the undergraduate years. That learning involves the ability to communicate in all four language macroskills: listening (e.g. lectures), speaking (e.g. seminars), reading (e.g. library research) and writing (e.g. essays and exams). Research, in particular, involves writing as the medium of communication and this is usually the most difficult skill to master.

There is also the research process itself. Ballard and Clanchy (1991b: 72) point out that students who have 'survived' an Honours or Masters course know what to expect. Overseas students may have extensive research records in their own country, but be unprepared for the independence and aloneness. Their 'existence is indeed solitary, nasty, brutish – and long drawn out'. In this situation, inadequate English language ability is difficult to diagnose, especially if the student does not acknowledge that support is needed, or expresses it as a research or cross-cultural problem.

Inconsistent entry pathways for overseas students make it impossible to discern whether the required language levels are always satisfied. Even if satisfied, the entry tests focus on proficiency and not on other required skills and knowledge in subjects utilizing highly complex language and specific reasoning and research skills. Ballard and Clanchy (1991b: 71) suggest that such postgraduates do badly when placed in undergraduate courses with ESB students to fill in the gaps because these courses are seldom suited to the particular needs of NESB postgraduate students. A low achievement in the course reinforces a sense of shame and lack of confidence. These students 'are better served by a focused and well directed course of instruction or reading' which is culturally embedded in the Western academic tradition.

Given financial restrictions in the tertiary sector, the question is what type of course best serves the needs of these students?

Support strategies: debates in the field

NESB students have diverse backgrounds. These may include pre-tertiary and/or undergraduate study in an Australian institution. In such cases, students are clearly better equipped for postgraduate study than overseas students whose tertiary entry in Australia is at the postgraduate level. Clearly, the support services available to undergraduate and postgraduate students, experienced and inexperienced English-language speakers, must be differentiated.

Our research indicates a trend towards systematizing support at the undergraduate level. Data collection involved, first, surveying each university via the Internet; second, contacting all Australian universities by telephone regarding post-entry courses on offer in communication and English language for international students; third, collecting introductory materials; and fourth, identifying key models (Todhunter 1996). The working party also collected relevant literature in the field, university reports and student numbers in our own university. We then analysed the models and trends and devised a course for our own students.

NESB and international students, as groups, registered similar levels of dis/satisfaction with support services, although the statistics do not analyse needs for diagnostic purposes. We therefore returned to the international students who listed language proficiency, cultural/academic adjustment and support time as issues.

The incipient trend in Australian universities is a move from preparatory English language courses, through a range of adjunct services pre- and post-entry, to credit-accruing subjects, primarily at first year. Most universities with international/NESB students offer the first two options. Some universities have also recently initiated the third option, credit-accruing subjects which precisely target the problems of English language proficiency, academic requirements and time. This is done by using an English for Academic Purposes approach, incorporating study, communications and employment skills, and systematizing support in academic subjects so as to save time outlaid on ad hoc, one-to-one or adjunct assistance. This approach also offers NESB students a more comprehensive, relevant and useful degree programme.

Credit accrual is important because it removes the the notion of a deficit model, contextualizes learning and provides student networks, so alleviating loneliness. The Griffith University report (Parra 1995: 21) claimed that international students 'agreed that decontextualized English language support is of limited value when students are pressured to respond to more immediate assignment and examination demands'. This negative response to a centralized study skills model attached to elements such as student services reinforces the benefits for students of courses for credit as part of their degree.

The literature highlights certain problems with the centralized study skills model. The centralized model is seen as isolating skills, especially language skills, from course content (Marshal 1982, quoted in Parra 1995: 21). The credit-accrual approach, conversely, links skills and content.

A second problem relates to Western academic expectations. Many of our international students and an increasing number of NESB Australian students come from Asia. Thus Ballard and Clanchy (1991b: 12–18) claim that Australian students move along a continuum from reproductive (primary/secondary) to more analytical and critical approaches to knowledge (late secondary/tertiary) and, finally, to 'the creation of "new" knowledge' through speculation and hypothesis (postgraduate). Alternative Asian traditions, they argue, have the same continuum but reproductive, more passive attitudes dominate even at the postgraduate level. This stereotype is under criticism. For example, Biggs (1996b: 40) questions the equating of reproductive with rote or mechanical learning and claims that Confucian-based cultures prefer a 'constructivist' approach with 'a stronger preference for high-level, meaning-based learning strategies'. He cites studies which show that Asian students regularly score higher than United States students in standardized tests, particularly in maths. This confirms problems with delinking language/study skills from meaning-based course content.

Support services: undergraduate

Our research showed a progression in university support services for NESB students at the undergraduate level. Over the last ten years, support has increased from preparatory programmes only through adjunct models towards centralized, generic and credit-bearing subjects. The University of Melbourne (CCS & ESL 1995), which appears to have moved furthest along this path, states that its mission is to:

> establish itself as an internationally recognized model for teaching and research with a strong commitment to supporting the academic progress of the University's international and NESB students, as well as to fostering a culture of excellence in English language expression.

The university's research links context with themes, such as computer literacy as a communication skill, the required language skills, learning strategies and content-based instruction.

The University of Melbourne offerings were taken as one of four models in our research. A first finding was that students require credit-accruing subjects which are not only skills-based but also content-based. This is, theoretically, the approach of Kramsch (1993) and, practically, that of the University of Melbourne, which offers centralized, generic sets of subjects to supplement discipline-specific programmes, support classes for undergraduates and postgraduates, and individual tutorials. Centralized and adjunct models run in tandem. The centralized model is run by a new Centre for Communication Skills and ESL (CCS & ESL), established in 1995 after a

1994 review. It offers four credit-bearing subjects in ESL (for NESB and international students) and five credit-bearing subjects in communication, including technical and technological, skills (for ESB students or those with a minimum IELTS score of 7). Except for one subject, *all* are offered in both semesters. The objectives are academic and not remedial. Other universities offer less extensive and less structured but nevertheless similar credit-bearing subjects.

This finding informed our curriculum design for a Communications (English Language) major for international students at the first stage of their degree. Skills include exit and entry language proficiency ratings (e.g. IELTS 6.5 to 7.5–8); communication in various contexts (such as the university) and registers (such as disciplinary and vocational); technological communication; and study skills.

A second finding relates to meaning-based learning in academically sound subjects. The relationship of 'content' familiarity to language ability and development is one of the programme evaluation themes at the University of Melbourne's new Centre. While skills acquisition is clearly an objective in any support subject for NESB students, content is crucial. Kramsch (1993: 3–4) states: 'One of the more tenacious dichotomies in foreign language education is that of skills versus content. Language is viewed as a skill, a tool that in itself is devoid of any intellectual value.'

She writes that language teachers want to get their students talking and writing while 'depth and breadth of thought belong to other subjects'. We believe, first, that talking and writing should involve depth and breadth; second, that the history, nature and working of English as an international language (science, business, diplomacy and technological communications) and regional language supplies embarrassingly rich content; and third, given the nature of our students, that the communications objective should include a further dimension of intercultural communication so that students explicitly link back to their native cultures as they learn to explore 'third places' of their own.

An undergraduate programme, structured around three years of study, is thus conceptualized around English as an international and regional language which displays a range of communication strategies, depending on the medium, context, culture, and – sometimes – vocation or discipline. For example, returned international student graduates may use English in business negotiations with foreigners or for further study. Therefore, the skills and knowledge should not only transfer across subjects within a university syllabus but also extend to lifelong learning. The teaching method therefore encourages a gradual process of moving towards independent learning, a major feature of postgraduate study.

A possible array of subjects has been suggested, with a strategy to increase competent use of information and communication technologies. In one sense, this is a marriage of the University of Melbourne's Communication Skills and ESL subjects, but with explicit academic content and themes. Suggested subjects in a Communications (English Language) major are:

- *First year:* English in the World Today; English in the University (Study Skills);
- *Second year:* Cultural and Commercial Communications; Science and Technology in the World Today; Communication and Organizational Behaviour; Language and Power (including rhetoric, negotiation, etc.);
- *Third year:* Communication through Computers and the Media; Intercultural Communication and the Internet.

Such a major fills a lacuna in present university offerings. While LOTE subjects may touch on all the above issues pertinent to the language and culture studied, we have discovered no such structured course on English as a means of communication in the world today. This is surprising given the importance of English and the number of international and NESB students in Australia. Indeed, tentative discussions with various stakeholders have generated excitement – not just approval – for such a support strategy for NESB students.

Support strategies: postgraduate

Undergraduate support services are clearly important for the quality of postgraduate students. NESB graduates may go on to postgraduate study and so benefit from systematized support services – if they need it – in their undergraduate training. Thus Melbourne University's strategy is an investment in quality future postgraduate students. The problem of adequate support, however, remains for those students who have not had access to such services or who enter university in Australia at the postgraduate level. The latter include international students.

A recent Department of Employment, Education, Training and Youth Affairs (DEETYA) study undertaken by the International Development Program (IDP) Education Australia (Tideman 1996) reported that international students in 1995 comprised 8.4 per cent of the total student population and provided 6.6 per cent of total university income. The Australian International Education Foundation (Peacock 1996: 2) believes that, with effective strategies, these earnings may double to $4 billion a year by 2001. The IDP report (Tideman 1996: 36) stated:

> After some hard lessons in some earlier phases, Australia has mature international student programs . . . and is host to 4 per cent of the world's international student population. The most common reason students choose Australia is for quality.

Postgraduate students, including those from overseas, require quality supervision and support services. Indeed, a Japanese academic who successfully completed postgraduate study in Australia confirmed this when she said that international postgraduates choose 'to come here' precisely to learn Western research techniques and traditions, 'so don't be too soft'.

Nevertheless, as we have argued, postgraduate support services are not as developed as those for undergraduates. Griffith University, for example, has a professional editor for postgraduates, an initiative much praised by other universities. But the trend will probably follow that of undergraduate support: towards systematization through course offerings. Melbourne University is, again, probably one of the most organized in terms of centralized postgraduate support. ESL support classes are open to undergraduates and postgraduates and include reading and writing up research for postgraduates only. A further short course, Written Communications Skills for Postgraduates, is offered at a more advanced level.

The rationale for systematization is the same as for undergraduates. Leaving all support arrangements to the supervisor is unfair and unreliable, for both student and academic, as well as time-consuming. Centralized postgraduate support courses diagnose problems early, facilitate student networking, pool the talents of experienced supervisors and save time.

Ballard and Clanchy (1991b: 70–2) list some of the problems specific to overseas postgraduates, such as being 'more firmly bound within their own educational traditions', different capacities for independent study and perhaps confusion about 'the relationship between supervisor and student'. The same problems would apply to recent immigrants. Ballard and Clanchy categorize these problems as either technical or cultural, and they apply particularly to social sciences and humanities postgraduates who are expected to work independently, whereas science students may be gradually acculturated through teamwork in laboratories.

Ballard and Clanchy (1991b: 87) conclude that the role of a supervisor is a 'demanding' one, particularly when cross-cultural issues intervene. The parental aspects of the role may be particularly difficult and foreign to many Australian academics. Our own student surveys have, however, pointed to language proficiency as a major issue. As with undergraduates, communication in English about research – whether findings or problems – is central to the learning process.

Therefore, as with undergraduates, a rationale exists for a centralized, contextualized and meaning-based course on English Communication for Research Purposes. This lessens the supervisor's parental role, diagnoses and helps overcome English language problems at an early stage, and allows student networking to alleviate loneliness, particularly in the humanities and social sciences. It may be either voluntary or credit-bearing if it is part of a Masters by coursework programme.

However, it cannot be structured as a stage following an undergraduate major. This is because, as stated above, the language proficiency entry level is approximately the same for undergraduates and postgraduates. It must also be sufficiently focused on postgraduate research purposes.

We therefore devised two postgraduate subjects called English for Research Purposes (ERP). They accrue credit at the Masters coursework level. Using a research process model developed by Nancy Viviani, the first subject asks, 'What is research?' as a prerequisite to the second subject, 'Doing my [own]

Table 11.2   Example ERP module

(Intensive I: 10 credit points) **Task-based: What is research?** **Techniques and skills using models**

Classwork: 30 hours

Lines of inquiry

1. *What is research?* Introduce Darwin's *Origin.* Why is the work significant for the field?
2. *Library, citation, bibliography, plagiarism, copyright.* Darwin's introduction/s. The case of Wallace.
3. *What is an argument/thesis?* Darwin as above. Rewrite introduction, use of modalities.
4. *Approaches: descriptive, critical, analytical, etc.* The language of Darwin; the research process.
5. *Introductions and conclusions.* A textual analysis of Darwin's introduction and conclusion.

Guided independent work

6. *Group seminar presentation and written paper.* Students to formulate their presentation topics and work in pairs, culminating in a student-run seminar at the end of the course.

research'. The first subject ends with a group seminar presentation and written paper; the second with a mini-conference. Students, as Kramsch (1993) states, learn to manipulate language to empower their own work.

While language use and strategies are therefore important, we also decided to teach this through a classic research text, Darwin's *Origin of Species.* This is a beautifully written scientific text, but the English is somewhat old-fashioned and therefore provides an excellent basis for rewriting in relevant modern idioms. Furthermore, Darwin's story narrates one example of the research process, including competition with Wallace, and the final book includes a literature review, summaries and so on. Because of its topic, style and impact on our understanding of life, it is a significant text in all fields and cultures, such as the Chinese. This allows the intercultural theme of the undergraduate major to continue in the postgraduate course with students exploring the ways their own culture used Darwin's work or used key concepts from it. Or students may wish to extend key concepts into their own particular disciplines – for example, competition in international business. The main point is that the subjects are meaning-based around a core classical text in our own and other cultures.

This example of approaches is just one of many exciting paths that could be followed to teach Western research skills and traditions to NESB postgraduates. In the process, there is less reliance on the supervisor. Students are also better placed to form networks to adjust to both academic demands and a new culture at the beginning of their study programme and to find help for various stages of study, especially writing up. In short, there is a clear need to systematize postgraduate, not just undergraduate, support services through focused and creative course offerings. These supplement, rather than replace, other support services.

Table 11.3   Example ERP module

(Intensive II: 10 credit points) **Task-based: Doing my research** **Defining a research topic: The Viviani model**

Classwork: 30 hours (same as Intensive I)

Lines of inquiry

1. *Introduction: What to look at? The model?* The topic, research question, area and field.
2. *Justification: Why?* Literature review and debates.
3. *Methodology: How?* Various research methods.
4. *Theory.* Developing an explanatory framework drawing on key debates in the field.
5. *Pulling it together.* Students write up a research project outline of their own.

Guided independent work

6. *A mini-conference: 'speech and written events'.* Students conduct their own mini-research conference. Topic chosen in collaboration with class members as part of team research; individual papers determined by students in collaboration with teachers. Experts invited.

Conclusion

This chapter has mapped trends in undergraduate support services for NESB students in Australian universities as a forerunner to identifying postgraduate requirements. The services include preparatory, remedial, adjunct and, more recently, credit-bearing academic courses. Whether deliberately or coincidentally, these help those students who later undertake postgraduate studies. For those NESB students who enter universities at the postgraduate level or who have not had access to undergraduate support in a university, there is a need for a similar range of support services at the postgraduate level. Few universities, however, have developed focused courses for NESB postgraduates.

The present system of leaving much of the welfare and cultural adjustment of NESB students to the supervisors alone is an unfair burden on academic staff, and cannot provide maximum benefit for the students' academic and personal development. It may also leave international students, in particular, with unpleasant memories of overseas study.

Acknowledgements

This research was conducted under a small School of Languages and Applied Linguistics grant awarded to the author in the Faculty of Asian and International Studies at Griffith University, Brisbane. Dr Penny McKay in the Department of Language and Literacy, Queensland University of Technology, acted as a consultant. Maureen Todhunter gave editorial and research assistance and was a member of the working party. Other members of the working party were: Lynette Bowyer, Deputy Director, Centre for Applied Linguistics and Languages (CALL), Griffith University; Debra Hoven, Lecturer, Faculty of Asian and International Studies; and Helen Cherry, Research Assistant.

Part 4

Practical Responses

12

Information Technology and the NESB Research Student

Allan Ellis and Renata Phelps

Introduction

Tertiary educators and postgraduate students can no longer ignore the role of technology in learning and research. As Lee (1995: 1) states, 'few areas of research, teaching or scholarship now remain untouched by developments in information technology'.

In its broadest sense, the term 'information technology' (IT) encompasses the vast range of tools which humans have used in their management of information, from wooden styluses and wax tablets to satellite communication systems, or the global pool of computers that make up the Internet. In the academic environment, it could include books, records, libraries, audiovisual materials and telecommunications technologies. However, in its more contemporary sense, IT tends to assume definition from computing disciplines and hence encompasses not only hardware and software, but the documentation, support and training necessary to render the hardware and software fully effective in performing tasks undertaken by users.

From this more specific definition, it is possible to form a concept of IT within higher education institutions which includes:

- all *electronically mediated tools* for storing, transferring, managing, searching, presenting, creating, accessing and exploring information. The most common current format of such technologies is digital;
- the *supporting structure* of staff, material resources, reference resources and protocols needed to enable staff and students to use those tools productively. This structure facilitates access to technologies, training, information processing and storage, telecommunications services, and software support and evaluation;
- the *integration* of these tools and supporting structures with the needs of staff, students and administrators. This involves ascertaining and evaluating patterns of use and need amongst users and maintaining an institutional commitment (including financial) to providing students and staff with

adequate access and guidance in appropriate academic applications. It also involves monitoring and fostering the healthy growth of IT on campus by formulating, promulgating, implementing and reviewing information technology policies and fostering interaction between libraries, media services, computing services, technical services and academic departments.

This chapter aims to address issues surrounding the adoption of information technologies specifically by non-English speaking background (NESB) postgraduate students. The first section of the chapter will deal with the opportunities provided to researchers, and specifically to NESB research students, by various electronically mediated tools. We then go on to examine some of the specific challenges which need to be addressed in terms of the second and third aspects of IT, particularly as they relate to NESB students and their supervisors.

Opportunities

Information technology, according to our definition, takes many diverse forms. It encompasses applications for research preparation, data collection and analysis, dialogue and interaction as well as for research presentation. Many of these applications can greatly enhance the quality and efficiency of research conducted by postgraduate students and enhance the dissemination of research findings.

Writing assistance

One of the major difficulties facing NESB students is the linguistic construction of their theses. Editorial assistance becomes a major factor for supervisors and other support staff, with many NESB students expecting their supervisors to perform a major editorial role for them. This is a time-consuming added responsibility for the supervisor and many object or refuse to perform this role to the level that the NESB student expects. At many universities, an additional 'learning assistance' staff member is employed to assist NESB students to develop the grammatical skills necessary for their academic writing.

For the NESB student, word processing programs can also assist in overcoming many writing difficulties. By utilizing computers for all their jottings and notes, research students can significantly decrease the amount of work that remains later in thesis writing. Cut-and-paste editing provides considerable efficiency in thesis writing. Spell-checkers, thesauruses and grammar checkers are now commonplace additions to word processing software and can be of immense value in providing editorial assistance; the ability to build customized dictionaries allows the specialist researcher to modify these programs to recognize technical terms; grammar checkers, while slow and somewhat tedious, may offer assistance in alerting the NESB student to problems in their writing. While these programs will never substitute for human editorial assistance, English improvement and grammatical development, they can decrease the reliance of the NESB student on his or her supervisor and other study assistance staff.

For the research student in maths or the sciences, equation editors such as 'Mathematica' assist in writing mathematical formulae and many of these software programs are capable of producing 'live' formulae which actively perform the calculations they express.

Improvements in word processing and desktop publishing software, their decreasing cost and ready availability have raised expectations regarding thesis presentation. The use of such technology by the research student is today considered virtually essential in Australian higher education institutes. While many academics, as well as employers, consider word processing and typing skills to be essential, these skills are frequently under-addressed in terms of student skill development. Keyboard skills are a good investment for the researcher and readily available typing tutors can assist in developing these skills. Once such basic computer skills are developed, further utilization of IT in such areas as e-mail communication becomes extremely efficient.

Presentation assistance

Research students are frequently required to present their work to others in an oral form, either as part of their course requirements or at conferences, seminars or other functions. Software packages such as Microsoft Powerpoint can assist in the presentation of text and graphics (including graphs, diagrams and photographs), either by screen projection or by production of overheads. For the NESB student with limited English language skills, use of these programs can assist in visually clarifying concepts for an audience.

Bibliographical software

Bibliographical software can greatly assist researchers to manage their research-based literature efficiently and effectively. Such software not only assists in filing and retrieving references, but facilitates the writing process by creating bibliographies from in-text citations. With growing pressures on researchers to publish widely, apply for grants from several agencies and submit articles to multiple journals, the value of bibliographic software rises (Finn 1996). Many bibliographic software programs are now exploiting features of the Internet, allowing users to export and import records and to share libraries of references across networks. Results of literature searches performed through online databases can be imported directly into many of these bibliographical databases.

Data analysis software

Data analysis software packages, both quantitative and qualitative, are greatly revolutionizing researchers' work, creating efficiencies and accuracies hitherto impossible. It is important that supervisors are aware of such programs, their potential and limitations, so that they are able to advise postgraduate students on the appropriateness of such software to their research projects.

Many postpositivist researchers are hesitant to use computers for qualitative data analysis. However as Tesch (1990: 300) states, 'computers are not alien to "humanistic" ways of handling data. They merely mimic what qualitative researchers have done for decades as part of their work.' Qualitative research software performs such functions as text retrieval, coding, categorization and organization. More recently, relational database managers (RDBMs) have enabled not only the sorting and categorizing of data, but the linking of this data to theoretical categories, and the ability to modify these linkages as the analysis process progresses (Rodgers 1995: 368).

The Internet: a network of researchers

The Internet is a global network of computers linked together through telecommunications systems. One specific application of this network of hardware is the World Wide Web, which can be defined in a very basic sense as a set of protocols for information sharing over the Internet.

The WWW is a medium not only for text retrieval, but for access to graphics, animation and sound. While traditionally much of the researcher's information has been sought in text format, many multimedia resources can prove equally valuable, such as recorded interviews and movie footage.

Postgraduate research has often been described as a lonely activity. The Internet offers unprecedented opportunities for dialogue and interaction. Communication software such as e-mail, discussion groups and mailing lists can not only reduce the isolation of NESB students from their country of origin but create an international community of researchers.

E-mail can be a valuable additional medium for interaction between supervisor and research student. Contact is no longer reliant on scheduled meetings and both parties need not be on campus for interaction to occur.

'Listservs' are electronic mailing lists which provide opportunities for people to share questions, ideas and experiences about a particular topic with people around the world. Of particular interest to NESB educators are Web sites such as that of the University of California Linguistic Minority Research Institute which sponsors a number of discussion lists as part of its electronic networking project.[1]

Newsgroups are very similar to mailing lists; however, instead of e-mail, the newsgroups are read on a 'newsreader'. The EDNET Guide to Usenet Newsgroups provides a list of educationally focused newsgroups including, for the NESB student or educator, a large number of international related groups, language-focused discussions and a whole host of highly specialized academic and research groups.[2]

The Internet, then, provides NESB students with the opportunity to maintain communications with subject experts internationally, some of whom may speak their first language, or be in their home country. In this way, professional relationships can be established and maintained at an international level.

Newer technologies such as videoconferencing and Web-based conferencing mean that students and supervisors can move away from the written word and incorporate the many benefits of non-verbal communications in their interactions. Such communication technologies facilitate further enhanced communication with supervisors and other researchers in the field.

The World Wide Web: a rich source of information

The WWW is a powerful medium for both information retrieval and information dissemination. For the prospective international student, it can assist in identifying appropriate postgraduate programs and supervisors. Sites such as Australian University Research Contacts[3] provide contact details for research officers of Australian universities, including phone, fax and e-mail. Active university faculty Web sites can enhance postgraduate study and supervision and facilitate access to academics, supervisors and other students with similar research interests.

A further advantage of the WWW is illustrated by the National Graduate Research Database, sponsored by Southern Cross University in conjunction with the University of Melbourne Postgraduate Association.[4] This is a freely searchable database of postgraduate research being conducted within Australia. Student participation is voluntary but highly encouraged, with potential benefits including enhanced research collaboration, easy contact with other researchers via e-mail and phone and links to home pages of individual researchers or research groups, providing access to recent papers or topical information.

The World Wide Web: a support network for NESB students and supervisors

The WWW is a valuable medium for distributing information regarding the availability of resources for NESB students. The Australian National University's support pages for NESB students provide details of their University English Language Program (UELP),[5] and the University of Adelaide details information on its Integrated Bridging Program (IBP) for International Postgraduate Students.[6] Provision of such information through an internationally accessible medium such as the WWW allows prospective overseas students to determine whether particular universities provide the support services they desire and/or need.

Supervisors can also find resources on the Internet to help them in addressing issues regarding the supervision of NESB students. The 'Creating a Community of Scholars' Web site,[7] maintained by the Centre for Applied Language Research at Edith Cowan University, presents an interactive training package to assist academic staff in the management of tutorial classes and workshops where students come from a range of different cultural backgrounds and different life experiences.

The WWW can also provide access to valuable information concerning sources for research funding, including scholarships and research grants, tenders, prizes and awards. An example of such an Australian database is the SPIN database.[8]

Many organizational bodies offering funding for research also provide access to application forms and guidelines either by downloading from their Web site or by File Transfer Protocol (FTP) processes. For NESB students, this improved accessibility means that they may be able to locate and make application to appropriate funding bodies before arriving in Australia.

In a more general sense, many universities are now providing Web access to their research guidelines, regulations, codes of practice, ethics clearance procedures and forms, guidelines for supervision and thesis preparation. They are thus providing the opportunity for prospective international students to begin preparation of their submissions and enrolments in a timely and efficient manner.

Further writing support for NESB students can also be found on the Internet, with a vast array of multilingual dictionaries, thesauruses, glossaries and other reference works freely available to access and/or download.[9]

Critiquing of writing

Academics often express uncertainty about accepting students' writing by electronic delivery means (Phelps 1996: 81). These fears are somewhat surprising given that our postal system is just as likely to misplace assignments, or create delays in their delivery. Using electronic means for submission of students' work, supervisors are able to provide immediate confirmation of receipt and hence, if problems occur, resubmission is possible.

For growing numbers of postgraduate research students, many of whom are off-campus or may be overseas for extended periods, 'snail mail' represents an archaic and unnecessary delay in feedback. Prompt return of thesis drafts with quality constructive feedback is crucial, and greatly enhanced through electronic delivery. Software developed to facilitate paperless assignment submission (Hoe and Whale 1995) could be equally applicable to thesis editing.

Peer reviewing of drafts of research publications and theses is also possible using such technologies. Such methods have been used for some time in undergraduate coursework degrees, where, for instance, students use e-mail to receive and submit all assignments, anonymously evaluate each other's work, discuss lectures, concepts or problems, help each other with assignments, get instructor feedback on assignments, resubmit assignments, and request and receive individual help from the instructor.

The adaptation of such an approach with NESB students presents an opportunity for peer-assisted development not only of research content, but of language.

Online libraries, databases and published resources

The importance of resource access should not be underestimated as a concern for NESB students. At a workshop for NESB research students and their supervisors at Southern Cross University in 1996, students cited resourcing issues as their primary concern.

> Students felt that they faced an inability to access both home country literature and other external sources and that slow turnaround time for inter-library loans had a negative impact on their ability to research.
> (Shevellar and Heywood 1996: 4)

Online library catalogues and databases greatly increase accessibility to literature resources locally and internationally. Many of these databases are available in full text or have extensive abstracts. Access to such databases can be greatly facilitated via the WWW. It is important for both postgraduate students and supervisors to be familiar with the literature databases relevant to their research area, as well as to be aware of emerging information sources and sites on the Internet such as CyberStacks,[10] a unified collection of Internet resources categorized using the Library of Congress classification scheme. For the NESB research student, such sources can greatly facilitate the literature reviewing process. For overseas students intending to enrol in a course of study at an institute, such databases allow them to access specialized resources and hence develop a focused research plan before committing themselves to a particular path of study and travelling overseas.

Supervisors should be aware of the difficulties that NESB students may face in mastering 'Boolean logic' techniques necessary to use these databases effectively. Students with limited mastery of English may be hampered in their information-retrieval capabilities if they are not aware of appropriate synonyms for their search terms or if they do not have clear understandings of the linguistic factors surrounding indexing systems.

Use of technology for language development

Technology and computer-mediated communication (CMC) have been utilized in language development for some time. Examples of successful programs include the University of Arizona's *Spanish Basic Language Program* (Smith 1993), the University of Toronto's *Computer Writing Network (CWN)*

Project in East Asian Languages (Nakajima 1993) and Harvard University's videodisc project for ESL entitled *Who Should Do the Housework?* This last example illustrates how technology can assist NESB students to develop a cultural understanding of the country in which they study. International networking fostered through the Internet can further this capacity for language development.

Challenges

Despite these opportunities afforded to researchers by IT, it would appear that, in many academic environments, research students may not be effectively and efficiently utilizing these technologies. This section will discuss several factors which at present may be limiting the use of IT by postgraduate NESB students.

From the definition of IT detailed at the beginning of this chapter, we saw IT as encompassing both support structures for the use of these electronic tools and the integration of these tools and supporting structures with the needs of staff and students. There are many indications that limitations on the adoption of these technologies may be caused by a lack of attention to these latter two aspects of the IT definition.

At a workshop for NESB research students and their supervisors at Southern Cross University in 1996, NESB students argued that computer facilities were inadequate and that there was a lack of computer training and support, particularly for the Internet (Shevellar and Heywood 1996: 4). While computer access at Southern Cross University could be considered comparatively good, training in its use and promotion of its research potential may not be as adequate. International students are provided with a special two-hour session on computing when they begin their studies to assist them in mastering 'logging in' and networking issues. While this is highly valuable, there is a definite need at Southern Cross University, as at other universities, to provide both students and supervisors with ongoing training in specific research applications.

Multilingual considerations

The most urgent task associated with the internationalization of technology is the creation of multilanguage character sets (Chuguev 1996; Yong *et al.* 1996). Multilanguage computer systems and keyboards have been available for some time and their ready availability means that NESB students need not entirely forego their first language when computing in a new country. Computer language systems can be obtained by FTP from various computer manufacturers' FTP sites. The development of multi-character Web clients and servers is rapidly accelerating and indications are that the Internet will truly facilitate a move towards multilingual publishing. While print-based publishing techniques are highly limited in their ability for multilingual publication, an increasing number of Web sites and several search tools are presenting multilanguage interfaces to their users (Susaki *et al.* 1996).[11] As these authors state (1996: 354), the 'Internet supports a multitude of different languages, and it is only natural that users want to access information resources in their native tongue'.

Explicating expectations

Ballard and Clanchy (1991b: 16–21) devote considerable discussion to the differences in approaches to teaching and learning which occur between cultures. If the many opportunities which IT affords to research students are to be equitably available to NESB students, it is important that both supervisors and students are clearly aware of these opportunities and openly discuss the advantages and disadvantages of their application.

Quality of information and interaction on the Internet

There tends to be a sense amongst some academics that the quality of information available on the Internet is somehow inferior to that obtainable in print. There is no doubt that the Internet carries a body of information which varies greatly in nature and quality. The Internet is a tool not only for educational pursuit, but also for leisure, entertainment, business, marketing and propaganda.

All the information sources which researchers associate with 'quality' and which they would traditionally access through print-based means exist on the WWW. There are a rapidly expanding number of refereed and editorially reviewed academic journals available; there are sources for traditional literature (such as the Project Gutenberg Site);[12] there are sites for newspapers, conference papers,[13] statistics, research reports, working papers and government publications.

The immediacy of the Web can take information quality and currency one step further. Not only is information accessible as soon as it is written, but it is possible to access, via e-mail, writers who have submitted documents to electronic journals, challenging the ideas and concepts presented in their papers. Such techniques are being trialled by Sydney University's *Medical Journal of Australia*[14] and by the *Journal of Interactive Media in Education*,[15] among others. Readers are able to access the articles and reviewers' comments and make additional comments which may be incorporated by the author into the final article (Blue 1996). For researchers, these possibilities are without precedent. 'The wide range of electronic material available underlines the reality of the electronic medium and the need for more tools to cope with the ensuing information overload' (Bearman *et al.* 1996).

Further, the more informal the interaction taking place, the more subjective the information is likely to be. NESB students in particular must be alerted to the importance of selecting information carefully, filtering the subjective from the rigorous, and assessing quality in the midst of quantity.

Teaching critical approaches to information quality

Skills of critical evaluation of information are integral to study and research and one of the most valuable skills supervisors can foster in their research students is a critical approach to information. While these skills are essential on the Internet, they are certainly no less crucial in traditional information media. Some NESB students' cultural background and past experience have taught them that it is improper to raise criticisms and questions (Ballard and Clanchy 1991b: 17). It may thus be necessary for the NESB supervisor to explicate the need for critical approaches to information and assist students to develop these skills.

Acquiring and teaching strategies to cope with the quantity of information

Academics often express fears of 'losing control' of their knowledge base. For students as well, particularly at PhD level, who are expected to have a thorough knowledge of the literature in their area of study, the sheer volume of readily accessible information may prove overwhelming. This can certainly be so of NESB students, who may expect the teacher to 'provide clearly and without equivocation all the knowledge the students need in their course' (Ballard and Clanchy 1991b: 19).

Very little appears to have been written on this subject, and this perhaps raises a call for further research to be conducted into how teaching staff are coping with this 'information explosion'.

Compelling staff and students to use IT

Our informal discussions with staff have revealed concerns about 'forcing' technology usage on students. Similarly, we might question whether educators themselves should be expected to utilize such technology.

One issue relates to our expectations that Masters and PhD students be fully conversant with the literature of their discipline. The Internet has now become such a powerful information resource that we can no longer expect students to be familiar with this literature if they have not utilized the Internet. Information technology skills can, in this respect, be considered essential for the research student, and this raises, for NESB students in particular, the importance of incorporating some IT training in research programmes.

Adoption of new information technologies certainly varies between cultures. In accepting NESB students into Australian courses, educators must question whether local values should be imposed on students from other cultures. Some cultural groups, and in particular some postgraduate students who have left high managerial positions in their own country to pursue their studies, view computing as 'secretarial' work, expecting this role to be performed for them. Similar expectations are only now beginning to be broken down amongst academics. However, neither students nor academics can afford to relinquish responsibility for their information management. Not only do limited resources prevent this, but information access, management and organization are integral aspects of the academic environment.

In many countries, IT is part of the experience of studying for a degree. Many education systems embody the value of producing graduates equipped for contemporary society, including computer and network literacy.

Southern Cross University's 1996 *Information Technology Plan* has as its stated aim that all graduates of Southern Cross University will be computer and network literate. Thus there is an institutional commitment to students developing IT skills.

The move to the use of technology for learning and research embodies values for self-directed approaches to learning. Independent learning, however, does not come naturally to all students, regardless of culture, but is more widely adopted in some cultures than others.

Many students, such as those from Asian cultures, do not share the 'independent learning' approach, and prefer to be highly directed in their learning (Ballard and Clanchy 1991a). NESB students will not always adjust easily to the flexible, independent study which characterizes most postgraduate research degrees in Australian society. They may thus see encouragement to use technology to independently access information and/or other experts in their field, or to assist themselves with editing, as 'a sign that the teachers are negligent in their professional duties' (Ballard and Clanchy 1991a: 20).

In many universities, an increasing number of research students are studying at a distance. NESB distance education students are a group whose specific needs have been under-addressed. One of the few studies dealing with this group of students, while discussing undergraduate students, indicated that NESB students favour materials which are interactive in nature (Erben and Fagan 1995: 60). Information technology offers great possibilities in this regard. The issue remains, however, of how these students can be introduced to technologies to assist them in their research.

While the possibilities provided by technology present many opportunities for increased student support, particularly at a distance, it is well recognized that access to computer equipment does not in itself ensure that students will connect to electronic support services, even when technical assistance is available (Curtis *et al.* 1995). These authors point out that students will not use electronic services unless there is a clear advantage. Supervisors' expectations thus play a large and important role.

Given encouragement and access, many 'self-tutorial' Web sites are available to assist students to develop skills in using the Internet. An example of such a World Wide Web-based independent Internet instruction program is discussed by Wilson (1996).[16]

Intellectual property and copyright: old issues, new approaches

Academics, in confronting these new technologies – and in particular the Web – often express concern regarding intellectual property issues. Copyright has certainly been complicated by these new technologies, and while considerable debate and discussion on policy issues continues to arise (*Creative Nation: Commonwealth Cultural Policy* 1994; Dilanchian 1995; Leonard 1995), many issues remain unresolved. The Internet is also providing new challenges to academic writers in adapting conventions for bibliographic referencing to cater for this new medium.

However, as Ballard and Clanchy (1991a: 24–5) point out, overseas students can have great difficulty grasping the complexities of plagiarism and referencing, particularly if they are from a society which does not encompass Western constructions of plagiarism. As with other intellectual property issues, those associated with technology and referencing are best carefully explained to the student from a basis of sound cultural understanding.

Conclusion

We have illustrated the many opportunities which IT provides to improve the scope and efficiency of the work of NESB postgraduate research students and their supervisors. A number of barriers to the adoption of these technologies have been discussed, many of which relate to the areas of integration and support. It is vital that supervisors of NESB students realize the potential of IT for the support of their students, as well as for their research training, and for the students themselves to seize all opportunities to utilize IT for their personal and professional development.

Hypertext references

1. University of California Linguistic Minority Research Institute
   http://lmrinet.gse.ucsb.edu/
2. EDNET Guide to Usenet Newsgroups
   http://netspace.students.brown.edu/eos/usenet_plain.html
3. Australian University Research Contacts
   http://www.swin.edu.au/sgrs/ausresch.html
4. National Graduate Research Database
   http://www.webventures.com.au/ngrdb

5. Australian National University's Students of Non-English Speaking Background (NESB) Page
   http://www.anu.edu.au./ssc/ssc/NESB2.html
6. University of Adelaide's Integrated Bridging Program (IBP) for International Postgraduate Students
   http://www-etu.itd.adelaide.edu.au/leap/focus/postgrad/ibp.html
7. Creating a Community of Scholars, Centre for Applied Languages Research at Edith Cowan University
   http://www.cowan.edu.au/calr/home.html#cc
8. SPIN Database
   http://spin.web.unsw.edu.au/
9. For example, Index to Online Dictionaries
   http://www.bucknell.edu/~rbeard/diction.html
10. Cyberstacks
    http://www.public.iastate.edu/~CYBERSTACKS/
11. Savy Search Engine, presenting search facilities in more than 20 languages
    http://guaraldi.cs.colostate.edu:2000/form?lang=english
12. Project Gutenberg Site
    http://www.promo.net/pg/
13. University of North Texas WWW Archive for Conference Proceedings
    http://archive.lis.unt.edu/
14. Medical Journal of Australia
    http://www.library.usyd.edu.au/MJA/
15. Journal of Interactive Media in Education
    http://www-jime.open.ac.uk/jime/
16. World Wide Web Walkabout
    http://www.lib.mq.edu.au/www/welcome.html
17. Citation Guides for Electronic Documents
    http://www.nlc-bnc.ca/ifla/I/training/citation/citing.htm

13

Supervising NESB Students from Confucian Educational Cultures

Doug Smith

Whether it is a question of newspapers or Proust, the text has a meaning only through its readers; it changes along with them; it is ordered in accord with the codes of perception that it does not control. It becomes a text only in relation to the exteriority of the reader, by an interplay of implications and ruses between two sorts of 'expectations' in combination: the expectation that organizes a readable space (literality), and one that organizes a procedure necessary for the actualization of the work, a reading.

(de Certeau 1988: 170–1)

Clearly, students from educational cultures different from our own may have quite different expectations that organize the procedures for 'the actualization of a text'. In Western educational culture, at least at post-graduate level in the arts and the social sciences,[1] the process of actualization is ideally an epistemological one. Students are expected to research, analyse, problematize and synthesize a critical response to a specific self-designed problem. Consequently, reading – a large and important aspect of the research process – is expected to be a *critical* actualization of texts. Simply put, questions of how and why dominate in a search for an internal coherency in the arguments put forward. An analysis of the history of reading in cultures that have been influenced by Confucianism would highlight quite a different expectation of reading. There is clearly less emphasis placed on these epistemological questions and more placed on issues of the ethical outcomes of the reading process itself. Quite often the question posed by readers in such cultures is, 'What is the necessary outcome of this reading for my conduct?' In other words, in contrast to the epistemological motivations of reading in Western societies (gaining 'knowledge' from a text), the motivation of reading in Confucian-influenced societies is moral – it is ethically oriented.

This chapter has a number of aims. First, it aims to provide some background to the different approaches that students from Confucian-influenced educational cultures may bring to the reading and, hence, the research process. In doing so, it aims to make supervisors and teachers aware of a number of the important assumptions that determine outcomes for the 'Confucian' knowing process. Second, it outlines what impact such reading styles may have on the development of a critical approach within these students and then posits a number of suggestions supervisors may use to help students overcome these difficulties. Here the question of critical thinking is considered as, *inter alia*, a problem in intertextuality – that is, in the construction of the necessary 'fundamentals of scholarship' that are implied by the interplay between a series of texts that circumscribe a discipline or discourse.

This is controversial because many supervisors believe critical thinking is more an innate capacity than a variety of learned practices, and it is thus often left to the individual student's own initiative. However, if critical thinking is a skill which derives from academic socialization (itself part of a broader cultural orientation), it follows that the supervisor can play a role in developing this skill, particularly with NESB students whose cultural background indicates a different, less critical, more ethically based strategy of reading.

The amount of sustained reading demanded by the research process in the arts and social sciences is nearly always the first major academic hurdle faced by the NESB student. The biggest problem is usually insufficient English language to cope with the complexity and/or volume of this reading. This problem has been discussed in great depth elsewhere (see, for example, Ballard and Clanchy 1991a: 2), and does not concern us in detail here. However, the volume and complexity of the reading, in tandem with the problem of language, masks the fact that what reading the student *does* achieve may be done in a superficial and reproductive way. This will become apparent later in the research process, often requiring an intensive investment of time and energy on the part of the supervisor.

Given this lack of experience with critical processes, students need to be made aware of the specific requirements of their research activities and introduced in a systematic way to the specific research criteria and the appropriate methods in the very first stages of candidature. Supervisors, on the other hand, need to be aware that, although many NESB students have the capability to meet these criteria (Ballard and Clanchy 1991a: 11–17), they simply have no 'deep sense' of their meaning and significance. The first important step, therefore, is the realization at the beginning of the postgraduate's candidature that these problems may exist. It is to the specific cultural influences that may influence these approaches to reading that we now turn.

There are clearly many ways in which we approach texts. We do not read a car manual, the Bible, legal contracts, *Penthouse*, laundry dockets or Kant's *Critique of Pure Reason* in exactly the same way. Recent works on the history of reading have highlighted the many ways in which texts have been and can be actualized (see, for example, Manguel 1996). It was Augustine who suggested the way of reading that has dominated academic practice in the West. He suggested readers should be:

> . . . neither using the book as a prop for thought, nor trusting it as one would trust the authority of a sage, but taking from it an idea, a phrase, an image, linking it to another culled from a distant text preserved in memory, tying the whole together with reflections of one's own – producing, in fact, a new text authored by the reader.
>
> (quoted in Manguel 1996: 63)

For contemporary readers, this breakthrough style of reading has two important aspects. First, there is a clear emphasis on the idea that it is – at least in part – an individualizing act. The reader is now not to be merely passive, but to take on the role of an evaluating and creative subject. Second, and related to the first aspect, Augustine's prescriptions suggest that we are to take on an irreverence to the particular text by rendering it merely one of many. Texts are now not to be 'sage-like'. This type of reading clearly has strong resonances with the research processes with which Western university supervisors are very familiar – an original argument developed around a series of texts focused on a common problem. In this individualistic and democratic environment, differences in opinion are not only to be tolerated, but indeed actively encouraged. The role of the researcher is to construct a field of intertextuality through multiple sources – where texts are lined up in contrast or support with other texts from which original ideas and opinions can emerge. This field of literature, it should be noted, usually develops its own specific objectives, manoeuvres, grammar, vocabulary, assumptions and tests for veracity.

When we look to the subject of reading in the Confucian context of a country like China, we find quite a different set of practices. An English language history of reading in China is yet to be published. However, in a preliminary and general way, we can identify a number of the features of the practices of reading – and knowing in general – from that educational culture.

One of the major aims of education throughout Chinese history has been to 'combine the individual and the state into a harmonious whole' (Cleverly 1985: 3). This has traditionally meant that the individual – which we in Western cultures tend to see as an atomistic cognitive/creative one – is subservient to the collective. Of course, being critical is premised, to a large extent, on a notion of individuality that is defined by its difference from others. Within the Confucian tradition, on the other hand, individualism has been seen as impolite, even rude, and implied a sort of egoism verging on arrogance. Innovation, especially amongst the young, was seen as diverging from an approved mode of conduct, and disrespectful of tradition. Hence, at this basic level, Confucian society has never prized the basic requirements for the concept of a person as an atomistic and creative individual. In comparison to the West, originality was never privileged and the texts of antiquity were preferred over more contemporary ones (Price 1979).

This, of course, led to the belief that study was to focus almost entirely upon the study of the Confucian canon. The role of the scholar was to discover those rules set down in these texts, requiring an intensive study of the limited texts within the reference. Study was often rendered as commentary and exegesis rather than a synthesis of different views presented in the form of an individual argument. The role of reading was to (re)discover what the sage was saying, while the role of writing was to reveal the truth held in the text for a larger audience, rather than to argue with it. Education was to serve the continuation of the ruling dynasty, and the approved curricula were almost solely based on moralistic tracts that, in general, militated against forms of dissent. The aim of education was the simple transfer of knowledge and skills with emphasis on the conservation and reproduction of knowledge, at the expense of its extension and testing, through the avoidance of any explicit evaluations or judgments.

In addition, there has historically been a reverential attitude to texts in China and this has greatly affected the types of reading undertaken. There are two reasons why this is the case. The first concerns the importance of the texts themselves as part of the canon left through the ages by the sages to the Chinese people. Second, to learn the written language was a long and painstaking process that had to rely on rote learning of numerous individual characters. A number of authors have suggested that this learning, determined by the fact that each character had to be learnt by rote, contributed to a conservative and reproductive thinking tradition in China.[2] Those few who did master the written language became part of an elite that dominated Chinese political and educational life for over 2000 years. Zheng Qiao (1104–62) gives an indication of just how important these scholars were when he writes: '[T]he world is of the opinion that those who know Chinese characters are wise and worthy, whereas those who do not know characters are simple and stupid' (quoted in De Francis 1986: 1). This reverence for the written word signposts an attitude to learning in which the written word was in fact the goal of learning, rather than a mundane tool for learning.

One central difference between the Western and Confucian systems can be highlighted by asking the simple question, 'Is understanding an essential component of knowing?' Especially since the Renaissance, there have been influential schools of thought in the West that have argued it is. The major concerns for these important discourses have been philosophico-epistemological topics such as:

- the certainty of things, and whether truths could be doubted;
- the relationship between our conclusions and how we arrived at them;
- the relationship between knowledge and belief;
- the relationship between the 'competing arguments in favour of intuition, sense experience, and awareness of the laws of logic'; (Munro 1977: 28).

Yet another important set of questions has been:

- What is the relationship between the objects of study and our perceptions of those objects? and
- Do these objects exist outside our minds and experience? (Munro 1977: 28).

Study, then, demands a Cartesian-like understanding. Western scholarship stresses the distance between science and intuition, between the rational and the irrational, between the coherent and the incoherent and, therefore, between a passive reading and a critical one. These distances determine many of the strategies that underline the reading and research processes that we expect our students to bring to bear on their own projects. While many students from Western institutions are not interested in these questions themselves, they are integral to the epistemological approach that stresses logical coherency, the use of multiple sources and the necessity for relevant, coherent and scientific evidence.

An analysis of the discourses concerned with the practices of knowing in Confucian philosophy reveals that these topics are rarely significant. Within the Chinese tradition – while questions such as these were asked – the emphasis was directed more to questions such as:

- What can we learn through studying things that will tell us both how things are naturally structured to act and how they should act?
- What are the moral rules that help evaluate whether we are acting properly?

And importantly for our discussion here:

- What are the effects of this study or reading in terms of an ethical outcome or how does it enable the knower to know how to act properly? (Munro 1977: 28–9).

It would be incorrect to suggest that understanding did not play a role, but it would be an exaggeration to suggest that it was crucial to the most influential approaches within the Chinese tradition. There was simply no strong emphasis on those epistemological questions that dominate Western thought.

The Chinese scholastic method, on the other hand, continued to be essentially little more than the training of students to consider a text according to already established and officially approved ethical criteria. A sense of the logic of the universe was not important, and understanding, therefore, was not a requisite of knowledge, because the crucial knowledge lay in the ethical regimes of adapting behaviour to this natural logic. The aims of reading such as this were not to excavate a private significance in the text but to recite and compare the interpretations of acknowledged authorities, and thus become a 'better person'. It is clear for the traditional Chinese that a moral order did exist and study attempted to link the student with that order. Arthur Danto (1985: 386) clearly identifies moral order as the chief aim of the four Chinese philosophical classics. He writes that each of the books defines a 'way of life' and are 'like garments which have to be worn; if you do not put them on they are deeply empty and existentially shapeless'.

In some ways, this may not be so different from a number of the earlier approaches in the West. Reading in the Middle Ages and earlier had a similar ethical tenor (Manguel 1996: 76). The important issue is that, since the Enlightenment, the West has assumed that the reader has the ability to stand apart from the social processes being studied. This ability to break with the interconnectedness of things to know does not exist in any influential way in the Chinese tradition. For the Chinese, there has been relatively less distinction than in the West between knowing and feeling, between an epistemological and ethical reading. In contrast, much Western scholarship has endeavoured to overcome the problem of intuition, to find an objective position. Moreover, while many things have changed in contemporary China, there are still strong vestiges of these approaches in Chinese educational cultures.

What is the significance of this distinction in regard to reading attitudes for NESB students? My experience with students from these cultures is that their reading is dominated by an ethical approach to reading and knowing at the expense of a critical one. While NESB postgraduate students often understand that they are to be 'critical' – they have read it in study guides and 'how-to' books – they simply do not have a history from which a deep understanding of the term 'critical' can emerge. Their history has been determined by an educational culture that emphasizes the specific approaches to reading that we have discussed above, and which has engendered a passivity amongst its students that encourages the avoidance of any controversial issues. Independent learning is not promoted, lessons are didactic in the extreme, and students tend to rely on lecture notes and set texts for all their information. This is reflected in the fact that many of my own students, when asked to critique a particular account of history, respond with the querulous statement: 'How can I challenge history? History happened.'

Before we consider how supervisors are to foster critical approaches in NESB students, however, we need to define what we actually mean by the term 'critical thinking'. Ballard and Clanchy (1991a: 44), in their excellent introduction to Western education systems for Asian students, suggest that critical thinking, in broad terms at least, is a two-stage process where 'judgement . . . is arrived at through a process of systematic analysis and questioning'. The first process entails the:

- reduction of complex matters to their simplest elements; and
- examination of the relationships between them.

The latter questioning phase consists of 'adopting a *critical* attitude towards those elements by:

- questioning their meaning;
- evaluating the evidence for them;
- making judgements about their value or importance; and
- presenting those judgements in a persuasive and reasoned argument' (1991a: 60).

This definition offers a very good foundation for students starting their academic careers in Western universities. However, it does not go far enough for our purposes here, because it does not fully describe the requirements of critical thinking at postgraduate level. Clearly, the two aspects of the definition that need further clarification are 'critical attitude' and 'judgements about . . . value and importance'. It is these processes that are posited as the touchstone against which a definition of critical thinking is to find its purchase, yet these criteria themselves remain under-theorized, and hence are left to the student to decipher. So how do we make judgments about 'value and importance', especially if we come from a different culture – a culture where reading strategies look for quite different outcomes and 'correct' judgments are determined by values very different from our own?

Robert Ennis suggests that there are 12 possible criteria by which to evaluate whether an approach is critical or not. His concept of critical thinking is developed through a comprehensive analysis of the literature and critical thinking programmes in the United States. His 12 aspects of critical thinking are:

- grasping the meaning of a statement;
- judging whether there is ambiguity in a line of reasoning;
- judging whether certain statements contradict each other;
- judging whether a conclusion follows necessarily;
- judging whether a statement is specific enough;
- judging whether a statement is actually the application of a certain principle;
- judging whether an observation statement is reliable;
- judging whether an inductive conclusion is warranted;
- judging whether the problem has been identified;
- judging whether something is an assumption;
- judging whether a definition is adequate;
- judging whether a statement made by an alleged authority is acceptable (Ennis 1962: 84).

Students need to be made aware of these criteria as important kick-starters of a critical approach. But they still beg the question as to what critical thinking actually *is*. Ennis makes little attempt to suggest on what grounds we should make critical judgments. Although there is much that is useful here, we will have to look elsewhere for a comprehensive understanding of what critical thinking means at a postgraduate level.

Much of the discussion about critical thinking revolves around the issue of whether it is a generic skill or a skill that is discourse dependent. McPeck (1990) criticizes the standard generic approach to the teaching of critical thinking because it reduces all notions of critical thinking to argument analysis. By this he means that critical thinking cannot be reduced to a generic logic, because such a logic does not exist. McPeck (1990: 40) argues, rather, that there are a number of discourse-dependent logics and it makes no sense to teach critical thinking unless the teaching is delivered from within a particular discourse. There is no meta-thinking that has equal impact across discourses, but rather each field sets up its own language and syntax from which critical thinking gains its shape. Historians, economists, Marxists, biochemists, postmodernists critically analyse the content of texts with respect to already negotiated rules, routines and ruses. There is scope for dissent, but it is not until the student has assembled a considerable 'background in scholarship' and inculcated the important rules, routines and ruses of scholarship in a particular discipline or discourse that critical thinking can take place. McPeck argues that the establishment of these disciplinary knowledges increases the student's ability to communicate in the language of that discipline and, in fact, 'enable(s) one to think, and to engage in intelligent conversation, about problems which fall under the disciplinary domains'. It is these rules, routines and ruses which establish the criteria upon which we can adopt a 'critical attitude' and make 'judgements about . . . value and importance'.

The final aspect of our definition of critical thinking is imagination or creativity. Passmore (1967) suggests that, within the great academic traditions, imagination plays an integral part in the critical process. It is simply not enough to criticize, for two reasons. First, as Dewey has suggested, simply questioning everything would lead to 'a disconnectedness (which) may artificially generate dispersive, disintegrated, centrifugal habits' (quoted in Passmore 1967: 200). We need to understand the role of existing knowledge in organizing our thinking. Second, just to criticize leaves the job half-done. It is very common for overseas students who have not fully understood what it means to be critical to ignore the synthesis aspect of critical thinking, and merely criticize an author's works. Passmore argues that true critical thinking 'conjoins criticism and imagination in a single form of thinking where the free flow of imagination is controlled by criticism and criticisms are transformed into a new way of looking at things' by imagination (1967: 201). This imagination, though, is not to be entirely thought of as the capacity of a gifted individual, but rather premised on the confidence found in the mastery of scholarship and the role models provided in the student's environment.

Let us summarize what we mean by the process of critical thinking in the following way. The critical process is one in which the sorts of technical processes suggested above by Ennis, and Ballard and Clanchy, find meaning and significance through the particular strategies and knowledge bases of a specific discipline or discourse. This process, though, is not merely technical in nature, but contains a creative component that cannot really emerge with any consequence until the basic foundations of scholarship have been established. Given the particular approaches identified in the educational background of students from Confucian educational cultures, how are supervisors to inculcate such skills and attitudes?

My response to the question may seem insufficiently exciting – such is *our* own obsession with originality. However, there is no better environment – with a number of important qualifications – for the development of these skills than an open liberal style environment, one provided by the supervisor, in which the foundations of scholarship can be developed through the appropriate discipline knowledge bases. This scholarship should be supported by an open relationship where propositions can be questioned by both the student and the supervisor. Whether these skills are innate or can be learned, the foundations of scholarship need to be established for critical process to be meaningful. Much of what good supervisors have done within the liberal tradition in the past has been effective, especially in the area of providing guidance and acting as devil's advocate, as well as providing appropriate role models. We should realize that it is not a revolution that we need here – more a shift in emphasis.

The first important qualification is that the shift in emphasis is required because NESB students from Confucian cultures do not have a background from which these critical practices can emerge spontaneously. One shortcoming of traditional supervision has been to expect these students to be members of an elite group. With increased numbers of overseas students enrolling at postgraduate levels, we need to reassess who it is we are teaching. The aim here is not to adjust standards to meet more appropriately the existing skill levels of these students, but rather to provide support structures so they may meet these standards. In specific practical terms, how then do we need to adapt our current approaches for these students?

Clearly, reading widely is the first step. It would be a mistake, however, to send these students off to read widely to build a foundation of scholarship from which critical thinking can emerge – as we would do for our own local students. We have argued that their reading may, right from the beginning, consolidate the problem, rather than help solve it. The first step, then, is to initiate a critical reading programme – one which, while building the foundation of scholarship, also engenders an independent and active approach to learning.

I suggest that the first important steps to take in supervising these students is to make explicit the fact that, within our academic tradition, there are numerous valid and 'correct' approaches to solving problems – not just the one presented in any text. There is simply no one 'solve-all approach' to the issues that students confront at postgraduate level. This means that students will have to engage with series of texts rather than just one.

At the same time, students need to be very aware of the differences between substantive issues and the methodological processes used to study them. That is, they need to be aware of the epistemological issues that frame our approaches to research topics and their relationships with reality. It should be clear that models used to describe reality are not necessarily congruent with reality. It would also help for these students to understand how their ways of thinking/reading are perceived by Western supervisors – thus they have a clearly defined starting point.

Another possible approach is to have the student undertake an informal or formal guided reading course. A formal course may take a similar approach to that described by Knight and Zuber-Skerritt (1992), where the problems and methods in research are introduced systematically. The aim of such a course (a series of integrated lectures and workshops) is to present a history of the various ways in which the social sciences have tried to come to grips with specific epistemological problems. To a large extent, the role of the lecturer/tutor in this course is to play the devil's advocate in problematizing these various historical approaches as well as the student's own research processes (Knight and Zuber-Skerritt 1992: 211). At an informal level, supervisors may construct reading courses for their own students. These courses should be a systematic review of the literature that covers a variety of different approaches to the particular student's topic. Students should then be asked to evaluate these approaches, and to think about which approach they will take and why. Special emphasis should be placed on the development of an argument as to why the student has selected a particular approach. The emphasis here should be on a student-centred approach which aims to develop an independent and active learner rather than a passive and dependent one.

Finally, the supervisor and the student need to evaluate actively the student's performance throughout candidature. This should ideally be done together not only when specific problems arise, but regularly throughout the year. These sessions provide opportunities for further modelling to take place. The criteria set down by Ennis, and by Ballard and Clanchy, are very useful for these purposes. They provide a set of tangible practices that can be consistently referred to and which can be measured. Supervisors can provide a checklist of questions as a set of guidelines from which students can continually monitor their practices. Such a checklist may include questions such as whether the NESB student is:

- simply presenting descriptive factual information;
- merely summarizing other writers' ideas or theories;
- comparing and contrasting the information or ideas of one writer with another;
- arguing their own particular interpretation of the facts;
- merely criticizing the ideas of other writers;
- not recognizing problematic assumptions underlying certain concepts;
- accepting the meaning of statements given;
- accepting statements that contradict one another;
- confusing substantive and methodological issues;
- accepting the reliability of statements;
- accepting something as fact that really is an assumption;
- judging whether a definition is adequate.

It is apposite here to reinsert briefly the question of reading and draw it closer to the heart of critical thinking. To be critical, we have argued, students must develop a disposition or capability not to believe everything they read or hear. They also need to develop the appropriate knowledge base that will form a particular type of 'reflective skeptisim' (McPeck 1990: 40). This is because these knowledges have a specific logic and texture peculiar to that discourse. The knowledges, skills and confidences gained through the mastery of this intertextuality not only lay the foundation for

critico-creative approaches to emerge, but characterize them. This intertextuality, however, requires understanding of the discursive language in
which the texts within the discourse converse. It is here that most NESB
postgraduate students find their greatest difficulty. Even if their language is
competent enough to cope with the purely linguistic demands of the text,
much of the critical edge is lost because they are unfamiliar with the discursive context of the language used. I believe this is where clear differences
between language, knowledge and critical thinking dissolve because they
are so intimately linked. However, it is exactly here that students are to
develop the appropriate skills, attitudes and creative capabilities from which
critical approaches are to emerge at the postgraduate level.

There is a certain circularity here. Reading is the problem, but it is also
the answer. Reading will form critical scholars, but only if reading is done
in a critical manner. We have noted at length the non-critical outcomes of
a Confucian approach to reading. We could, of course, fall back into the
conservative position of claiming that the ability to carry out critical thinking is innate. This, however, would mean admitting defeat in terms of the
exact problem we are now wanting to solve – that is, what sort of strategies
can we develop to inculcate critical approaches in NESB students?

We have argued that reading is central to this process. This is the case
because the content of a discipline determines the appropriate forms of
reasoning, and reading is still the most efficient way of building the relevant
content. Therefore, supervisors need to be aware that there is a necessity to
break students out of non-critical reading habits early in the students' candidature by making the expected outcomes of reading explicit and making
them repeatedly. Students, then, need to be guided to the appropriate
reading strategies through direct intervention by the supervisor. The supervisor should direct the student to read first the key concepts of the discourse because they contain its intellectual power and integrity. The aim is
to develop a comprehensive knowledge base, a familiarity with the rationality of the particular discourse, and the reading skills necessary to manage
the discursive languages inherent in the discourse. This process is best
thought of as a spiral where the student's reading and her/his critical
approach develop through a dialogic process. Given the right conditions,
sufficient time and the appropriate role models, nearly all NESB students
will be able to move considerable distances towards an understanding of
the importance of reading in a critical way. Even ethical readers can become critical readers.

Notes

1. It is not meant that these epistemological questions are not important in other
   disciplines, but that these are the only ones that I can confidently speak about.
2. Again this is not to say this was the only form of thinking. There is considerable
   evidence, given the number of truly great scientific inventions of traditional
   China, to believe there were also strong traditions of innovative thinking as well.

14

Encouraging Student-directed Research and Critical Thinking in NESB Students

Christine Susan Bruce and Gerald Humphrey Brameld

Introduction

The ideas of supervisor- and student-directed research have long been part of the literature of postgraduate supervision. Some authors have noted the need for a shift from supervisor to student direction during the course of postgraduate study, whilst others have established that many supervisors do not take the varying needs of their students into account when establishing a supervisory style (Aspland and O'Donoghue 1994: 61). It is also a common observation, although not always accurate (Biggs 1996b), that NESB students have great difficulty in embracing the self-directed culture of postgraduate research that is an integral part of the tradition of Western universities.

There is some evidence that the problems experienced by students in the early stages of research are magnified in the case of these groups, making them highly dependent upon their supervisors (Ballard and Clanchy 1993). A recent study that explored the experience of Asian NESB students in Australia (McSwiney 1995) supplies quotations from interviews with students, such as the following, that support these observations. At PhD level, a student comments: 'My teacher is very lazy – he gives me no information . . . instead he expects me to go to the library and read it . . .' (McSwiney 1995: 32); after eight months in Australia a postgraduate remarks: 'Indian system suited better – teachers gave all information . . .' (McSwiney 1995: 112). Further, Ballard and Clanchy (1993: 70) suggest the need for strong supervisory guidance in the early months of a research programme and emphasize the need for a focus on critical thinking at this stage.

Unfortunately, varying expectations and cultural backgrounds amongst both students and supervisors sometimes lead to the development of less than happy circumstances. In the first part of this chapter we explore, through a case study, what can happen when that guidance is not provided and the expectations of a student and supervisor conflict. Here we retell the story of an event that forced one research unit to re-examine its understanding of the influence of varying expectations and cultural backgrounds. In the second part of the chapter we examine strategies which may help supervisors to encourage students explicitly to take a critical, and increasingly independent, approach to their work in the literature review and extended proposal phase. We also discuss some of the ways in which experienced researchers conceive of effective information use – ways that are centred around the need for critical thinking. Understanding some of these key approaches to working with information, and the adoption of strategies for critical thinking, may help students as they walk the path towards autonomy. This chapter is written around the following points.

• What happens when the expectations of the student and supervisor conflict (a case study)?
• How do various people involved respond (outcomes of a role-play)?
• What can exacerbate the situation where overseas fee-paying students are involved?
• What is the role of critical thinking and the path to autonomy in research?
• What strategies can help students with critical thinking?

The data we have used in writing this chapter were obtained in various ways. Material in the case study comes from the observation and experience of the authors. The responses of the actors in the case come from observations by the authors of real-life events, as well as a video, and the written responses of academic staff involved in a role-play. The descriptions of how experienced researchers rely on critical thinking come from interviews conducted for a study which analysed conceptions of information literacy amongst higher educators (Bruce 1996).

What happens when the expectations of the student and supervisor conflict?

Although all the names in the following case study are fictitious, the events did occur. When brought, via a workshop, into the public forum, they proved also to reflect the experience of participants from a wide range of universities. We now introduce the salient features of the case and then analyse the responses of 'actors' role-playing a meeting between various parties involved in an attempt to resolve the situation.

The events in this case study took place in the Centre for Transportation Engineering Systems (CTES), Department of Civil Engineering, Oxley University of Technology (OUT). The Centre had been operating for four years and was one of the high-profile centres within the Oxley University of Technology. Considerable energy has been expended in building the Centre to a stage where it was recognized nationally and internationally as a centre of excellence.

Dr Susan Jones, the supervisor, had been collaborating with the state railway authority for some years and had undertaken a number of collaborative research projects with them. She had received seed funding to allow her to employ a research assistant to produce a literature review on a topic related to long-term maintenance of the rail track. This review was used in a successful application to obtain Australian Research Council (ARC) funds to assist in conducting the research. All projected costs associated with the field experimentation were covered, but there were insufficient funds to employ a full-time research assistant.

Mustav and his family arrived in Australia from Transylvania with a government scholarship to cover fees and living expenses. He had been targeted by his government to move from industry to a university, but needed a PhD to be eligible. His government had had problems in the past with some students going overseas and not returning with additional qualifications and now included a clause in current contracts which required students to refund five times the scholarship allowances if they returned without a PhD. Mustav's professional activities in Transylvania were with the Railways Corporation and when Dr Jones proposed the railway project he immediately accepted it, as it appeared the most suitable, given his background.

One of the first steps taken by Dr Jones was to send Mustav to the Advanced Information Retrieval Skills (AIRS) course offered by the library at OUT. Dr Jones gave Mustav the list of references (over 200) produced by her research assistant, but did not give him either the literature review or copies of the specific articles, because she believed that as part of their development as researchers all her graduate students should produce their own literature reviews.

During the following months, Mustav had regular contact with Dr Jones but also had extreme difficulties in locating and critiquing the literature. He was concerned that his friend in the United States was given weekly reading lists together with copies of the relevant material, and Mustav felt that he was not receiving adequate supervision. When he approached Dr Jones about alternative forms of supervision she said, 'That's not the way it's done in Australia.' Dr Jones did, however, help Mustav with his written English by rewriting his six-monthly reports in a form acceptable to the research committee.

After 18 months, Dr Jones became concerned that her ARC project was in jeopardy and might not be completed on time. She gave Mustav an adverse report, recommending termination. At the same time, Mustav had become very concerned that he had not yet started any experimental work and felt that time was running out. He was surprised at the recommendation for termination, given that there had been no adverse comments on any of the previous six-monthly reports, and he became extremely distressed since the financial burden he faced if he returned without a PhD would cripple his family. He could not possibly hope to repay five times the allowances. In order to protect his own situation, Mustav wrote to his Embassy in Australia and complained about poor supervision and inadequate facilities.

When reading the student's six-monthly report, the Centre Director, Professor Brian Williams, was surprised that Dr Jones had recommended termination, especially when there had been no prior indication of difficulties. He saw Dr Jones as the Centre's most capable researcher, with an international reputation and a reputation for producing doctoral graduates of the highest standard. Professor Williams decided to convene a meeting with the student, supervisor and liaison librarian to determine:

• what had happened to this student; and
• what strategies could be implemented to retrieve the situation.

As Dr Jones was one of the key members of his research centre, Professor Williams did not wish to upset her unduly.

How do various people involved respond?

The meeting convened by Professor Williams was 'role-played' in a postgraduate supervision staff development workshop at Ballina in July 1996. The actors in the role-play took the parts of the Centre Director, the supervisor, the student and the liaison librarian. After completing the role-play and reflecting upon it, they were asked to record:

• the feelings of people involved;
• conflicts which arose;
• strategies suggested;
• future prevention strategies.

Table 14.1 summarizes the responses to these stimuli given by the various groups.

Most research centres or academic departments have a reference librarian assigned to support their information needs. These members of the research support structure often have higher degree qualifications and therefore understand the process of postgraduate study and supervision. They also usually undertake to induct new students into the processes of information retrieval and management which are subject to significant and continuous change. In doing so, librarians are likely to be committed to the principles of self-direction and lifelong learning. They may have experience in helping students to improve their information literacy, particularly in relation to developing their ability to think critically in the literature review process.

The individuals who played the librarian in the 'role-play' reported feeling *frustrated* in their attempts to assist. They had access to a range of resources which were likely to help the supervisor to work constructively with the student to encourage independent thinking. During the role-play, most of the 'librarians' were unable to gain the attention of the remaining members of the group, and so their potential contribution was lost. Some, however, did succeed in contributing to the discussion, and these became

Table 14.1 Summary of responses to stimuli

Feelings of people involved	Strategies suggested
Supervisor • frustration – inability to understand student's problem • anger – potential loss of credibility • annoyance at not being appreciated *Student* • anxiety/pressure and comparison • not being included in discussion • shafted • not a significant player • valued only for $$$ *Centre Director* • needed a more global and sensitive view of overseas students • frustration • concerned about university reputation • looking for strategies of support *Liaison Librarian* • frustrated at inability to talk about real problem • concerned about failure of student to master information retrieval skills • offered support whilst highlighting student's inadequacies	• change (principal) supervisor • use conference room (less interruption) • help from librarian • initial enrolment in a postgraduate programme • truth in recruiting • supervisor and librarian to work on the review frame and then librarian with student • tightened structure of supervision • recognition by supervisor of cultural mismatch • need for an associate supervisor • negotiate roles, discuss expectations, have clear outcomes • have clear university policy and practices for NESB students • improve IT facilities • improve communication • programme revision and evaluation • more workshops • social groupings • conciliation/mediation • terminate studies now rather than prolong them
Conflicts which arose	*Future prevention strategies*
• supervisor resentful of justifying actions to director • timelines • communication on different wavelength • expectations unclear (on both sides) • financial – both university and school • student expects director to solve problem by intervening • supervisor expects director to solve problem by supporting her • obligations to ARC • $$$ earner for centre • conflict of expectations	• peer groups • separate projects (ARC) from supervision • clear timelines; stricter timetables • discussions of roles and responsibilities (early) • more regular meetings • report six-monthly from library • postgraduate committee • policy on entry level of NESB students to be developed • increase NESB supervisory expertise

involved in the process of devising strategies to keep the student 'on target'. One group went so far as to suggest that a six-monthly report from the librarian would be useful in the first 12 months of enrolment. Such a step is likely to be of value where reference librarians take a close interest in PhD students or if they teach information skills coursework within the doctoral programme.

What can exacerbate the situation where overseas fee-paying students are involved?

Very strong threads in the role-play situation included the emphasis on the reputation of the university involved, and the perceived influence of students paying fees. The political agenda of the need to attract fee-paying students seemed to affect the situation adversely in a number of ways. The student reported feeling unvalued, except as a source of funds. Staff reported feeling pressured to retain and graduate the student despite his difficulties with language and research process. It appears that the focus on 'fees' in this situation leads to a loss of attention to academic standards and staff support. The supervisor in the role-play reported feeling anger that the feeling of the group was turning against him. Perhaps if guidelines existed about responsibilities of students as well as supervisors, and about termination of candidature, a more professional response – one that was not clouded by the dollars involved in the case – may have been possible. One of the 'actors' in the role-play commented afterwards that 'it was disgraceful that dollars had come into the picture and swayed the director and the librarian'.

In this case study, the Transylvanian Embassy wrote to the Centre Director setting out the complaint from the student and pointing out that they currently have over 600 doctoral students in Australia, this being the first at CTES. The Embassy recommended that the student withdraw from his studies, called on the OUT to refund all fees paid to the university in respect of the student and threatened to withdraw its support for students attending OUT in the future. This letter arrived while the Centre Director was attempting to resolve the conflict. Recent funding models exerted additional pressures. These placed a premium on PhD completions, especially in the calculation of the Research Quantum, and the $3000 which the department would receive was vital to its future.

Critical thinking and the path to autonomy in research

The need for students to assume responsibility for their postgraduate research is clearly explained by Phillips and Pugh (1994). Students need to become independent researchers as a result of the PhD process, demonstrating that they are worthy of being recognized as an 'authority'. Where supervisor-directed models prevail, this outcome is jeopardized and the journey to becoming an independent researcher shifts to the context of postdoctoral work. Advice to new students by Phillips and Pugh (1994: 2) is unambiguous:

> In doctoral education, you have the responsibility for managing your learning and getting yourself a PhD . . . the responsibility for determining what is required, as well as for carrying it out, remains firmly with you . . . You are under self-management, so it is no use sitting around waiting for somebody to tell you what to do next or, worse, complaining that nobody is telling you what to do next; in the postgraduate world these are opportunities not deficiencies.

If we are to meet students' expectations of 'receiving' an education of a high quality (Aspland and O'Donoghue 1994: 61), then we need to ensure that they have every opportunity to become independent researchers as a result of their postgraduate study. Focusing on critical thinking is an element of supervision which encourages independence of thought and, therefore, is likely to contribute to the development of autonomy. Earlier discussions of critical thinking in the research process that are likely to be useful to supervisors include Ballard and Clanchy (1991a: 44–61), Zuber-Skerritt and Knight (1986) and Zuber-Skerritt (1992a: 36–53).

Bruce (1996) provides some insights into the importance of critical thinking for researchers, and the processes that may be involved in taking a critical approach. Many of the researchers she interviewed described a critical, analytical approach to information as being central to their ability to develop a personal knowledge base in previously unfamiliar areas of discourse. Several examples are provided by respondents which explain what they mean by critical analysis. One engineering academic explains critical analysis as involving 'identifying gaps in knowledge, recognising conflicting schools of thought and assessing the reliability of research':

> I think there are a couple of areas that are important . . . to identify gaps in the current knowledge and searching through the information to find out where there is conflict between various groups of researchers or schools of thought or whatever it might be; and also searching through to see where there's just been a simple blunder which may appear through comparing results from different people. So I guess those three things are important there. It's not good enough just to read and say, yes, Smith and Jones said this, and Brown and Jackson said that and whatever. You have to be able to look at them and say, 'why did they say it', 'what's the basis on which they've made their observation' and perhaps 'why is that different from what Smith and Jones have said?'

An outcome of the critical approach identified by these researchers is the adoption of personal perspectives on the area of interest. Their descriptions of the process leading to the adoption of personal perspectives shed further light on the meanings they attribute to critical analysis; researchers describe it as 'a process of clarification and as researching your own thoughts'. Once a personal knowledge base has been developed, they explain that creativity, or intuition, must be exercised to enable knowledge to be extended or new insights gained. This creative element of the experience is described as a mysterious, intuitive process, particularly with regard to making connections between previously unconnected pieces of information:

> I think there's a creative relationship really . . . You can stuff yourself full of information and only be capable of regurgitating it, but actually to synthesise and relate it to other things . . . I find that just happens spontaneously, you make connections . . . I still find it a rather mysterious process, you start to see the connections, the relationships.

These essential components of the research process – critical analysis, the adoption of personal perspectives and knowledge extension – are not possible unless an appropriate foundation, based upon rigorous critical thinking, has been laid.

What strategies can help students with critical thinking?

Although critical thinking is clearly an important intellectual skill in postgraduate work, many students are likely to be able to relate to the experience of being told to think or write critically without being enlightened about what this means. Table 14.2 contains some resources produced to help students understand what is involved. Whilst students need to ensure that they approach information made available via new technologies with a critical eye, technology can also be used to facilitate critical thinking. Two products which we have found useful for this purpose are concept mapping software and bibliographic database management software.

Concept mapping software, such as VISIMAP (1996), can be helpful as an aid to organizing thoughts. Such software helps students to depict relationships between concepts graphically as well as automatically modifying the concept maps as they progress. They usually interface with common word processors. Concept mapping software can be used to:

- construct text (that is, develop headings and subheadings, embed paragraphs under headings, arrange and rearrange the structure at will); or
- deconstruct text (that is, develop maps to depict key elements of articles being analysed, discover relationships between sections of text or reveal the logical structure of arguments).

Bibliographic database management software helps students to organize notes and documents. Effective information management helps students to retrieve the material they need and to record relationships they see between documents. Students can use bibliographic software to help them

Table 14.2   Resources to aid critical thinking

What questions should I ask when critiquing an article?	*What does thinking critically mean?*
• Who is the author? • What is the motive for writing/doing the research? • For what audience is the author writing? • Does the author have a bias? • What research approach or data-gathering method was used? • What conclusions does the author arrive at? • Does the author satisfactorily justify the conclusions? • How does the study compare with similar studies? (Adapted from Engeldinger 1988)	• distinguishing between verifiable facts and value claims • determining the reliability of a source • determining the factual accuracy of a statement • distinguishing relevant from irrelevant information, claims or reasons • detecting bias • identifying unstated assumptions • identifying ambiguous claims or arguments • recognizing logical inconsistencies • distinguishing between warranted and unwarranted claims • determining the strengths of an argument (Beyer 1985)
Critically assessing Internet resources	*How could the following elements of a document help you determine its relevance?*
• Is your resource an example of vanity publishing or has it been through a rigorous review process? • What evidence is there to suggest that the resource is of high quality? • Who are the 'authors'? What are their credentials? • How current is the resource? Can you establish when it was last updated? • How easily accessible is the resource? • Is the resource stable? Is it likely to remain stable? • How well is the resource regarded? Do other people refer to it regularly? Can you identify how often it has been used? • Is the resource organized in some way? Is there a contents page, an index? An abstract or other summary to communicate the nature of the content? (Adapted from Tilman 1996)	• key terms in the title • the language (technical or otherwise) used in the title • the author's name • the author's institution • the name of the journal, or publishing house • the type of document, e.g. conference paper • the abstract or executive summary • the subject headings • chapter titles It is the mind of the researcher that endows a document with *relevance* by conceiving a way in which it, or even a small part of it, fits into his or her emerging research scheme . . . (Stoan 1991). [A document] user is continuously assessing the value of information and interpreting a citation in order to learn and shape the research problem (Park 1993).

analyse the information they gather by assigning index terms (that is, establishing words or phrases that indicate what the document is about), assigning classification (that is, establishing codes to indicate what major area of interest the document belongs to) and writing abstracts (that is, creating notes which reveal the relevance of the document to the research).

Conclusion

In this chapter we have explored events which may unfold when problems associated with the early stages of postgraduate supervision are compounded in the case of NESB students. We have also argued that autonomy in the research process can be encouraged, for all groups of students, from the earliest stages, via an emphasis on critical thinking. None of the material we have included in this chapter solves the difficulties we encounter in the supervision process. However, it may provide insights into the experience of some NESB students and those who work with them, and some ideas for improving our management of the critical thinking that must be part of the research process.

Acknowledgements

We wish to thank the attendees and convenors of the workshops on postgraduate supervision of NESB students held at Ballina, New South Wales in 1996 for making this chapter possible. Special thanks must go to the small team that consented to be videotaped during the role-play session at the conference.[1] They not only participated enthusiastically, but also committed their thoughts and feelings about their roles to videotape afterwards. Finally, we thank our postgraduate students for providing us with challenges in the area of making explicit some strategies for critical thinking.

Note

1. This video, part of a series released from the workshop, is available from WoRLD Institute, Southern Cross University. Contact Pam Price, GCM, Southern Cross University, Lismore NSW 2480, Fax 617 266 212717 or e-mail pprice@scu.edu.au for details on this series and others available on postgraduate supervision.

15

Thesis Planning and Writing: A Structured Approach

Jim Sillitoe and Glenda Crosling

Often, in the final stages of a student's research programme, supervisors of international and NESB students are confronted with unconventionally structured, seemingly incoherent drafts of theses from students who have hitherto demonstrated considerable potential for carrying out complicated research methodology. The supervisor's dilemma is then how to deal with such work without compromising either ethical and quality standards or the dignity and self-confidence of the student. In many cases, inadequate mastery of English grammar and syntax is the major problem, and the usual processes of editing, in a developmental way, can produce a thesis of reasonable quality.

However, there are a significant number of cases where difficulties in thesis production can be attributed to unexamined or inexplicit expectations about thesis construction and presentation in the Western university system – where neither supervisor nor NESB student has clarified these expectations. In the instances which concern us, even though the students may be writing in English and using terminology and phraseology which are familiar to Western readers, they may be applying organizational and writing patterns from their first language. When the students' writing is based in cultural and discourse conventions borrowed from their first language and culture, the writing can often have a considerably different structure and logic to that required by Western universities. Consequently, the resulting mismatch of understandings can result in a reader who is attuned to Western conventions experiencing, at best, a sense of strangeness or difference in the written work, at worst confusion and incomprehension.

Clearly, this situation works to the detriment of NESB postgraduate candidates in examination of their theses, and the situation is not alleviated by recourse to spellchecking and grammar analysis. In Western education, a thesis is expected to be linear, embodying a sense of progression and continuity as it moves from the general to the specific, and from the problem to the resolution. This overall pattern is also expected within sections of the thesis, and a reader expecting linear organization may find such alternative organizations confusing, especially when these occur both over the length of a thesis and within sections of it.

Another related area where intercultural differences in discourse conventions may intervene in NESB students' thesis planning and writing is in the organization of ideas. Whereas the preference in Western cultures generally is for linear and direct presentation and development of complex concepts, this does not seem to be the case with other cultures and languages. For example, the preference in Asian cultures is for indirection and viewing the topic from various perspectives (Kaplan 1966). In Vietnamese culture, it is expected that the various aspects which have some bearing on the issue will all be examined, rather than coming straight to the point (Nguyen 1990). In Arabic discourse, the preference is for parallel constructions at the sentence level and repetition of main ideas, with the aim of achieving an overall sense of balance (Ostler 1987; Farquarson 1988). Western readers may be frustrated by the sense of repetition and circularity produced by the use of these features in a thesis.

There is also evidence that, when writing in Japanese, Chinese, Thai and Korean, a delayed introduction of the purpose of the piece is often used. Because this style of writing does not strictly follow either inductive or deductive lines of organization, which are 'buried in the passage' (Connor 1996), such writing can be perceived by Western readers to be directionless.

Furthermore, in thesis writing at the postgraduate level, the Western expectation is that students will express a sense of authority in their work and thus explicitly comment on, analyse and interpret information from other sources. If relevant, students should also refer to their own findings to support their knowledge claims. There is a demand in research theses that relationships between ideas and the way that empirical evidence supports the student's propositions be expressed clearly and unequivocally. Unsubstantiated claims or unjustified statements are treated severely by examiners, since they throw the whole basis of the thesis into question. As a consequence, in most disciplines, what is acceptable as a research thesis has a critical approach to the literature, a methodology which has inherent mechanisms for ensuring both internal and external validity of collected data, and modest but clearly defensible knowledge claims.

Again, conventions from other languages and cultures can intervene at this level where there appear to be differences across cultures in the responsibilities of writers to their readers. The expectation in English discourse is that the speaker or writer is responsible for making clear to the reader the direction of the piece of writing and for making explicit the link between ideas. Hence transition and discourse markers are used at the local and global levels to guide the reader in regard to the organization of the links between ideas, giving overall cohesion to the piece and making transparent the logic and analysis which underpin the assertions and conclusions of the thesis. Conventions in other languages, however, differ. For instance, it is reported that, in Japanese, the responsibility is for the *reader* to make the cognitive links within the text (Hinds 1987). In contrast to Western writers, it seems that Japanese writers like to give 'dark hints' and to leave behind 'nuances' (Suzuki, quoted in Hinds 1987). Also, in Japanese writing, transition markers 'may be more subtle and require a more active role for the reader' (Hinds 1987). The effect of this is that when a reader is reading English with a Japanese sub-structure, the incompatibility of the assumed (Western) and actual (Japanese) systems makes the text incomprehensible.

The Finnish language is another example where it appears that the convention is for writers to suggest ideas rather than to spell them out openly. Such practice is said to emanate from a sense of politeness towards the reader – that is, the writer is expected to demonstrate respect for the reader's ability to deduce aspects of the argument which are considered obvious (Mauranen 1993).

There are also more subtle cultural understandings which have implications for the possibility of students to comment critically on published works in their thesis. Osterloh (1987) argues that readers from Third World countries have been educated in a system which does not discriminate between the author and the content of the message. There also appear to be similar difficulties in reading and, consequently, writing critically for Arab students. The suggestion is that this reluctance to produce critical work emanates from a cultural respect for the sanctity of the text (Farquarson 1988). As a consequence of this close relationship between the person and their statement, argumentation – even in scholarly works – takes on a different perspective, since it has a special defined social role. A Middle Easterner, for instance, is consistently polite within his or her own culture, even to people who are disliked. Parker (1987) argues that this view also prevails in writing where it would be unusual for a Middle Easterner to commit a critical judgment of anyone to paper.

Related to this different approach and sensitivity to commenting on other persons' work are the cultural variations which have been noted in the construction of arguments or providing proof for assertions (Leki 1992). Whereas in English the preference is for supporting statements with evidence in the form of facts, statistics and illustrations, in other cultures the conventions may be for the use of evidence in the form of analogies, appeal to intuition or shared communal wisdom.

In the light of this wide range of understandings of the writing process which students now bring to the postgraduate area, it is our contention that, with NESB postgraduate students, it is an important responsibility of the supervisor to make explicit the required structure and epistemological understandings of a thesis early in the student's candidature. In parallel, we feel that beginning students need to clearly understand their roles as postgraduate students as 'apprentices' to the disciplinary communities they are seeking to enter. Such a perspective has significant implications for the role of the researcher/supervisor who, in most situations, is the most influential person in the research student's education, and who must take on the added role of explicitly demonstrating and explaining aspects of academic conventions.

For example, we think it is useful to indicate to students that it is usual for a literature review to overview the field of study generally, then move to the area which is the focus of investigation, and finally expose the problem or gap in the field of study which the research addresses and which is the basis of the thesis. Within this review, published work is dealt with critically, and the project is clearly located within a conceptual and theoretical framework. As the thesis draws toward its conclusion, any knowledge which has been exposed by the research must be explicitly discussed, and sufficient evidence should be provided to convince the reader of the authenticity of the knowledge claims. Notwithstanding the specific conventions of various disciplines, this pattern is familiar in most university faculties. However, it should be recognized that, even contained within this brief statement, there are ideas which many students – even those from English speaking backgrounds – find challenging. When they are further overlaid with the implicit understandings brought by students from their first culture, the necessity for clarification of processes involved in writing for research clearly becomes more urgent.

We believe that such discussions between supervisor and research student about thesis structure will not only avoid problems with writing at a point where a considerable amount of material may have already been assembled, but will also significantly improve the development of the research project. In the formative stages of the work, a student often needs to discuss ideas and present half-formed thoughts to a supervisor or peers, and if communication is a problem, then the student cannot fully benefit from developmental advice and criticism. This is particularly evident in seminars and research discussions, where NESB students are often placed under enormous pressure just to deliver a coherent spoken piece in front of a critical audience.

We have found that, during the process of supervision, one way to acquaint such students with the expected conventions underpinning their written work is to utilize pictorial representations or diagramming of thought processes and relationships between concepts. The importance of visualization, we suggest, cannot be underestimated at this level. Myer (1986) suggests that visualization is a powerful way to facilitate coherent, critical thought. He describes visualization as an attempt to draw a diagram of the process which is going through the worker's mind, giving a concrete representation, as far as possible, of what can be fairly abstract thought processes.

Linked arrays of conceptual schemes were developed by Novak and Gowin (1984) into what they termed 'concept maps', which have found many uses in teaching and learning situations. The production of a concept map is a way of making visible the thoughts and relationships which are often only partly formed in the mind, and which are therefore difficult to communicate in spoken words or writing. The 'spaces', such as tacit linkages between ideas which can often be hidden in verbal exchanges, become immediately apparent in visual form. Each concept and its relationship with the others is forced into explicit focus, and can be examined in full without losing the overall picture.

Again, there is a clear implication here for NESB students. If the underlying concepts, which in the research area are often complex and detailed, have not been organized in a linear fashion in a way which can be quickly and unambiguously apprehended by the Western listener, the added process of translation to spoken word or written prose will further obfuscate the ideas.

Also, at the beginning stage in the supervision process, pictorial representations can be made of the project that the candidate is engaged in, locating it within the context of the disciplinary community. The roles and responsibilities of all parties involved in the production of the thesis (the student, supervisor, examiner and other students) can be explained in relation to the final product. Thus, even at this early stage, the need to provide support for assertions can be drawn out. These are important understandings which underpin the process of research.

We suggest that there are several other advantages of using concept maps in the context of postgraduate research. First, as Grinder (1991) has pointed out, visual modality, compared with auditory or kinaesthetic modalities, is the most powerful way of communicating and organizing complicated ideas, and is often the preferred mode of university-educated people. It allows rapid cross-linking of ideas, and also allows for implications and contradictions in ideas to be quickly recognized. In geometric terms, a visual display is two-dimensional, allowing movement across and between ideas, whilst verbal communication is one-dimensional and unidirectional. In a pictorial display, the control of the discussion can become shared, whilst in a verbal presentation, control can often remain with the speaker. A further advantage for NESB candidates at this stage, where concepts and their linkages are being clarified, is that the focus and pressure is taken off the students' need to use language where they often feel less confident than native speakers. In the less confronting climate produced by pictorial representation, close scrutiny of concepts and assertions, and the support which is necessary for them, can occur.

Second, at a psychological level, the production of a concept map can aid in decentring the discussions from the student and attention can be focused upon the communication medium. This overcomes the problem of *ego defence*, which is often a feature of verbal exchange at the research level. By having a whiteboard available during the discussion, concepts and the relationships between them can become depersonalized, allowing flexible and wide-ranging contributions to be recorded. Such isolation and depersonalization of concepts, especially those presented in published work, enable the development of objective analysis and scholarly criticism to occur.

Finally, during the early attempts by the student to form a concept map, indirect perceptions and expressions of relationships – which are typical of an early stage in synthesis of information – are made visible. When these aspects are being discussed, the supervisor and student can restructure ideas in a more direct and linear form. If subtle exploration of the genesis of the less appropriate first attempts is made, this is an ideal time to point out the expectations in Western discourse and, if relevant, draw comparisons

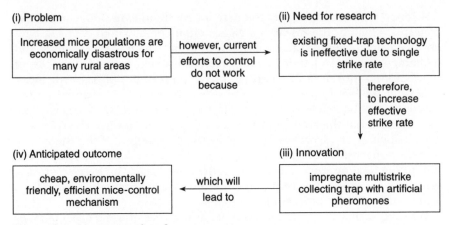

Figure 15.1 Linear template for concept map

with conventions of first language and culture. It is also an ideal time for the supervisor to verbalize and demonstrate the discourse markers and transitions which are expected to guide the Western reader. These phrases or words can then be inserted in the concept map at relevant points and further emphasize the direct and linear pattern which is expected.

There are many ways in which this process might be demonstrated to students, but we have found that, in the early stages of thesis development, a simple and effective way of focusing the discussion is to invite the student to answer four basic questions about their project which gives a 'linear template' that can be drawn on a whiteboard. These questions are:

1. What is the problem which has stimulated the research?
2. What is the need for the research?
3. What is the innovative part of the project?
4. What are the anticipated outcomes of the work?

When these questions have been answered, the project can then be summarized in about 50 words. In this way, during a discussion of about an hour, several useful understandings about academic discourse can be achieved. Figure 15.1 is a hypothetical example which has been used to demonstrate this technique.

The figure shows the attempt to visualize a research project in which it is proposed to build a better mousetrap. From this diagram, which is usually a fairly rough device which is not published, can come a concise statement of the project. This is often a critical step in a research presentation, either at a seminar or discussion of the project, later in a candidature or even at the draft production stage of the thesis. This task of preparing a brief, concise statement of a research project presents a significant barrier to many students. In many cases, the inability to prepare such an overview is an indication that the student may have difficulty in keeping the thesis writing under control, both at the macro- and micro-level. Notice how the following summary follows closely the linear thought pattern of the concept map.

> In rural areas, mice populations are increasing and current fixed-trap technology is ineffective. To increase the effective strike rate, multi-capture traps will be treated with pheromones (sexual attractants). Appropriate compounds will be isolated by the method of Disney (1989) and synthetic analogues prepared. Apparatus and chemicals are environmentally friendly, inexpensive and efficient.

From this simple example, it can be seen that each major step in the research process has been separated out for individual discussion, and can be subjected to fine scrutiny and criticism. As indicated earlier, during the close discussion of specific details of the project, the map allows a 'global' view of the project to be held at all times. As we work in the visual mode, changes in one part of the project which have wider implications to other parts can be quickly recognized and dealt with. Also, the relationship between the various parts of the project is made explicit. It also forms a template into which sections and sub-sections of information can be inserted as the research process proceeds.

The relevance to thesis preparation, we suggest, is fairly obvious. At an early stage in the student's candidature, the demonstration of the structuring of a project using a simple example can allow the student to prepare, stepwise, a simple description of the structure of his or her project and to summarize in his/her own mind the focus for his/her work. This can allow the supervisor to ensure quickly that the linear development of ideas is occurring and that the justification of knowledge claims is being attempted. In addition, the focus of discussion can be placed upon one area of the research without losing sight of the context in which the details are embedded.

Later, using this same mapping technique, a simple thesis structure can be rendered in diagrammatic form and the relationship between the various sections can be made explicit. This mapping can occur for the whole thesis, a chapter or a small section. A summary of the map can form a rudimentary table of contents, which can then be kept to guide the writing and editing process. In our experience, students often keep this map continually visible as they write, as a reminder of the direction the thesis is taking.

Concluding remarks

Many students experience discomfort and lack of confidence in projecting their early conceptions of their research work – feelings which are compounded for NESB students who do not have the same levels of facility with English conventions as their native English speaking fellow students. Since these students are reluctant to involve themselves in extended discussions about language conventions, structural problems often only become evident in the thesis-writing stage, where first-language conventions can make the production of an acceptable Western thesis even more difficult.

The use of pictorial representations of ideas in the form of a concept map or similar device takes the pressure off the students' verbal resources and provides a less threatening context for the explication of Western norms and conventions of thesis writing and production, particularly in the early stage of the research project.

The use of such a structured approach to supervision of NESB students appears to be one way of assisting, in a developmental way, the production of acceptable quality theses and, in an important way, increasing the quality of the postgraduate experience.

References

Altbach, P.G. (1991) Impact and adjustment: foreign students in comparative adjustment. *Higher Education*, 21(3), 305–23.

Armitage, C. (1996) Degrees of doubt. *The Weekend Australian*, 31 August–1 September, review.

Aspland, T. (1995) Windows into the supervision of overseas students. Paper given to Australian Association for Research in Education Conference, Wrest Point Casino, Hobart, 26–30 November.

Aspland, T. and O'Donoghue, T. (1994) Quality in supervising overseas students?, in O. Zuber-Skerritt and Y. Ryan (eds) *Quality in Postgraduate Supervision*. London, Kogan Page.

Australian Science and Technology Council (1994) *The Networked Nation*. Canberra, Australian Government Publishing Service.

AVCC (1994) *Universities and Their Students: Expectation and Responsibilities*. Melbourne, AVCC.

Back, K., Davis, D. and Olsen, A. (1996) *Internationalisation and Higher Education*. Canberra, Australian Government Publishing Service.

Ballard, B. (1995) Some issues in teaching international students, in L. Conrad and L. Phillips (eds) *Reaching More Students*. Brisbane, Griffith Institute for Higher Education.

Ballard, B. and Clanchy, J. (1988) *Studying in Australia*. Melbourne, Longman-Cheshire.

Ballard, B. and Clanchy, J. (1991a) *Study Abroad: A Manual for Asian Students*, 2nd edn. Kuala Lumpur, Longman.

Ballard, B. and Clanchy, J. (1991b) *Teaching Students from Overseas*. Melbourne, Longman.

Ballard, B. and Clanchy, J. (1993) Supervising students from overseas: a question of attitude, in David J. Cullen (ed.) *Quality in PhD Education*. Canberra, Australian National University.

Bearman, M., Vanzyl, A. and Cesnik, B. (1996) Lessons learned in publishing an electronic journal. Paper given to AusWeb96 – Second Australian World Wide Web Conference, Conrad Jupiters Hotel, Gold Coast, 7–9 July. <http://www.scu.edu.au/ausweb96/educn/bearman/paper.html>

Becher, T. (1989) *Academic Tribes and Territories: Intellectual Enquiry and the Cultures of Disciplines*. Milton Keynes, Society for Research into Higher Education and Open University Press.

Berchem, T. (1991) The internationalisation of higher education: the German perspective. *Higher Education,* 21(3), 297–304.

Beyer, B. (1985) Critical thinking: what is it? *Social Education,* 49(4), 270–6.

Biggs, J. (1993) From theory to practice: a cognitive systems approach. *Higher Education Research and Development,* 12(1), 73–86.

Biggs, J. (1996a) Western misperceptions of the Confucian-heritage learning culture, in D. Watkins and J. Biggs (eds) *The Chinese Learner: Cultural, Psychological and Contextual Issues.* Melbourne, Comparative Education Research Centre, University of Hong Kong and Australian Council of Educational Research.

Biggs, J. (1996b) Report on a series of workshops on the Asian learner, RMIT, by G. Healy, 'Notions of Asian learning "unfounded"'. *The Australian,* 16 October.

Biggs, J. (1996c) Don't stereotype Asians. *The Australian,* 12 September, letters to the editor.

Blue, T. (1996) Caught in the net. *The Australian,* 3 April.

Boud, D. (1993) Experience as the base for learning. *Higher Education Research and Development,* 12(1), 33–44.

Brislin, R.W., Cushner, K., Cherrie, C. and Young, M. (1986) *Intercultural Interactions, a Practical Guide.* Vol. 9, Cross-cultural Research and Methodology series. New York, Sage.

Brown, R. (1992) *Key Skills for Writing and Publishing Research.* Brisbane, Department of Primary Industries.

Bruce, C.S. (1994) Research students' early experiences of the dissertation literature review. *Studies in Higher Education,* 19(2), 217–29.

Bruce, C.S. (1995) A reflective approach to reviewing the literature, in O. Zuber-Skerritt and S. Pinchen (eds) *Third Manual for Conducting Workshops on Postgraduate Supervision.* Brisbane, Griffith Institute for Higher Education.

Bruce, C.S. (1996) Information literacy: a phenomenography. Unpublished PhD thesis, University of New England, Armidale.

Bulletin of Information for TOEFL (1996) Princeton, NJ, Educational Testing Service.

Campus Review (1996) Special report, 4–10 September.

Carter, H. and Harland, T. (1996) *Contract Law in Australia.* Sydney, Butterworths.

CCS & ESL (Centre for Communication Skills and English as a Second Language) (1995) Course information handout. Melbourne, CCS & ESL, Melbourne University.

Chincotta, D. and Underwood, G. (1996) Mother tongue, language of schooling and bilingual digit span. *British Journal of Psychology,* 87, 193–208.

Choi, M. (1997) Korean students in Australian universities: intercultural issues. *Higher Education Research and Development,* 16(3), 263–82.

Chuguev, K.V. (1996) Multilanguage and multicharset Web server. Paper given to INET '96, the 6th Annual Conference of the Internet Society, Montreal, Canada, 25–28 June. <http://www.isoc.org/isoc/whatis/conferences/inet/96/proceedings/a5/a5_1.htm>

Clarke, J. (1994) *The Teaching and Learning in Tertiary Education (T&LiTE) Project. A Report Prepared for the Teaching and Learning Committee, Queensland University of Technology by the Research Concentration in Cognition in Learning and Development, School of Learning and Development.* Brisbane, Queensland University of Technology.

Cleverly, J. (1985) *The Schooling of China.* Melbourne, Longman.

Commonwealth of Australia. Creative Nation: Commonwealth Cultural Policy (1994). <http://www.nla.gov.au/creative.nation/>

Connor, U. (1996) *Contrastive Rhetoric: Cross-cultural Aspects of Second-language Writing.* New York, Cambridge University Press.

Cryer, P. (1996a) Training research students and supporting supervisors through self-study materials customised for the research students. *The Graduate,* 2(2), 44–52.

Cryer, P. (1996b) *The Research Student's Guide to Success.* Buckingham, Open University Press.

Cryer, P. (1997) Handling common dilemmas in supervision, in *Issues in Postgraduate Supervision, Teaching and Management.* Guide No. 2. London, SRHE *The Times Higher Education Supplement.*

Cryer, P. (1998) Beyond codes of practice: dilemmas in supervising postgraduate research students. *Quality in Higher Education,* 4(3), 229–34.

Crystal, D. (1996) *English as a Global Language.* London, Cambridge University Press.

Curtis, D.D., James, D. and Julian, J. (1995) Supporting computer-mediated communication: who needs it? Paper given to conference, Distance Education: Crossing Frontiers, 12th Biennial Forum of the Open and Distance Learning Association of Australia, Vanuatu, Central Queensland University, Rockhampton, September.

CVCP (1996) *Recruitment and Support of International Students in UK Higher Education.* London, CVCP.

Danto, A. (1985) Postscript: philosophical individualism in Chinese and Western thought, in D. Munro (ed.) *Individualism and Holism: Studies in Confucian and Taoist Values.* Ann Arbor, University of Michigan Press.

Davies, R. (1996) Academia as Roman holiday. *The Times Higher Education Supplement,* 26 April.

de Certeau, M. (1988) *The Practice of Everyday Life.* Berkeley, University of California Press.

De Francis, J. (1986) *The Chinese Language: Fact and Fantasy.* Honolulu, University of Hawaii Press.

Denicolo, P. and Pope, M. (1994) The postgraduate's journey – an interplay of roles, in O. Zuber-Skerritt and Y. Ryan (eds), *Quality in Postgraduate Education.* London, Kogan Page.

Department of Employment, Education, Training and Youth Affairs (1997) *Selected Higher Education Student Statistics.* Canberra, Australian Government Publishing Service.

DeVos, G. (1992) *Social Cohesion and Alienation: Minorities in the United States and Japan.* San Francisco, CA, Westview Press.

Dilanchian, N. (1995) *Civilising Australia's Electronic Frontier: Public Policy and Information Infrastructure.* <http://snazzy.anu.edu.au/CNASI/pubs/OnDisc95/docs/ONL09.html>

Elsey, B. and Kinnell, M. (1990) Introduction, in M. Kinnell (ed.) *The Learning Experience of Overseas Students.* Buckingham, SRHE and Open University.

Elton, L. (1985) Teaching and tutoring overseas students, in S. Shotnes (ed.) *The Teaching and Tutoring of Overseas Students.* London, UKCOSA.

Elton, L. (1994) Staff development in relation to research, in O. Zuber-Skerritt and Y. Ryan (eds) *Quality in Postgraduate Education.* London, Kogan Page.

Elton, L. and Pope, M. (1992) The value of collegiality, in O. Zuber-Skerritt (ed.) *Starting Research: Supervision and Training.* Brisbane, Tertiary Education Institute, University of Queensland.

Engeldinger, E.A. (1988) Bibliographic instruction and critical thinking: the contribution of the annotated bibliography. *RQ,* 28(2), 195–202.

Ennis, R.H. (1962) A concept of critical thinking. *Harvard Educational Review*, 23(11), 81–111.

Erben, T. and Fagan, S. (1995) Being a non-English speaking background (NESB) student and distance education: understanding a process of in- and ex-clusion. Paper given to conference, Distance Education: Crossing Frontiers, 12th Biennial Forum of the Open and Distance Learning Association of Australia, Vanuatu, Central Queensland University, Rockhampton, September.

Fairclough, N. (1989) *Language and Power.* New York: Longman.

Farquarson, M. (1988) Ideas for teaching Arab students in a multicultural setting. Paper given to Annual Meeting of the Teachers of English to Speakers of Other Languages, Chicago, July.

Farquhar, M. (1996) English for research purposes: A workshop on designing curricula for NESB postgraduates. Paper given to Supervising Postgraduates for Non-English Speaking Backgrounds, Balliwar, Southern Cross University, NSW, 29 June–3 July.

Felix, U. and Lawson, M. (1994) Evaluation of an integrated bridging course on academic writing for overseas postgraduate students. *Higher Education Research and Development*, 13(1), 59–69.

Finn, R. (1996) *Bibliographic Software: Adding New Features, Becoming Web Savvy.* http://www.the-scientist.library.upenn.edu/yr1996/july/tools_960708.html

Francis, A. (1993) *Facing the future: the internationalisation of post secondary institutions in British Columbia. Task Force Report.* Vancouver, British Columbia Centre for International Education.

Gallois, C., Giles, H., Jones, E., Cargile, A. and Hirohi, O. (1995) Accommodating intercultural encounters: elaborations and extensions, in R. Wiseman (ed.) *Intercultural Communication Theory.* London, Sage Publications.

Gardner, M. (1994) *Griffith University Learning Assistance Program Report,* Volume 1. Brisbane, Griffith University.

Gardner, R.C. and Lambert, W.E. (1972) *Attitudes and Motivation in Second-Language Learning.* Boston, MA, Newbury House.

Giddens, A. (1991) *Modernity and Self-identity: Self and Society in the Late Modern Age.* Stanford, Stanford University Press.

Ginsburg, E. (1992) Not just a matter of English. *HERDSA*, 14(1), 6–8.

Gore, J. (1993) *The Struggle for Pedagogies: Critical and Feminist Discourses as Regimes of Truth.* London, Routledge.

Green, B. and Lee, A. (1995) Theorising postgraduate pedagogy. *The Australian Universities Review*, 38(2), 40–5.

Greenaway, D. and Tuck, J. (1995) *Economic Impact of International Students in UK Higher Education.* London, CVCP.

Grinder, M. (1991) *Righting the Educational Conveyor Belt.* Portland, Metamorphous.

Gumperz, J. and Hymes, D. (eds) (1986) *Directions in Sociolinguistics: The Ethnology of Communication.* Oxford, Blackwell.

Harris, M. (1996) *Review of Postgraduate Education – Consultative Document.* Higher Education Funding Council for England/Council of Vice-Chancellors and Principals/Standing Conference of Principals (HEFCE/CVCP/SCOP), Bristol.

Harwood, A. (1994) A research student's perception of the supervisory role, in P. Denicolo and N. Fielding (eds) *Handbook for Research Supervisors.* Guildford, University of Surrey.

Hashemi, M.R. (1992) Analysis of academic discourse: insights for teaching grammar. Paper given to conference, 'FLTI' (Foreign Language Technological Institute), Tabriz-Baku, Iran, July.

Hesselgrave, D.J. (1979) *Communicating Christ Cross-Culturally.* Grand Rapids, Mich, Zondervan Publishing House.

Hinds, J. (1987) Reader versus writer responsibility: a new typology, in V. Connor and R. Kaplan (eds) *Writing across Languages: Analysis of L2 Text.* Reading, Addison-Wesley.

Hockey, J. (1991) The social science PhD: a literature review. *Studies in Higher Education,* 16(3), 319–32.

Hockey, J. (1994) New territory: problems of adjusting to the first year of a social science PhD. *Studies in Higher Education,* 19(2), 177–90.

Hodge, B. (1995) Monstrous knowledge: doing PhDs in the new humanities. *Australian Universities' Review,* 38(2), 35–9.

Hoe, P.S. and Whale, G. (1995) Paperless assessment: using multimedia and hyperlinks to improve the commentary in assignments, in H. Maurer (ed.) *Educational Multimedia and Hypermedia, 1995.* Proceedings of ED-MEDIA95, AACE (American Association of Computer Education), Charlottesville, VA.

Hore, T. (1993) Learning: theories in practice. *Higher Education Research and Development,* 12(1), 1–3.

Hymes, D.H. (1972) Introduction, in J. Cazden and D.H. Hymes (eds) *Functions of Language in the Classroom.* New York, Teachers' College Press.

Illing, D. (1996a) Saturated market blamed for overseas student slump. *The Australian,* 10 July.

Illing, D. (1996b) Study refutes NESB 'disadvantage' label. *The Australian,* 13 March, a report on a study of higher education participation rates of NESB students of different backgrounds, by I. Dobson, B. Birrell and V. Rapson, published in *People and Place,* March.

International English Language Testing System (1996) *The IELTS Handbook.* Cambridge, University of Cambridge, British Council and IDP Education Australia.

James, R. and Beattie, K. (1995) *Expanding Options: Delivery Technologies and Postgraduate Coursework.* Canberra, AGPS.

Jones, J. (1979) *Education in Depth.* Hong Kong, Swindon.

Joo, C.T. (1996) The idealised stereotype of an overseas student experience, *Campus Review,* 2–8 October, p. 12.

Jordan, G. and Weedon, C. (1995) *Cultural Politics: Class, Gender, Race and the Postmodern World.* Oxford, Blackwell.

Kaplan, R. (1966) Cultural thought patterns in intercultural education. *Language and Learning,* 16, 1–20.

Kennedy, K.J. (1995) Developing a curriculum guarantee for overseas students. *Higher Education Research and Development,* 14(1), 35–46.

King, M. and Margetson, D. (1995) *A Guide to Higher Degree Supervision,* 2nd edn. Brisbane, Griffith Institute for Higher Education.

Klineberg, O. and Hull, W.F. (1979) *At a Foreign University: An International Study of Adaptation and Coping.* New York, Praeger Publishers.

Knight, N. and Zuber-Skerritt, O. (1992) Problems and methods in research – a course for the beginning researcher in the social sciences, in O. Zuber-Skerritt (ed.) *Starting Research – Supervision and Training.* Brisbane, Tertiary Education Development Institute (TEDI) University of Queensland.

Knight, N.J. (1995) Theory and discourse in research: implications for supervision of research students in the social sciences, in O. Zuber-Skerritt (ed.) *Frameworks for Postgraduate Education.* Lismore, Southern Cross University Press.

Kramsch, C. (1993) *Context and Culture in Language Learning.* Oxford, Oxford University Press.

Lakoff, G. and Johnson, M. (1980) *Metaphors We Live By*. Chicago, University of Chicago Press.

Leder, G.C. (1993) Constructivism: theory for practice? The case for mathematics. *Higher Education Research and Development*, 12(1), 5–20.

Leder, G.C. (1995) Higher degree research supervision: a question of balance. *Australian Universities' Review*, 38(2), 5–8.

Lee, R.M. (ed.) (1995) *Informational Technology for the Social Scientist*. London, UCL Press.

Leki, I. (1992) *Understanding ESL Writers: A Guide for Teachers*. Portsmouth, Boynton-Cook.

Leonard, P.G. (1995) *Beyond the Future: Multimedia and the Law*. <http://snazzy.anu.edu.au/CNASI/pubs/OnDisc95/docs/ONL10.html>

Little, A. (1988) *Learning from Developing Countries*. London, Institute of Education, University of London.

Loke, K.-K. and Howell, F. (1995) Stranger in a strange land: teaching in an alien culture, in L. Conrad and L. Phillips (eds) *Reaching More Students*. Brisbane, Griffith Institute of Higher Education.

McGarry, K. (1990) Doing a thesis: the loneliness of the long-distance runner. *Assignation*, 7(2), 13–16.

McLaughlin, D. (1996) School teaching and higher education: a Papua New Guinea case study. *Teaching in Higher Education*, I(1), 105–25.

McMichael, P. (1993) Starting up as supervisors: the perceptions of newcomers in postgraduate supervision in Australia and Sri Lanka. *Studies in Higher Education*, 18(1), 15–16.

McPeck, J.E. (1990) *Teaching Critical Thinking*. New York, Routledge.

McSwiney, C. (1995) *Essential Understandings – International Students, Learning, Libraries*. Adelaide, AUSLIB Press.

Manguel, A. (1996) *A History of Reading*. London, Harper Collins.

Mann, S.J. (1992) Telling a life story: issues for research. *Management Education and Development*, 23(3), 271–80.

Mauranen, A. (1993) Contrastive ESP rhetoric: metatext in Finnish English economics texts. *English for Specific Purposes*, 12, 3–22.

May, M. and Bartlett, A. (1995) 'They've got a problem with English': perceptions of the difficulties of international postgraduate students, in T. Crooks and G. Crewes (eds) *Language and Development*. Canberra, Indonesia Australia Language Foundation.

Mehran, G. (1992) Social implications of literacy in Iran. *Comparative Education Review*, 36(2), 194–211.

Minichiello, V., Aroni, R., Timewell, E. and Alexander, L. (1995) *In-depth Interviewing: Principles, Techniques, Analysis*, 2nd edn. Melbourne, Longman.

Morris, D. (1978) *Manwatching*. New York: Panther Books.

Moses, I. (1984) Supervision of higher degree students – problem areas and possible solutions. *Higher Education Research and Development*, 3(2), 135–65.

Moses, I. (1985) *Supervising Postgraduates*. HERDSA Green Guide No. 3, Kensington, Higher Education Research and Development Society of Australia.

Mullen, C. and Dalton, J. (1995) The dance of becoming educated/socialized teacher–researchers. Paper given to 7th Biennial Conference of ISATT, Brock University, Canada, September.

Munro, D.J. (1977) *The Concept of Human Nature in Contemporary China*. Ann Arbor, University of Michigan Press.

Myer, C. (1986) *Teaching Students to Think Critically*. San Francisco, Jossey-Bass.

Nakajima, K. (1993) Computer writing network project in East Asian languages, in J.V. Boettcher (ed.) 101 Success Stories of Information Technology Use in Higher Education. Princeton, NJ, McGraw Hill.

National Postgraduate Committee (1995) *Guidelines for Codes of Practice for Postgraduate Research*, 2nd edn. Troon, Ayrshire, Brandon House.

National Tertiary Education Union (1998) *A Code of Ethics*. Melbourne, NTEU.

Nguyen, C. (1990) Barriers to communication between Vietnamese and non-Vietnamese. Paper given to Fifth National Conference of the Network for Intercultural Communications. Crosscultural Communication in the 1990s, La Trobe University, September.

Nightingale, P. (1992) Writing about research in the humanities and social sciences, in O. Zuber-Skerritt (ed.) *Manual for Conducting Workshops on Postgraduate Supervision*. Brisbane, Tertiary Education Institute, University of Queensland.

Novak, J.D. and Gowin, B. (1984) *Learning to Learn*. Oxford, Oxford University Press.

Oberg (1958) Culture shock: adjustment to a new cultural environment. *Practical Anthropology*, 7, 177–82.

Okorocha, E. (1996a) Cultural clues to student guidance. *The Times Higher Education Supplement*, 7 June.

Okorocha, E. (1996b) Some cultural and communication issues in working with international students. *Journal of International Education*, 7(2), 31–8.

Okorocha, E. (1996c) The international student experience: expectations and realities. *Journal of Graduate Education*, 2(3), 8–84.

Okorocha, E. (1997a) Counselling international students. *Journal of Race and Cultural Education in Counselling*, 12, 26–7.

Okorocha, E. (1997b) Supervising international research students, issues in postgraduate supervision, in *Teaching and Management, Guide No. 1*. London, Society for Research into Higher Education/*The Times Higher Education Supplement*.

Okorocha, E. (1998) A study of overseas students' experience in UK higher education and issues that affect counselling and working with them. Unpublished PhD thesis, University of Surrey.

Osterloh, K. (1987) International differences and communication approaches to foreign language teaching in the Third World, in J. Valdes (ed.) *Culture Bound*. Cambridge, Cambridge University Press.

Ostler, S. (1987) English in parallels: a comparison of English and Arabic prose, in U. Connor and R. Kaplan (eds) *Writing Across Languages: Analysis of L2 Text*. Reading, Addison-Wesley.

Park, T.K. (1993) The nature of relevance in information retrieval: an empirical study. *Library Quarterly*, 63(3), 318–51.

Parker, O. (1987) Cultural clues to the Middle Eastern student, in J. Valdes (ed.) *Culture Bound*. Cambridge, Cambridge University Press.

Parra, D. (1995) *Gaps in Learning Assistance Provision at Griffith University*, Volume 2. Brisbane, Griffith University.

Passmore, J. (1967) On teaching to be critical, in Richard Peters (ed.) *The Concept of Education*. London, Routledge and Kegan Paul.

Peacock, R. (1996) *Australian International Education Foundation Quarterly Report*, 2(2).

Pedersen, P.B. (1991) Counselling international students. *Counselling Psychologist* 19, 10–58.

Phelps, R.A. (1996) Information skills and the distance education student: an exploratory study into the approaches of Southern Cross University distance educators to the information needs of external students. Unpublished Masters thesis, Deakin University.

Phillips, E.M. and Pugh D.S. (1994) *How to Get a PhD: A Handbook for Students and Supervisors*. Milton Keynes, Open University Press.

Postgraduate Information Handbook (n.d.) Brisbane, Department of Asian Languages and Studies, University of Queensland.

Price, R.F. (1979) *Education in Modern China*. London, Routledge and Kegan Paul.

Prosser, M. (1993) Phenomenography and principles and practices of learning. *Higher Education Research and Development*, 12(1), 21–33.

Ramsden, P. (1993) Theories of learning and teaching and the practice of excellence in higher education. *Higher Education Research and Development*, 12(1), 87–98.

Reynolds, C.H. and Smith, D.C. (1990) Academic principles of responsibility, in William W. May (ed.) *Ethics and Higher Education*. New York, Macmillan.

Rodgers, B.L. (1995) NUD.IST software for qualitative data analysis. *Management Learning*, 26(3), 367–70.

Roman, L. (1992) The political significance of other ways of narrating ethnography: a feminist materialist approach, in M. Le Compte, W. Milroy and J. Preissle (eds) *The Handbook of Qualitative Research in Education*. San Diego, Academic Press Incorporated, HBJ Publishers.

Ryan, Y. and Zuber-Skerritt, O. (1998a) *First Manual for Conducting Workshops on Postgraduate Supervision*. Lismore, WoRLD Institute.

Ryan, Y. and Zuber-Skerritt, O. (1998b) *Second Manual for Conducting Workshops on Postgraduate Supervision*. Lismore, WoRLD Institute.

Ryan, Y., Zuber-Skerritt, O. and Pinchen, S. (1998a) *Third Manual for Conducting Workshops on Postgraduate Supervision*. Lismore, WoRLD Institute.

Ryan, Y., Zuber-Skerritt, O. and Schevaller, L. (1998b) *Fourth Manual for Conducting Workshops on Postgraduate Supervision*. Lismore, WoRLD Institute.

Salmon, P. (1992) *Achieving a PhD – Ten Students' Experience*. Stoke-on-Trent, Trentham Books.

Sandeman-Gay, E. (1995) How Iranian postgraduate students learn Australian-style written academic discourse, four case studies. Unpublished Masters thesis, University of Wollongong.

Sandeman-Gay, E. (1996) Different approaches to supervisor support of international postgraduate students: the question of academic discourse. Paper presented at the Higher Education Research and Development Society of Australia (HERDSA), Different Approaches: Theory and Practice in Higher Education, Perth, WA, 8–12 July.

SERC (Science and Engineering Research Council) (1989) *Research and Supervisor: An Approach to Good Supervisory Practice*. SERC, London.

Shevellar, L. and Heywood, E. (1996) Report on a workshop for non-English speaking background (NESB) research students and their supervisors at Southern Cross University. Unpublished Report, Faculty of Education, Work and Training, Southern Cross University.

Shotter, J. (1993) *Cultural Politics of Everyday Life*. Buckingham, Open University Press.

Smith, D.E. (1990) *The Conceptual Practices of Power: A Feminist Sociology of Knowledge*. Boston, Northeastern University Press.

Smith, K.L. (1993) Computer-mediated communication and learning environments for Spanish as a second language students, in J.V. Boettcher (ed.) *101 Success*

Stories of Information Technology Use in Higher Education. New York, McGraw Hill. (Also available at <gopher://ivory.educom.edu/11/stories.101>).

Smith, R. (1989) Research degrees and supervision in polytechnics. *Journal of Further and Higher Education,* 13(1), 6–83.

Solomon, R. (1971) *Mao's Revolution and the Chinese Political Culture.* Berkeley, University of California Press.

Southern Cross University (1996) *Information Technology Plan.* Lismore, Southern Cross University.

Speier, A. (1990) Development of a predeparture preparation course for national staff of the PNG University of Technology going for overseas studies. Unpublished Diploma Project, Diploma in the Practice of Education, University of Surrey, Guildford.

Stoan, S.K. (1991) Research and information retrieval among academic researchers. *Library Trends,* 39(3), 238–57.

Strauss, A. and Corbin, J. (1992) *Basics of Qualitative Research: Grounded Theory Procedures and Techniques.* Newbury Park, Sage.

Susaki, S., Hayashi, Y. and Kikui, G. (1996) Navigation interface in cross-lingual WWW search engine, TITAN. Paper given to AUUG '96 and Asia-Pacific WWW '96, World Congress Centre, Melbourne, 18–20 September.

Tambiah, S.J. (1990) *Magic, Science, Religion and the Scope of Rationality.* Cambridge, Cambridge University Press.

Taylor, E. (1994) Intercultural competence: a transformative learning process. *Adult Education Quarterly,* 44(3), 154–74.

Taylor, G. (1993) A theory of practice: hermeneutical understanding. *Higher Education Research and Development,* 12(1), 59–72.

Terry, L. (1995) Teaching for justice in the age of the *Good Universities Guide,* reviewed in *Australian Universities Review,* 38(2), 75–6.

Tesch, R. (1990) *Qualitative Research: Analysis Types and Software Tools.* New York, Falmer Press.

The Australian Higher Education Supplement (1998) 12 August, p. 33.

Tideman, D. (1996) International students make up 8.4pc of total. *The Australian,* 23 October.

Tilman, H. (1996) *Evaluating Quality on the Net.* <http://www.tiac.net/users/hope/findqual.html>

Tjok-a-Tam, S. (1994) Learning in action: developments in management education. Unpublished PhD thesis, University of Surrey, Guildford.

Todhunter, M. (1996) Teaching English language for academic purposes at Australian universities. Unpublished paper, Griffith University, Brisbane.

VISIMAP (1996) Visimap home page. <http://www.coco.co.uk>

Volet, S. and Ang, G. (1998) Culturally mixed groups on international campuses: an opportunity for inter-cultural learning. *Higher Education Research and Development,* 17(1), 5–23.

Volet, S. and Renshaw, P. (1996) Chinese students at an Australian university: adaptability and continuity, in D. Watkins and J. Biggs (eds) *The Chinese Learner: Cultural, Psychological and Contextual Issues.* Melbourne, Comparative Education Research Centre, University of Hong Kong and Australian Council of Educational Research.

Watkins, D. and Biggs, J. (1996) *The Chinese Learner: Cultural, Psychological and Contextual Issues.* Melbourne, Comparative Education Research Centre, University of Hong Kong and Australian Council of Educational Research.

Wilson, K. (1996) World Wide Web Walkabout: a subject-oriented program for teaching and learning the Internet. <http://www.scu.edu.au/ausweb96/educn/wilson/paper.html>

Wilson, Richard W. (1970) *Learning To Be Chinese: The Political Socialization of Children in Taiwan.* Cambridge, MA, MIT Press.

Wolpert, L. (1993) *The Unnatural Nature of Science.* London, Faber and Faber.

Wright, J. (1991) Left to their own devices. *The Times Higher Education Supplement,* 6 December.

Yong, L.K., Wee, T.T., Govindasamy, N. and Chee, L.T. (1996) Multiple language support over the World Wide Web. Paper given at INET'96, the 6th Annual Conference of the Internet Society, Montreal, Canada, 25–28 June. <http://www.isoc.org/isoc/whatis/conferences/inet/96/proceedings/a5/a5_2.htm>

Zuber-Skerritt, O. (1992a) *Action Research in Higher Education: Examples and Reflections.* London, Kogan Page.

Zuber-Skerritt, O. (1992b) Major issues and concerns, in O. Zuber-Skerritt (ed.) *Manual for Conducting Workshops on Postgraduate Supervision.* Brisbane, Tertiary Education Development Institute, University of Queensland.

Zuber-Skerritt, O. (1993) Improving learning and teaching through action learning and action research. *Higher Education Research and Development,* 12(1), 45–58.

Zuber-Skerritt, O. and Knight, N. (1986) Problem definition and thesis writing: workshops for the postgraduate student. *Higher Education,* 15(1–2), 89–103.

Zuber-Skerritt, O. and Knight, N. (1992) Problem definition and thesis writing – workshops for the postgraduate student, in O. Zuber-Skerritt (ed.) *Starting Research: Supervision and Training.* Brisbane, Tertiary Education Institute, University of Queensland.

Zuber-Skerritt, O. and Ryan, Y. (1994) *Quality in Postgraduate Research Supervision.* London, Kogan Page.

Zwingmann, C.A. and Gunn, A.D.G. (1983) *Uprooting and Health: Psycho-social Problems of Students from Abroad.* Geneva, World Health Organization.

Index

The Society for Research into Higher Education

The Society for Research into Higher Education exists to stimulate and coordinate research into all aspects of higher education. It aims to improve the quality of higher education through the encouragement of debate and publication on issues of policy, on the organization and management of higher education institutions, and on the curriculum and teaching methods.

The Society's income is derived from subscriptions, sales of its books and journals, conference fees and grants. It receives no subsidies, and is wholly independent. Its individual members include teachers, researchers, managers and students. Its corporate members are institutions of higher education, research institutes, professional, industrial and governmental bodies. Members are not only from the UK, but from elsewhere in Europe, from America, Canada and Australasia, and it regards its international work as among its most important activities.

Under the imprint *SRHE & Open University Press*, the Society is a specialist publisher of research, having over 70 titles in print. The Editorial Board of the Society's Imprint seeks authoritative research or study in the above fields. It offers competitive royalties, a highly recognizable format in both hardback and paperback and the worldwide reputation of the Open University Press.

The Society also publishes *Studies in Higher Education* (three times a year), which is mainly concerned with academic issues, *Higher Education Quarterly* (formerly *Universities Quarterly*), mainly concerned with policy issues, *Research into Higher Education Abstracts* (three times a year), and *SRHE News* (four times a year).

The society holds a major annual conference in December, jointly with an institution of higher education. In 1996 the topic was 'Working in Higher Education' at University of Wales, Cardiff. In 1997 it was 'Beyond the First Degree' at the University of Warwick and in 1998 it was 'The Globalization of Higher Education' at the University of Lancaster. The 1999 conference will be on the topic of higher education and its communities at UMIST.

The Society's committees, study groups and networks are run by the members. The networks at present include:

Access	Mentoring
Curriculum Development	Postgraduate Issues
Disability	Quality
Eastern European	Quantitative Studies
Funding	Student Development
Legal Education	Vocational Qualifications

Benefits to members

Individual

Individual members receive:

- *SRHE News*, the Society's publications list, conference details and other material included in mailings.
- Greatly reduced rates for *Studies in Higher Education* and *Higher Education Quarterly*.
- A 35 per cent discount on all SRHE & Open University Press publications.
- Free copies of the Procedings – commissioned papers on the theme of the Annual Conference.
- Free copies of *Research into Higher Education Abstracts*.
- Reduced rates for the annual conference.
- Extensive contacts and scope for facilitating initiatives.
- Free copies of the *Register of Members' Research Interests*.
- Membership of the Society's networks.

Corporate

Corporate members receive:

- Benefits of individual members, plus:
- Free copies of *Studies in Higher Education*.
- Unlimited copies of the Society's publications at reduced rates.
- Reduced rates for the annual conference.
- The right to submit applications for the Society's research grants.
- The right to use the Society's facility for supplying statistical HESA data for purposes of research.

Membership details: SRHE, 3 Devonshire Street, London
W1N 2BA, UK. Tel: 0171 637 2766. Fax: 0171 637 2781.
email: srhe@mailbox.ulcc.ac.uk
World Wide Web: http://www.srhe.ac.uk./srhe/
Catalogue: SRHE & Open University Press, Celtic Court,
22 Ballmoor, Buckingham MK18 1XW. Tel: 01280 823388.
Fax: 01280 823233. email: enquiries@openup.co.uk